MIKE CHARLTON / J.

P9-BYB-699

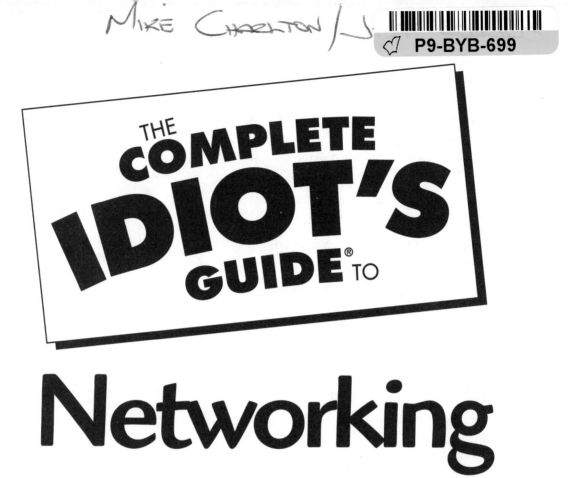

THE
COMPLETE
IDIOT'S
GUIDE® TO

Networking

Second Edition

by Bill Wagner and Chris Negus

que®

A Division of Macmillan Computer Publishing
201 W. 103rd Street, Indianapolis, IN 46290

The Complete Idiot's Guide to Networking, Second Edition

Copyright © 1999 by Que Corporation

International Standard Book Number: 0-7897-1802-2

Library of Congress Catalog Card Number: 98-86326

Printed in the United States of America

First Printing: February 1999

02   01   00   99   4   3   2

Trademarks

Warning and Disclaimer

Executive Editor
Christopher Will

Development Editor
Kate Shoup Welsh

Managing Editor
Brice Gosnell

Project Editor
Kevin Laseau

Copy Editor
JoAnna Kremer

Illustrator
Judd Winick

Indexer
William Meyers

Technical Editor
Kackie Charles

Proofreader
Benjamin Berg

Interior Design
Glenn Larson

Cover Designer
Mike Freeland

Layout Technician
Heather Hiatt Miller

Contents at a Glance

Contents

10 Case Study: Building a Windows SOHO System   141

Part 4 Maintaining and Administering Your Network   157

11 Networking VIP: The System Administrator   159

About the Author

Bill Wagner currently runs an Internet security consulting company. His sordid past includes NetWare, Linux, and UNIX system administration. Bill lives on the southern California coast with his wife, Michelle, who has been certified Y2K compliant.

Chris Negus has written about the UNIX system, networking, and the Internet for more than a decade. As a consultant, Chris worked at AT&T Bell Labs, UNIX System Labs, and Novell on UNIX system development. Chris's recent books include *Internet Explorer 4 Bible*, *Netscape Plug-ins for Dummies*, and contributions to *Using UNIX* and *UNIX Unleashed*. Chris lives in Salt Lake City with Sheree, Caleb, and Seth.

Dedication

Bill Wagner

In memory of Lewis Herschler: soldier, political scientist, and all-around cool cat.

Chris Negus

In memory of Joan Negus, the world's greatest astrologer, baseball coach, and mom.

Acknowledgements

Bill Wagner

The following persons were indispensable: Chris Negus, Michael Mikaleczko, David Sale, David Pennells, David Fugate, Margot Hutchison, and Marty Rush.

Additionally, I'd like to acknowledge a superb editing team: Chris Will, Kate Welsh, Dean Miller, Kackie Charles, and all the folks at Que.

Chris Negus

I'd like to thank Sheree for putting up with rushed deadlines, bringing Seth into the world, and marrying me (not necessarily in that order).

Tell Us What You Think!

As the reader of this book, *you* are our most important critic and commentator. We value your opinion and want to know what we're doing right, what we could do better, what areas you'd like to see us publish in, and any other words of wisdom you're willing to pass our way.

As the Executive Editor for the Operating Systems team at Macmillan Computer Publishing, I welcome your comments. You can fax, email, or write me directly to let me know what you did or didn't like about this book—as well as what we can do to make our books stronger.

Please note that I cannot help you with technical problems related to the topic of this book, and that due to the high volume of mail I receive, I might not be able to reply to every message.

When you write, please be sure to include this book's title and author as well as your name and phone or fax number. I will carefully review your comments and share them with the author and editors who worked on the book.

Fax: 317-581-4663

Email: opsys@mcp.com

Mail: Executive Editor
          Operating Systems
          Macmillan Computer Publishing
          201 West 103rd Street
          Indianapolis, IN 46290 USA

3, 2, 1, Go!

Computer networks lead the list of today's hottest technologies. Networks are everywhere, invisibly supporting the flow of money, products, and ideas around the world. Every day network capacities grow, allowing more information to be sent faster and to more places.

The Internet, in particular, has brought computer networks into public consciousness. However, despite the fact that millions of people use the Internet, few know how the Internet works. Even fewer know how private networks could serve their homes and businesses. This book is aimed at the brave souls who want to look under the covers to learn about today's computer networks.

You may already know how to display a Web page from the Internet. But have you thought about how a computer network can turn a handful of lonely employees into a workgroup? Have you considered how memos once lost in the mailroom can be transmitted instantaneously to anyone in your company? It's not just memos that can be shared, but everything from database records, to application programs, to printers, scanners, and other hardware devices.

Believe it or not, the power of computer networks is not beyond your reach. Gone are the days when men in white coats living behind glass walls controlled all networks. It would have made those men's propellers spin to see into the future, to look at what you can do today with a few network cards and some wire. Setting up your own high-performance local area network (LAN) is easy, inexpensive, and doesn't require a computer science degree.

Whereas a few years ago many organizations were getting their first computers, today you would be hard pressed to find an organization with only one computer. Computers are about as common in the workplace as typewriters once were. Connecting them has now become a primary goal of anyone who wants to make computer resources work together more efficiently.

Which brings us to why you might want to read this book. We've tried to break the subject of computer networking down into two basic concepts: how computer networks work and what you can do with them. From our descriptions you'll understand how networks are structured (architectures) and what makes them go (protocols). We'll also teach you what you need to make and maintain your own computer network.

What you learn here about networking will not only make you smarter, it will also make you a hit at cocktail parties. You'll actually be able to chat intelligently about the difference between the Internet, intranets, and extranets. Terms such as TCP/IP and client/server will roll off of your tongue. You'll understand why anyone who's anyone would want his or her own network.

Although this book can serve the namedropper in all of us, it's even more valuable if you want to get your hands dirty building a network. How would you begin to create your own network? First, you would need to figure out what your network needed to do. Then it wouldn't hurt to understand a bit about how networks are organized (topologies) and connected (cabling).

Next, you might want help understanding and choosing network hardware, network computer systems, and network software. So that you don't feel like a teenager walking into a used car dealership with a pocketful of babysitting money, we tell you how to shop for the best networking deals and where to find free—or inexpensive—networking software.

As networks grow and technology changes, you will need to know how to manage the evolution of your networks. Information in this book lays out the roles of system administrator for maintaining networks, as well as describing how to upgrade your networking hardware and software.

Once your network is up and running, your main concerns become keeping the network safe and fixing problems that might crop up. For keeping computing resources safe, we have a chapter that covers security issues. Furthermore, if things go wrong, you can refer to our troubleshooting chapter for ideas on how to find solutions.

In all of this, we have tried to present networking essentials in easy-to-understand terms. We hope you can learn a lot and have some fun doing it. If you have any questions or comments about the book, feel free to drop us an email. We'll do our best to get back to you.

> Bill Wagner
> bwagner@altavista.net
>
> Chris Negus
> chris.negus@cwix.com

Part 1

What Is a Network and Why Do You Need One?

You've been getting along just fine without a network. The tin cans and string between your and your employees' offices work great. Paper airplanes are fine for distributing memos. "If it ain't broke, don't fix it," you always say...

...Okay, so you have a sneaking suspicion that communication in your organization could be more efficient. The chapters in this part can help you understand what a network is and how it might help bring you and your people out of the horse-and-buggy era.

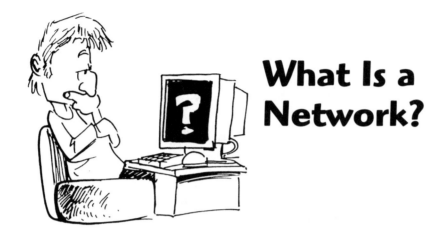

## Chapter 1

What Is a Network?

> ➤ Learn what a network is
>
> ➤ Various types of networks
>
> ➤ Advantages and disadvantages of networking

In today's business environment, the words *network* and *networking* are tossed around pretty liberally. These terms are so popular, in fact, that they've now become staple ingredients in ad campaigns!

However, even after absorbing all the media hype you can stand, you may be still be wondering what a network is. This chapter will answer that question in detail.

What is a Network?

Webster's New World Dictionary defines a *network* as

> …any arrangement or fabric of parallel wires, threads, etc., crossed at regular intervals by others fastened to them so as to leave open spaces; netting, mesh…

That definition is accurate and precise, but doesn't really explain a network's function. Let's remedy that.

A network has two chief characteristics:

> ➤ Interconnectivity
>
> ➤ The capability to facilitate communication

Let's briefly examine these two qualities.

Interconnectivity

The computing biz is full of fifty-cent words, and *interconnectivity* is one of them. What does it mean? Interconnectivity is a term used to describe anything that's tied together at many points (such as a grid).

To visualize that, think of American freeways. If you've ever watched a news traffic report, you've seen our freeway system filmed from helicopter—dozens of metropolitan freeways tied together by interstate highways. During rush hour, these thoroughfares are a snarled mess.

Our freeway system is a perfect example of interconnectivity in action. In it, highways intersect, allowing you to drive from Los Angeles to New York. Along that route, other folks (from still other cities) can also connect and travel to countless destinations in between. This is interconnectivity on a grand scale. Not only are these highways connected (some intersect with others), but they are *interconnected* (you can get anywhere by hopping from one freeway to the next and so on).

Computer networks work in a similar fashion. However, instead of relying on a patchwork of roads, computer networks rely on a patchwork of wires. These wires connect machines to one another.

To learn more about interconnectivity (and how networks are strung together) please refer to Chapter 4, "Network Topologies."

The Capability to Facilitate Communication

A network's second important characteristic is the capability to facilitate communication. In networks, machines "talk" to one another and perform various tasks including

➤ Transferring files from machine to machine

➤ Distributing email or messages

➤ Remote printing

Such communication is accomplished by packaging your data into small units. These units are sent across the network (by wire) to other machines.

In essence, then, a network is this: A series of computers that can communicate with one another by virtue of their interconnectivity.

What Are Networks Good For?

As you'll soon read, there are many different network types. Some perform specialized tasks while others serve more generalized purposes. However, in the broadest sense, all networks perform the same function: data transport.

There are several reasons to have a network:

To learn more about how computers communicate, please see Chapter 5, "System Architectures and Protocols."

➤ *Resource sharing*   In a network, users at different workstations can share the same printer, modem, or Internet connection.

➤ *Security*   Networks (as you'll soon learn) have advanced security features. These features allow you to incisively permit or deny users access to your data.

➤ *Organization and centralization*   Networks allow you to centralize databases so that users in different departments can access the same data. This eliminates the need to store copies of your database on each and every machine.

➤ *Communication and convenience*   Networks provide easy communication solutions such as email, messaging, and online collaboration.

Chances are, even the smallest business can benefit from a network. Through networking, businesses can perform "one-stop" transactions where billing, accounting, inventory, and management are entirely integrated. As each transaction occurs, all facets of the business are updated simultaneously. (At least, that's the theory. As you'll soon discover, we're not quite there, but almost.)

Types of Networks

There are many different network types. Types discussed in this chapter include

To learn more about what networks can do for you, see Chapter 2, "Why Do You Need a Network?"

➤ Local area networks (LANs)

➤ Controller area networks (CANs)

➤ Metropolitan area networks (MANs)

➤ Wide area networks (WANs)

➤ The Internet (the network of networks)

Let's briefly examine the advantages and disadvantages of each network type.

How many machines must you have before your system is deemed a network? Only two (though most network environments contain dozens or even hundreds of machines).

Local Area Networks (LANs)

Local area networks are normally confined to a single building or office (hence the term *local*). Essential components of a LAN are

➤ *Servers* Servers are machines that centralize data, management, security, or all three. System administrators or those with some degree of authority typically control servers.

➤ *Workstations* Workstations are machines on which network users do their work.

➤ *A network operating system* Network operating systems are operating systems specifically designed for networking. As such, they are capable of transmitting data over networks.

➤ *Communication links* Communication links are software and hardware designed to facilitate data transport.

To learn more about peer-to-peer networking, see Chapter 3, "Types of Networks."

As mentioned, these four components are essential elements of a LAN. However, LANs are not limited to these alone. In fact, LANs support many other devices, including printers, copiers, fax machines, and so on.

Your LAN's size will be determined by your particular needs. In small LAN schemes, you can sometimes take advantage of peer-to-peer networking, which allows workstations or PCs to interact without a centralized server. Such networks are generally less expensive, easier to establish, and far more manageable. In fact, peer-to-peer networks are ideal for small businesses.

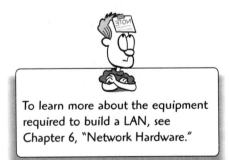

To learn more about the equipment required to build a LAN, see Chapter 6, "Network Hardware."

Chances are, you'll be building a LAN; if so, rejoice. Most mainstream software manufacturers have taken great pains to make small-business networking a snap. In particular, Microsoft, Novell, and Apple have refined easy networking to an art. In most cases, you can find everything you need to build an Ethernet LAN at your local computer store.

What the Heck is an Ethernet?

Ethernet is a LAN technology (originally developed by Xerox) that connects computers and transmits data between them. Data is packaged into small units called *frames* or *packets* and sent over wires. Today, Ethernet is the world's most popular networking technology (especially for small-to-medium sized networks).

Why do they call it Ethernet? Well, that's a strange story. Here's one version: Even 100 years ago, scientists believed that the emptiness between planetary and stellar bodies (the nothingness we call "space") actually contained an invisible substance called *Ether*. That theory has since been proven wrong (so wrong that in scientific circles, the term is now used in tongue-and-cheek fashion to characterize any weak explanation for phenomenon we don't understand, as in "Oh, it must be the Ether!") Because Ethernet was a fascinating (and to some, a puzzling) development, engineers coined the term *Ethernet*.

Pros of Local Area Networks

The following are pros of LANs:

➤ LANs offer efficient data transport between departments.

➤ Users can efficiently share network resources.

➤ LAN equipment is widely available and relatively inexpensive.

Cons of Local Area Networks

The following are cons of LANs:

➤ Heterogeneous LANs are rare. Networking different operating systems can involve a steep learning curve.

➤ Peer-to-peer LANs (the most common in small business) lack centralization, and their management is therefore difficult.

➤ Many LANs use proprietary protocols. Thus, you may encounter difficulty when meshing together LANs of disparate design.

Controller Area Networks (CANs)

Controller area networks (CANs) are quite specialized: They're designed for high-speed error checking, and are heavily insulated against electrical interference. For these reasons, CANs are often deployed in the automotive and aerospace industries (where communication transmissions typically coexist with equipment that emits electrical impulses).

In particular, CANs have formidable error-checking capabilities. In fact, the connection between CAN hosts and CAN networks is extremely tight—so tight that error checking can occur at the processor level. In this environment, nearly every message (and every shred of data) is checked for errors.

However, although CANs are fortified and precision-oriented, their fastidiousness comes at a heavy price. Unrelenting error checking eats substantial processor power, and this translates to slower transfer rates (even across high-speed transport media). For this reason, CANs are now specially designed to differentiate between messages that absolutely must be error checked and those that don't.

As you might suspect, CAN management and maintenance is complex and highly specialized. In fact, CAN administration and maintenance is so specialized that CAN experience may not necessarily qualify you for servicing other more garden-variety networks.

You'll probably never have occasion to use (or even see) a CAN. Today, CAN technology is employed most often for use with automobiles. For example, CANs are used to conduct computerized diagnostics, engine management, brake system control, fuel injection control, and so forth.

Pros of Controller Area Networks

The following are pros of CANs:

➤ CANs offer speed and exceptional reliability.

➤ CANs are resistant to electrical interference.

➤ CANs leave little room for human error.

Cons of Controller Area Networks

The following are cons of CANs:

➤ CANs aren't practical for human networking.

➤ CAN management represents a steep learning curve.

Metropolitan Area Networks (MANs)

Metropolitan area networks (sometimes called *campus networks*) are designed to transport data over large but still localized geographical regions. MANs are therefore suitable for networking a town, city, or university.

Most recently, MANs have employed fiber-optic cabling or other high-end digital media. These transport technologies offer incredible speeds, which is why MANs are often used at universities to connect departments for messaging, information transport, server sharing, and even collaborative computing.

Collaborative Computing

Collaborative computing is where folks work on the same project simultaneously, even though they're separated by considerable geographical distance. For example, imagine three architects reviewing blueprints together. Before collaborative computing, those architects had to be located in the same office (or if they weren't, they'd be looking at a fax). Collaborative computing changes all that. Today, those architects can be in different buildings and still work on their blueprints simultaneously and interactively. And because all participants can simultaneously see and alter the same data, they can collaborate more quickly and efficiently. This is collaborative computing at its best.

MANs, therefore, cover much more ground than LANs. LANs typically cover several offices in a single building; in contrast, a MAN can network several buildings, or even several campuses. This brings us to an interesting point: One MAN can be used to network several LANs together. That is, each campus might have its own LAN, and a MAN can be used as the glue between them.

If this sounds confusing, think back to our freeway analogy. If networks were freeways, LANs would be routes or minor highways, whereas MANs would be major freeways (but still not interstates). This analogy is quite accurate, because in most cases, MANs rarely extend beyond city limits.

MAN technology is becoming more popular. In fact, universities across the country have combined their efforts to network small cities. This process is tritely referred to as *MAN'ing* (as in, "I'm going to MAN that city," or, "Are you guys MAN'ed yet?") The University of Missouri and Southwest Missouri State University, for example, recently MAN'ed an entire city. If you ever drive cross-country and see heavy, shielded cabling attached to telephone poles, you may be driving along the perimeter of a MAN.

11

The MAN from Philadelphia

A good example of a MAN is the Commonwealth of Pennsylvania's Metropolitan Area Network (CPMAN). Designed to network government offices near the state capitol, CPMAN currently networks some 25,000 computers at speeds 10,000 times faster than standard modem links (at only 3% the cost of traditional telecommunication-based networking, meaning that the Commonwealth of Pennsylvania saved nearly $1 million annually by converting to MAN technology).

Pros of Metropolitan Area Networks

The following are pros of MANs:

➤ MANs are fast and efficient. In fact, many state agencies used new MAN technology to reduce their annual expenses by as much as 90%.

➤ MAN technology is on the bleeding edge and promises to change the future of networking.

Cons of Metropolitan Area Networks

The following are cons of MANs:

➤ MANs are rarely open to the public.

➤ MANs are large and difficult to maintain.

Wide Area Networks (WANs)

Wide area networks (WANs) cover enormous ground, connecting together schools, corporations, institutions, cities, and even countries. Typically, WANs are used to centralize data distribution. For example, consider a company in Chicago that manufacturers widgets. Suppose that company also has satellite offices in Los Angeles, New York, Orlando, and Honolulu. How can that company centralize its database but still propagate up-to-date information to all branch offices? The best solution is to employ a WAN.

To implement such a WAN, the company connects its offices via *landlines*, special telephone lines that provide high-speed transmission of data between states.

Here, it's useful to backtrack to our freeway analogy again. In that analogy, if LANs are minor thoroughfares and MANs are major freeways, WANs are interstate highways. Indeed, a WAN could easily be composed of several interconnected MANs, which in turn hold together dozens of LANs.

Wide Area Networks that are out of this world

If you'd like to check out WANs in action, go here:

`http://bernoulli.gsfc.nasa.gov/ebnet/Topologies/current_1297.asp`

This Internet site houses an interactive, clickable map of various WAN connections between research centers at NASA, the Jet Propulsion Laboratory, and other space research sites. If you click individual locations, the Web server will show you what hardware and software is in use at the specified location. Altogether, it's a great place to learn more about WAN networking.

Pros of Wide Area Networks

The following are pros of WANs:

➤ WANs can network thousands of machines.

➤ WANs move huge amounts of data that would otherwise be difficult to transport.

➤ WANs allow your firm to operate on a global level.

Cons of Wide Area Networks

The following are cons of WANs:

➤ WANs require extremely expensive hardware and software.

➤ WAN connectivity charges are steep.

➤ WANs are difficult to manage, often requiring whole teams of technicians.

The Internet: A Network of Networks

Finally, there's the largest network of all: the Internet. Often called the *network of networks*, the Internet is worldwide. To illustrate the Internet's structure, we need to go back a few years.

In 1962, anticipating a possible atomic disaster (and no doubt troubled by the Cuban Missile Crisis), the U.S. Air Force charged a small group of researchers with a formidable task: creating a communication network that could survive a nuclear attack. Their concept was revolutionary: a network that had no centralized control. If one (or 10, or 100) of its nodes were destroyed, the system would continue to run. In essence, this network (designed exclusively for military use) would survive the apocalypse itself (even if we didn't).

At the time, no such network had ever been constructed and, therefore, researchers were left to use their imaginations (and did they ever!). From that rather nebulous beginning, a network called the Advanced Research Projects Agency Network (or ARPAnet) emerged. ARPAnet was primitive, not even closely resembling the Internet of today. It consisted of four computers linked by telephone to various academic institutions (Stanford Research Institute, the University of Utah, the University of California at Los Angeles, and the University of California at Santa Barbara).

By 1975, however, ARPAnet had grown considerably. What started as a fledgling think-tank study had mushroomed into a fully functional communication system. So, in that year, the U.S. Defense Communications Agency (later the Defense Information Systems Agency) assumed control of the network and if Fate had not intervened, things would have remained just so.

Instead, the years that followed brought many changes. For a time, Internet access was available only to military, academic, and research personnel. During those Dark and Middle Ages, privileged folks did much to improve the Internet's efficiency, but their work went unnoticed by the world at large. Only in the early 1980s was the Internet exposed to daylight. From that point on, changes occurred rapidly.

Sometime between 1982 and 1985, the Internet as we now know it was born. The number of hosts increased to several hundred, and it seemed to researchers even then that the Internet was massive. Sometime in 1986, the first freely available public access server was established on the Net. It was only a matter of time—a mere decade, as it turned out—before humanity would storm the beach of cyberspace; a previously hidden world, teaming with information, would soon come alive with the clamor of merchants peddling their wares.

By 1990, the number of Internet hosts exceeded 300,000. For a variety of reasons, the U.S. government released its hold on the network in this year, leaving it to the National Science Foundation (NSF). In turn, the NSF instituted strong restrictions against commercial Internet use. However, in 1991, amidst debates over cost (operating the Internet backbone required substantial resources), NSF suddenly relinquished its authority, opening the way for commercial entities to flood the Internet.

The rest (as you will soon read) is history. To date, the Internet is the largest and most comprehensive structure ever designed by humankind. Providing widespread interconnectivity through the international telephone system, today's Internet is a superhighway populated by thousands of WANs, MANs, LANs, and even personal computers. Indeed, the term *Information Superhighway* is an apt (if somewhat trendy) label. In short, the Internet is massive.

Still Other Networks

Although the aforementioned network types are the most traditional, new technologies are constantly emerging. For example, it was recently theorized that WAN costs could be dramatically reduced if only the Internet could be used as the transport medium.

VPNs

This led to the development of *virtual private networks* or *VPNs*. These are private, isolated networks that use the Internet as a communication conduit. Using such a network, companies save hundreds of thousands (and sometimes millions) of dollars on leased line fees. Unfortunately, VPN technology is in its infancy, and security issues still exist. After all, you're sending your private, sensitive, corporate data over a public network. If built-in VPN security features fail, your trade secret information could be exposed to the world.

To learn more about network security issues, please see Chapter 13, "Security."

Intranets

Later, you'll also read about *intranets*. Intranets are small, self-contained, microcosmic versions of the Internet. Using an intranet, you can make your help desk available to all departments via Web browsers (such as Netscape Communicator or Microsoft Internet Explorer). Essentially, in an intranet, your network behaves exactly like the Internet does.

You might be wondering why anyone would want their network to emulate the Internet. Actually, there's an excellent reason: interoperability. (Oh no, another 50-cent word!) *Interoperability* is a term that describes any system in which machines of diverse architecture realize similar results. In other words, in an intranet, users can access data through the same procedure no matter what machine they use (whether an IBM compatible, a Macintosh, or a UNIX system).

To learn more about intranets, see Chapter 17, "Intranets, Extranets, and the Internet."

However, we're getting too narrow in our classifications. The word *intranet* is a fancy name for any LAN that runs Internet communication protocols. When it comes right down to it, that's all an intranet really is.

15

Where Are These Networks?

So, you've read about several different network types. Now, you're probably wondering where these networks are used. You're probably also wondering which network type is best for you. Don't worry—we address that issue later in great detail.

In fact, networks are everywhere, though they may not always be readily apparent. To give you a sense of how pervasive networks truly are, we've prepared a short list. Networks are used for all the following purposes:

➤ Cable and satellite networks deliver news and entertainment to your television.

➤ CAN networks probably run your car's steering, braking, heating, cooling, and diagnostic systems.

➤ MANs deliver electricity to your home.

➤ LANs manage storage, pricing, stock, and tracking procedures in supermarkets, drug stores, hospitals, and warehouses.

In nearly every important concern (from online electronic library catalogs to criminal records systems), networks play a major part in our lives. And the advent of the Internet will only increase the network's role.

For example, many companies are now networking to reduce cost. One popular method is to allow employees to telecommute. This is where employees work from home, using personal computers. In the past, such programs were simply too expensive (largely due to connection charges). The Internet has changed all that because it provides inexpensive connectivity.

Where To From Here?

This book should prepare you for most networking environments, taking you from the very simplest networking tasks all the way to network administration. However, before we embark on that journey, we still have a few basics to cover.

In this chapter, we defined what a network is. In Chapter 2, "Why Do You Need a Network," you'll examine why you need a network and what networks can do for you.

The Least You Need to Know

Right now, the least you need to know about networks is this:

➤ A network is a series of computers that can communicate with one another by virtue of their interconnectivity.

➤ Any system that interconnects two or more computers is technically a network.

➤ Networks facilitate communication either over short distances (office-to-office) or over wide geographic areas (country-to-country).

➤ You can use networks to streamline your business.

➤ As the Internet becomes popular, networking will become essential in business (and perhaps personal life).

## Chapter 2

Why Do You Need a Network?

In This Chapter

➤ Understand the kinds of computer resources you can share on a network.

➤ Learn how networks can facilitate communication and collaboration.

➤ Understand how administrators can efficiently manage computer resources via a network.

If you have more than one computer in your home or business, you can benefit from a network. Why? Because, as your Mom probably told you, "It's nice to share." With a network, your islands of computers and information become communities of shared resources. Great cost and time efficiency can be gained with a computer network. Printers, modems, and backup devices can easily be shared, resulting in lower costs and easier maintenance. Software applications can be stored and distributed from a few places on the network instead of on every computer.

With a network, the administration of computers in an organization can be centralized. A network administrator can efficiently manage groups of computers, leaving users free to focus more on their work than on keeping their computers running. So if you have recently found yourself running from computer to computer to get your work done, a computer network might be the solution that keeps you in your seat.

SneakerNet: The Low-Tech, Non-Network Non-Solution

Those who don't connect their computers in a network sometimes resort to a *SneakerNet* as a means of sharing computing resources. With a SneakerNet, you use other computer resources by copying your files onto floppy disks and running them down the hall (wearing sneakers is preferable—hence the name). Then you typically kick the computer's owner out of his chair so you can use his printer, application program, or whatever on your files. With a real network, you can get the job done faster, and without annoying your friends.

Why Create Your Own Network?

Creating your own computer network brings together the computing resources in your home, business, or organization in a way that saves money and increases efficiency. Unlike the Internet, in which you are a visitor to others' resources, your own network offers you the capability to:

➤ Selectively share your computer hardware and software throughout your organization.

➤ Control the security of your computer resources.

➤ Efficiently upgrade and maintain your computers.

➤ Offer an environment where people can easily exchange information and collaborate on projects.

In addition to encouraging your people to share resources, having a private network also enables you to obtain the benefits of large public networks such as the Internet. Often a private network offers a connection to the Internet so local users can access the World Wide Web. To protect the boundary between the private and public network, you can add a *firewall* to limit the traffic across that boundary. With a firewall, anonymous outside users might not have access to the computers behind the firewall. However, your users can probably browse the Web freely.

The bottom line is that when you create your own network, you can decide what resources are shared and who can share them. In most cases, that means striking a balance between making resources available to users on the local network and safe from users outside the local network.

Sharing Resources

When you bought your first PC, whether for work or play, no doubt you soon found that you needed a printer to print documents. Next you probably added software packages to do finances or play games. Then you might have added a backup device to protect your data and a modem to reach the Internet. When a second computer arrived at your door, you faced the prospect of purchasing the same set of add-ons again. A network can limit what you have to spend by enabling you to share hardware devices, application programs, and even the space on your hard disk.

Sharing Hardware

One of the primary uses of a *local area network* (*LAN*) in a small office is to share hardware devices. With proper security in place, sharing hardware devices on *wide area networks* (*WANs*) can be very useful too. (For example, you can print a report for someone at the home office while you are at a branch location.) Here are some of the devices you'll most likely want to share:

➤ Printers

➤ Backup devices

➤ Modems

Sharing Printers

Instead of buying cheap printers for every PC in the office, you can buy a couple of high-speed, high-resolution printers that can be accessed from the network. On the whole, you'll save money and your users will get higher-quality documents printed faster.

Printers can either be added directly to the network or attached to a computer and made available to other users on the network. Typically, the computer's owner needs to advertise the availability of the printer before users from other computers can use it. Once the printer is available, users select it from a list of printers when they go to print a document.

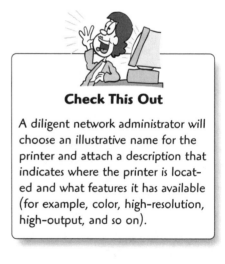

Check This Out

A diligent network administrator will choose an illustrative name for the printer and attach a description that indicates where the printer is located and what features it has available (for example, color, high-resolution, high-output, and so on).

Check This Out

Often a clerical worker is assigned to keep the paper trays and ink cartridges full, freeing other workers to focus on their work. Freeing most workers from computer maintenance is a major advantage to using networks; you'll notice that this is a recurring theme throughout this chapter.

Sharing Backup Devices

You only have to lose important files because of a disk crash or errant erasure once to understand the importance of backing up your files. For most people, backing up files means copying their most important work on to floppy disks and tossing the disks in a desk drawer. However, when the data on your computer is more critical than old copies of letters to Aunt Martha, keeping that data safe requires a more structured approach. Sharing one or more backup devices on a network is a great way to begin solidifying your backup plans.

Having one backup device (or set of devices) used for backing up data from lots of computers results in cost savings. Time savings can come from taking the backup process out of the hands of the user and making it an administrator's job to set the schedule and run the backups.

With a LAN for a small business, you can probably use a common Iomega Zip Drive or Jazz Drive (capable of backing up 100MB or more at a time). Tape devices are common backup media for large computer installations.

What Does Backup Mean?

To back up your data means to make an additional copy of that data on some medium so that if the original is destroyed, a copy still exists. Often, copies are made on portable media (tapes or removable disks) so that they can be stored safely offsite.

Because your data files are constantly changing, backing up critical information is an ongoing process. Automated backups over a network can make backups painless (and invisible) to users.

Sharing Modems

Although most computers come with built-in modems these days, most houses and small business are not equipped with multiple telephone lines for computer communications. It won't do much good for everyone to have a modem if only one person at a time can dial out to the Internet. If the computers in your home or business are connected to a LAN, it can be cost-effective to route all Internet traffic from your location through a single modem. Here's how it works:

➤ Each computer on the LAN is configured so requests to the Internet are directed to a single computer on the LAN.

➤ The single computer is configured as a router—routing communications between the LAN and the Internet.

➤ Traffic between the router and the Internet is sent over the computer's modem, possibly connected to ISDN, frame relay, or other high-speed connections.

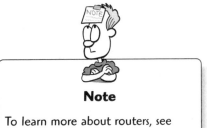

Note

To learn more about routers, see Chapter 6, "Network Hardware."

By purchasing a single high-speed modem, you can save a few dollars on each computer and have a faster connection to the Internet. Also, after you have dialed in, the connection is accessible to everyone on your LAN. The following figure illustrates a configuration where multiple PCs on a LAN can connect simultaneously to the Internet via a single modem.

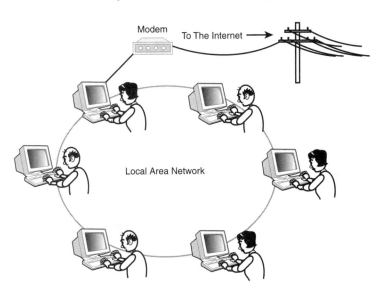

Modem   To The Internet

Local Area Network

Routing LAN Internet traffic through a modem.

Sharing Software

Purchasing, installing, and maintaining the applications your users employ on their computers can be both costly and time consuming. With your network in place, you can potentially run software from any computer connected to the network. This can have several benefits:

Check This Out

A higher-speed Internet connection (higher than 28.8Kbps or 56Kbps) usually requires expenses beyond the cost of the modem; your phone company will charge to bring a high-speed line to your place, and your ISP might charge extra to support the higher speed.

➤ You can possibly purchase fewer copies of the applications you need. Some programs use floating licenses, which enable a certain number of users to use a program at a time. Check with the licensing agreement that came with the software to see what your limitations are.

➤ You can save yourself the trouble of installing the program on every computer on a network and conserve the disk space the application uses on each computer.

➤ When an application needs to be upgraded, you can change it in fewer locations. Every user who runs that program automatically picks up the latest copy of the program.

Mechanisms for sharing applications among computers on the network typically fall into one of the following categories:

➤ *Microsoft Windows environments*   Because networking came as an afterthought to Windows operating systems, application sharing is not inherent to the design of Windows. Instead, Microsoft offers *NetMeeting*—an add-on to the Internet Explorer suite that contains application-sharing functions. Besides offering the capability to share programs, application sharing enables several users on different computers to collaborate using the same program simultaneously.

Check This Out

There are versions of the X Window System that run on Microsoft Windows systems. This allows applications running on UNIX servers to be displayed and used from Windows environments.

➤ *UNIX and the X Window System*   Most computers that run UNIX as their operating system use the X Window System (or X for short), an interface that is designed to share applications on a network. X controls the graphical user interface used by UNIX. Beyond that, however, X provides a framework that allows applications to potentially run on any computer on a network, and then be displayed and worked with by any other computer display on the network.

➤ *Application servers*   Dedicated application servers (such as Novell's NetWare servers) can be used to store applications that are actually run from a PC or workstation. A user simply connects to the server and runs the application as though it were stored on the local hard disk.

When sharing application programs on a network, there are a few issues that you might find confusing at first: where a shared application is actually running and the resources to which the application has access. This is best illustrated with an example of sharing an application between two UNIX systems. Let's say that a word-processing program is stored on computer A and is launched by a user on computer B. When the program is launched, it runs on computer A and merely appears on computer B's display. As a result

➤ The program uses the CPU from computer A. If the processor on computer A is slow, the user on computer B might wonder why the program is running so slowly when there is no other activity on computer B. Likewise, if the server is more powerful (which is often the case), a program might actually run faster over the network than it does locally.

➤ Files accessed and modified by the program take computer A's view of the file system. So, for example, if the user on computer B tries to save a file, the user might be surprised to see a pop-up window that shows the files and folders that exist on computer A.

➤ The application appears in a window on the user's display screen. Using the mouse and keyboard, the user can work with the application as though it were running locally. (The fact that an X application is running remotely is in most ways transparent to the user.)

If you think about it, the X Window System not only provides an opportunity for sharing applications, it also offers a means of distributing computer resources at the same time. So, for example, a less powerful or overburdened computer can draw on other computers' CPUs and file systems to obtain better performance.

Besides those methods for sharing software mentioned previously, there are a variety of third-party solutions you can use to distribute and run software using a network. One example is Novell's Z.E.N.Works, which provides a mechanism not only for distributing applications over the network but also for automatically updating application software to hundreds of users.

Techno Talk

If a shared application is graphics intensive (such as a drawing program), it might run slower over the network than it does locally. However, an application that is CPU-intensive (for example, one that crunches numbers) can run faster over a network if the remote computer is more powerful than the local one.

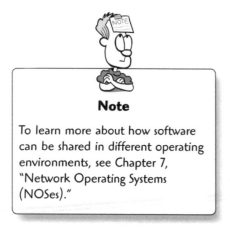

Note

To learn more about how software can be shared in different operating environments, see Chapter 7, "Network Operating Systems (NOSes)."

Sharing Files, Folders, and Disk Space

Besides expanding the computer hardware and software available to you, a network can expand your file system. In theory, any computer you can reach on the network can open its file system to you, enabling you to access its files and use its storage space.

Without a network, you are probably used to saving your files on a local hard disk (often the disk labeled C: on Microsoft Windows systems). By accessing file servers—such as a NetWare server—remote file systems can be represented by additional drive letters that, given proper permissions, enable you to retrieve or save files as though they exist locally.

Other methods for sharing file systems include the Network File System (NFS) feature that is available from most UNIX systems. With NFS, remote file systems can be connected right into a local file system tree. As a result, you probably won't even know whether the files you are using are local or remote—unless you are the network administrator.

Communicating and Collaborating

When you are connected to a network, communication can flow freely between the users on that network. Not only can you send messages to others, you can also interact with others in real-time. For example, you can take part in live chats, participate in conferences, or share applications simultaneously.

Electronic Mail (Email)

One of the first, and still very popular, uses of computer networks was to send email. Type a message, enter an address, and click Send to have your message delivered to one or hundreds of users who reside in any place that can be reached by your network. Using an email reader, users can open mail messages, read them, save them, respond to them, forward them, and remove them.

The first email messages were quite simple, consisting of typed words created with simple text editors and read with character-based mail readers. Over the years, new features have been added to most email programs. New email programs for creating and sending email now include features that help it integrate with the Internet's World Wide Web. Here are some examples:

➤ *Attachments*   One of the first major enhancements to email enabled users to attach additional data files to a mail message. Besides the typed message, the mail message can now include a graphic file, audio file, word-processing document, and so forth.

When you receive a message with an attachment, you might see an icon such as a paper clip alongside the message. Click the paper clip to select the file, and the mail reader probably gives you a choice of either opening the attachment or saving it to your hard disk. Because data within a mail message can be associated with a particular MIME type, your computer can choose the appropriate application (graphics reader, audio player, and so on) to handle the data.

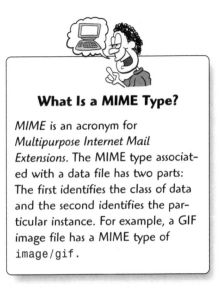

What Is a MIME Type?

MIME is an acronym for *Multipurpose Internet Mail Extensions.* The MIME type associated with a data file has two parts: The first identifies the class of data and the second identifies the particular instance. For example, a GIF image file has a MIME type of `image/gif`.

➤ *Web Content*   Within the body of a mail message, many mail composers/readers enable you to include HTML code. Therefore, instead of just creating a plain text message, you can include most anything that can appear on a Web page. For example, you can use colors, different font sizes and types, and images in your messages.

Clicking links within an email message can open a Web browser automatically and display the target of the link. Therefore, you can send an email telling a friend to check out your new Web page and include the address of the page in the message. When your friend receives the message and clicks on your under-lined Web address, the page opens.

Check This Out

Because not all email readers can handle HTML, it is not appropriate to include HTML in all messages. For example, if you are submitting a message to a public newsgroup, some of the users who subscribe to the group might be using a text-only mail reader.

Newsgroups

Newsgroups create forums for discussing nearly any topic imaginable among people on a network. USENET, the public mechanism used to distribute newsgroup messages on the Internet, contains more than 17,000 newsgroups—and it's growing larger every day. Private organizations with their own networks can support their own news servers, which can be used to share data among members of the organization (such as information about company projects, health plans, or events).

Collaboration

Some applications are designed to enable you to communicate *live* with other users on your network. Many of these programs, such as online chat rooms or games, are mostly for fun, whereas others, such as conferencing, can be used for serious business. Here are some applications that enable you to work or play with real live people on the network:

➤ *Live chats*　Chat rooms (also referred to as message boards) enable you to type messages that appear to everyone who has entered the "room." Anyone can respond to messages in the chat area by simply typing their own messages. A private network can use chat rooms to carry on conversations among members of an organization. These conversations can take the form of typed forums for topics of interest to the organization. On the Internet, however, there are literally thousands of chat rooms, most of which are related to a particular topic. For example, you can find chat rooms to discuss counter-terrorism, the Green Bay Packers, or *Gilligan's Island*.

➤ *Games*　As long as there have been computer networks, there have been games to play over them. (The creators of USENET newsgroups were big on exchanging chess moves online.) Today, the range of games available for network play is staggering. For traditional gamers, there are online games of Chess, Bridge, Hearts, and more. For high-tech gamers, there are 3D animated war and strategy games that can be played against others on a network. Examples of high-tech games include Doom, Quake II, and Total Annihilation. If you have a LAN in your home, you can square off against your family members in the games of your choice. Many freeware and shareware games are available.

➤ *Conferencing*　For business, conferencing is one of the most practical applications of computer networks. Both audio and video conferencing facilities are readily available for use over standard networks such as the Internet. Using software products—such as Microsoft NetMeeting—and adding a video camera and microphone, you can conference with anyone on a network that is similarly equipped. Because there are computer conferencing standards in place today, you can use a variety of products to communicate in a single conference. As an alternative, Internet User Locator Service (ILS) directory servers provide central locations for getting conference participants together. A user can sign on to an ILS and appear on a listing showing people who are ready to conference. Conference members can then select that user listing and sign on to the conference.

➤ *Whiteboards* By running whiteboard software, a group of users on a network can view an identical whiteboard window. Using a mouse and keyboard, anyone connected to the shared whiteboard can type words, draw, or add graphics to the whiteboard for anyone to see. With bundled software such as NetMeeting, whiteboards can be used with audio, video, or chat software to carry on conversations in addition to the whiteboard diagrams.

➤ *Internet telephony* Internet telephony products can be used to make telephone calls over the Internet that cost nothing more than the cost of your Internet connection. The first Internet telephony products provided PC-to-PC calls. Newer products, however, enable you to call real telephones from your PC without incurring long-distance charges.

Centralized Administration

As easy as using computers and software has become, some maintenance is still required to keep computer equipment up and running. Sharing computer resources on the network can remove the responsibility for maintaining those resources from most of the users on the network.

By assigning a network administrator to your network, many computing tasks can be centrally managed. As a result, the network users can focus on the work they have to do for your organization, rather than on how to get their computers to work the way they want. Here are some of the ways that resources on a network can be centrally managed:

➤ *Network backups* By centralizing a schedule for backing up the computers on your network, each user can forget about having to back up his or her own data. An administrator can manage a large backup medium (perhaps handling gigabytes of data at a time), and a backup schedule can back up data over the network once a week, every day, or every few hours (depending on the importance of the data).

➤ *Computer configuration* Complex computer configurations can be managed by the network administrator so that each computer is automatically set up to work on the network and have the organization's look and feel. Here are a couple of examples of how a computer's configuration can be updated over a network:

> ➤ On a network containing UNIX computers, a feature called bootp allows each client computer to automatically gather most of the information it needs to run on the network each time the computer starts. Updated information about domains and servers can be obtained each time a client boots up.

> ➤ With Netscape's Netcaster, an organization can distribute a complete desktop interface. The interface can set the background, icons, and menus that appear on every desktop. So, for example, desktops can be continually updated so that the latest company information is only a click away.

➤ *Software distribution*   Software that users need to do their jobs can be down-loaded automatically to their computer (or added to application servers that are easily accessible). The larger an organization is, the more savings can be obtained by distributing software centrally instead of installing at each physical computer. (Some of the issues involved in software distribution were described in the section titled "Sharing Software.") From an administrator's standpoint, central software distribution means that everyone gets the latest software, using the safest security measures, without a lot of running around.

➤ *Security policies*   Information is the lifeblood of most organizations. Customer data, product specifications, and inventory information need to be stored safely and often need to be accessed widely. Rarely do you want the only copy of important company information on someone's PC. Centrally managing file servers and databases of information enables a company to set security policies that meet the company's requirements. This means providing user passwords, firewalls (to control access from outside the local network), and different security levels.

Where To From Here?

After reading this chapter, you have a better idea about what you can do with a network. In particular, you understand how networks save money by enabling you to share computing resources (printers, disk space, software, and so on) and increase efficiency by allowing for central administration.

Chapter 3, "Types of Networks," describes the different types of networks you can choose. For each type of network (peer-to-peer and client/server), the relative advantages and disadvantages are discussed. This information will help you choose the kind of network that is best for you.

The Least You Need to Know

Right now, the least you need to know about what you can do with networks is this:

➤ You can save money by sharing hardware devices, such as printers and backup media, among several computers.

➤ You can use software applications that reside on other computers.

➤ You can save and access files that are stored on other computers.

➤ You can communicate with other people using features such as electronic mail or newsgroups.

➤ You can collaborate with other people using live chats, audio/video conferencing, and whiteboards, and by playing multi-user games.

➤ You can control groups of computers to efficiently manage data backups, computer configurations, software distribution, and security policies.

Part 2
Learning the Network Terrain

A network is like plumbing: You just connect some pipes and attach them to your favorite appliances. Pretty soon, everything will flow in the right direction to the right places.

Okay, so a network might be a bit different from plumbing. With networks there are topologies, architectures, and protocols representing how they are constructed. Instead of pipes and valves you have cables, routers, and hubs connecting everything. Furthermore, instead of sinks and tubs you have desktop computers, server computers, printers, and other devices sending and receiving stuff on the network.

Chapters in this part describe the different components that fit together to form computer networks.

## Chapter 3

Types of Networks

> ➤ Learn about common network types.
>
> ➤ Learn the pros and cons of different network models.
>
> ➤ Learn what networks can do and how they do it.
>
> ➤ Learn how to establish a basic network.

My, how things have changed! Before networking was first invented, transferring data from one machine to another was a major event.

In the computer Stone Age, for example, direct file transfer wasn't an option. Instead, when technicians wanted to duplicate their work from one machine to the next, they had to manually re-enter it.

Later, computer scientists took a giant step forward: the punch card. This was a small card on which you could record information by punching holes in it. Machines could read the patterns of those holes and thus, punch cards introduced a simple (or not so simple) method of storing and transferring data. (Of course, it took hundreds of punch cards to store one program and woe to you if you dropped them. If the cards were shuffled out of sequence, you were out of luck.)

Next came the infamous tape system, the kind you've probably seen in science fiction films: thick, unwieldy reels of tape attached to machines so large, they filled an entire room.

In all these scenarios, file transfer was a major pain. Looking back now, it's incredible how far we've come in just 30 years. On the average day, billions of files are transferred over the Internet. Often, users initiate those transfers with ease, with the click of a mouse.

So, this much is true: Networks have revolutionized our way of doing business. They make data exchange easy and occasionally even fun. More importantly, however, networks allow us to increase our productivity and efficiency, and in doing so, they save us money.

The problem is, before you actually build your network, you must first choose the network type that's best for you. This is no easy choice, either. Some networks are perfect for large-scale enterprises while others are more suitable for small businesses. This chapter will help you make that decision.

The Two Network Types

The two most common network types in use today are

➤ Peer-to-peer networks

➤ Client/server networks

Each works differently, and each has certain advantages over the other. In this chapter, you'll learn about those advantages and which network type will most effectively satisfy your needs.

Peer-to-Peer Networks

Peer-to-peer networks are typically small (10 workstations or fewer) and are nearly always local area networks (LANs). Their chief characteristic is this: They have no centralized server and, therefore, no centralized control.

Instead, in peer-to-peer networks, each workstation has roughly the same capabilities as its peers. In this respect, peer-to-peer networks offer you the bare minimum: the ability to share files, peripherals, and other resources.

Advantages of Peer-to-Peer Networks

The principal advantages of peer-to-peer networks are *simplicity* and *economy*—simplicity because peer-to-peer networks take only minutes to establish, and economy because the requisite hardware and software are quite inexpensive. Buy a few PCs, Windows 98, and a network kit—typically four Ethernet cards and a hub—and you're good to go.

In a peer-to-peer network, printers, scanners, and fax machines can be shared, as shown in the following figure. Thus, any connected peer can access remote peripherals. This allows a user at Workstation 3 to print from a printer connected to Workstation 1.

Likewise, all workstations can share directories and files. Therefore, a user at Workstation 3 can transfer files from Workstation 1, as shown in the second following figure.

To learn more about networking hardware (like hubs and network cards), see Chapter 6, "Network Hardware."

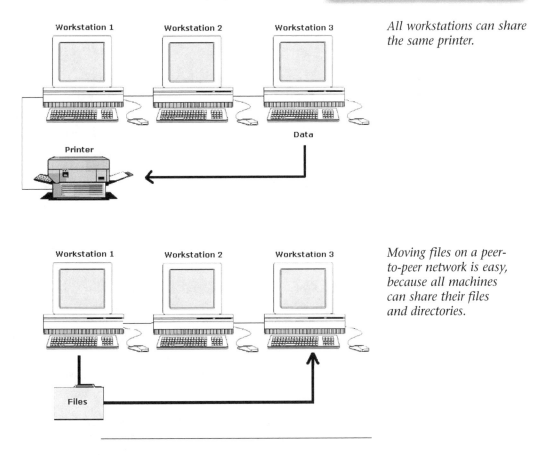

All workstations can share the same printer.

Moving files on a peer-to-peer network is easy, because all machines can share their files and directories.

In these respects, peer-to-peer networks give you the most networking bang for your buck. To set up such a network takes less than an hour. To learn how, see Chapter 10, "Case Study: Building a Windows SOHO System."

Disadvantages of Peer-to-Peer Networks

The principal disadvantages of peer-to-peer networking are physical limitations and lack of centralized control.

The physical limitations in peer-to-peer networks are stringent. For example, all workstations must be located in the same general area, such as in the same office or, at the very least, in the same building. For this reason, peer-to-peer networks are employed chiefly by small businesses.

We might have given you the impression that peer-to-peer networks cannot be networked with the world at large. That's not entirely true. In fact, it's possible to tie several peer-to-peer networks together using remote communication. Thus, one peer-to-peer network in one building can send information to a similar network in another. This is accomplished through telecommunication, a subject we examine closely in Chapter 16, "Enabling Telecommuting." However, it is true that each peer-to-peer network is a single entity and rather self-contained. (By default, such networks were not intended for long-range communication).

Another disadvantage of peer-to-peer networks is the lack of centralized control. This leads to two serious problems:

➤ *Limited resource potential*   Since there's no dedicated server to handle file and print sharing administration, peer-to-peer networking may not be practical for intensive file transfer/storage or heavy printer-sharing applications.

➤ *Management and security issues*   Because there's no centralized security or administration authority, peer-to-peer networks are difficult to manage. If you exceed 3–5 users with this type of network, management can become confusing and downright unwieldy.

The degree of trouble you'll encounter is directly related to your network's size. For example, consider enforcing a security policy in a peer-to-peer network. To do so, you must configure user restrictions on each individual workstation. If you have 100 workstations, that could take all day. (Think about that, walking from machine to machine, performing an identical task, over and over again.) At that point, it's probably better to switch to a client/server network.

Client/Server Networks

In client/server networks, workstations rely on data and services from one or more centralized servers. These servers can control various systems including applications, printing, communication, and administration.

Client/Server Semantics

The term *client/server* actually originated in the programming community. It refers to a programming model where a single server—typically an application—can distribute data to many clients. (For example, the relationship between a Web server and Web clients or *browsers*.) Many network applications and protocols are based on the client/server model. However, in recent years, the terms *client* and *server* have been more generally applied to machines that run either client or server software. The distinction is now minor (because the more recent interpretation is in wide use).

Advantages of Client/Server Networks

The principal advantages of client/server networks are centralization, security, and logging capabilities. Let's talk about these for a moment.

Centralization

Centralization is a powerful advantage for several reasons. First, it allows easier and more efficient management. This is especially true in reference to file storage. By enforcing centralized file storage, you proof your system against even the most disorganized employees.

The truth is, even folks who are exceptionally organized in other areas of their life may lack organization in their computing. I would estimate that 80% of all computer users have useless files cluttering their root directory. Worse still, most users have such files scattered across their hard disk drives. (You know the drill. They install a game, find that it doesn't work, and forget to uninstall it. Or worse, they give their directories ambiguous names, names that don't even remotely reflect their purpose.)

In a centralized file-management environment, *you* control file and directory names, locations, sizes, and so on. The drawback to this, of course, is that you're responsible for organization.

To learn more about network security (and how client/server networks help implement it), see Chapter 13, "Security."

Security

Another key advantage of client/server networks is increased security. Most client/server environments have discretionary access control, which allows you to incisively grant or deny access to files, directories, and resources based on user, host, time, or date.

For example, you can specify that Joe User can access the SYS:ETC directory only from his own workstation (and then only between the hours of 8:00 a.m. and 5:00 p.m.) In peer-to-peer networking, this type of stringent security policy cannot be enforced (or at least, not without purchasing and installing third-party security suites).

Logging

Finally, client/server networks typically have excellent logging facilities, allowing you to debug your network sessions. This is in contrast to most peer-to-peer configurations, which by default keep few or even no logs.

Disadvantages of Client/Server Networks

➤ *Centralization*   While centralized resources and management are definite advantages, if your servers go down, so does your productivity. Clients rely on the server for data. In most cases, if the server dies, your clients die with it. For this reason, you should always have several, full-featured workstations on hand.

➤ *Complexity*   Client/server networks are more difficult to configure and administer. This can add to your cost (for example, you may have to train your staff).

➤ *Expense*   Server operating systems, software, and hardware are more expensive than their peer-to-peer counterparts.

A Brief Look at the Client/Server World

For the moment, let's abandon the advantages and disadvantages of client/server networks in favor of how such networks are designed. We'll begin with clients.

Clients

Clients are PCs or workstations on which users run applications. Clients rely on servers for resources, such as files, devices, and even processing power. Many times, a client is nothing more than this: an application or machine designed specifically to access data that is centrally housed on a server.

There are many types of clients, including

➤ Thin clients

➤ Diskless clients

➤ Fat clients

➤ Workstations

Let's take a look at each one now.

Thin Clients

Thin clients are machines or processes that have only the bare minimum in localized software. Their express purpose is to interact with a centralized server. Whenever thin client users need to run a program, they download that program from the server. Such thin clients are used in networks where servers perform all the data processing. In this respect, thin clients are a throwback to the dawn of networking.

In the old days, networks were controlled by mainframes—powerful, centralized machines that could perform millions of tasks per second. Since data processing was done on the mainframe alone, users didn't need much horsepower. Instead, they used terminals: machines specially designed to communicate with mainframes. Terminals lacked hard disk drives, floppy disk drives, or other storage devices. In fact, terminals even lacked application software. Instead, they housed the bare minimum: firmware necessary to establish a network connection. Today's thin clients are only slightly more functional, and could be aptly characterized as fancy terminals.

What Is Firmware?

Firmware is software that's embedded in a chip on the motherboard. (In other words, firmware is a permanent fixture and doesn't need a hard disk to run.) The term is appropriate because firmware is technically both hardware and software. If you've ever used the BIOS or CMOS on a PC, you were dealing with firmware.

Thin clients offer some major advantages. For example, they're quite inexpensive, and not just in the short-term. Because thin clients are identically configured—and since they contain practically no adjustable components—their maintenance is a snap. (Moreover, users can't change the settings of a thin client and, therefore, they get no opportunity to foul things up!) This leads to lower Total Cost of Ownership.

Total Cost of Ownership (TCO) is the dollar amount a computer will cost you in its lifetime. (Machines don't really have lifetimes, of course. We simply use that term as a reference.) A machine's lifetime ends when it finally blows up, shuts down, becomes obsolete, or becomes permanently inoperable.

What Does It Mean in Dollars and Cents?

According to Gartner Group (a research firm), TCO for a PC is approximately $9,784. This figure encompasses both fixed and averaged variable costs, including purchase, administration, technical support, upgrades, and repair. In contrast, thin clients cost only one third that much.

To learn more about terminals and network computers, please see Chapter 6.

Right now, there's a strong thin client movement in networking. Many firms (Sun Microsystems and Netscape Communications, for example) are advocating thin client use, particularly in the UNIX world. In fact, Sun has developed specialized thin clients called *network computers*, or NCs. These machines are designed expressly to communicate with servers.

True thin client advocates are purists who feel that processor power and storage potential should be maximized. Thus, they promote total centralized computing. Their argument has more than a little merit: It's a fact that users rarely utilize more than 20% of their workstation's power and resources.

However, still another thin client school exists, and its chief evangelists are Microsoft and Intel. Their view is more moderate, perhaps, advocating beefier, not-so-thin clients. These machines differ from their purist counterparts in one important way: The beefier clients tend to have more software installed. Microsoft probably sees network computers as a potential threat. Hence, it has developed solutions that resemble network computer functionality but still build Microsoft software into the equation.

Either way, thin clients are only practical for large enterprises and here's why: Small businesses typically use commercial-off-the-shelf (COTS) applications such as Microsoft Word and Excel. Thin clients generally cannot run these applications, and those that run miniaturized, "networked" versions only offer limited functionality. Small business users need more, including local applications, local CD-ROM systems, local storage, and so on. Thin clients are most useful for networking proprietary systems, such as those used in retail or in production environments.

Also, populating your office with thin clients can expose you to problems with resource availability. For example, if the server's down, a thin client is useless. Remember that thin clients rely almost entirely on their server, even for the simplest task.

Finally, thin clients—while offering low TCO—are not as inexpensive as they first appear. This is because thin clients usually rely on proprietary communication protocols and can therefore interface only with a proprietary server. And while thin clients are cheap, their servers usually aren't. Therefore, a total thin client package can be expensive. In all, thin clients are really a corporate solution.

To learn more about TCO, maintenance, upgrades, and long-term costs, please see Chapter 15, "Upgrading and Expanding the Network."

Diskless Clients

Diskless clients are machines that have neither software nor networking firmware installed. Instead, they rely on floppy boot disks. The disks load tiny software modules into memory that establish a connection between the diskless client and the server. Such configurations are rare these days.

Diskless clients reached their heyday in the early 1990s, particularly on the Novell NetWare platform. If anything, the major advantage of diskless clients is that they're incredibly inexpensive. For example, you can establish a diskless client using a 386 with 8MB of RAM. So long as you're accessing NetWare only (and running DOS-based applications on the server), your 386 will fly.

Diskless clients also exist in the UNIX world. However, these don't rely on boot floppies. Instead, older UNIX workstations (SPARCstations in particular) house firmware that can communicate with a boot server over the network.

Diskless clients are cheap networking tools. However, the disadvantage of diskless clients is pretty fundamental: They have no storage and rely exclusively on the server.

Fat Client Scenarios

Fat client scenarios are a bit different. In the fat client scenario, data might still be stored on a server, but applications that manipulate that data reside on the local machine. Fat clients, therefore, move users away from centralized computing.

You can technically refer to any PC or workstation as a fat client. However, there are several firms that actually manufacture *bona fide* fat clients. These are machines that have infinitely more local software than thin clients but still not as much as PCs. Confused yet?

Workstations

The term *workstation* has two meanings, one traditional and one contemporary. Let's examine each.

The traditional definition of a workstation is a microcomputer that's designed expressly to run a UNIX variant. UNIX is a network operating system created by Bell Labs in 1969, and ultimately used to create the Internet. Learn more about UNIX in Chapter 7, "Network Operating Systems."

Traditional workstations are expensive (often costing five figures or more), and run on RISC chipsets. Here are some popular models:

➤ *The Indigo by SGI*   Indigos (from Silicon Graphics, Inc.) are used primarily in the film industry and deliver eye-popping graphics like those seen in *Jurassic Park* and *Titanic*. Check out the Indigo family product line at `http://www.sgi.com`.

➤ *The SPARCstation by Sun Microsystems*   SPARCstations are famous for their capability to process thousands of network requests per second. Hence, they're a favorite among Internet service providers. Find out more about SPARCstations at `http://www.sun.com`.

➤ *The Digital Alpha*   Alphas are 64-bit, high-performance workstations that offer 500+ MHz performance and 3D graphics. Find out more about Alphas at `http//www.digital.com`.

Is It Worth Taking the RISC?

RISC stands for *Reduced Instruction Set Computer*. Computer chips manufactured to RISC specifications use more simplified basic instructions, which eliminates overhead during data processing. For this reason, many folks argue that RISC-based processors are faster than their competitors.

An example of a RISC processor is the Alpha processor, from Digital Equipment Corporation. Alphas deliver extremely fast 64-bit computing and are typically one to two years ahead of other chips. For example, 500MHz Alphas were available in 1997 while most other chips topped out at 300MHz.

UNIX folks take their workstations seriously. In fact, they'll argue to the death that only UNIX microcomputers deserve to be classified as workstations. If you want to have some fun, tell a UNIX user that you're really enjoying your Macintosh workstation. Then stand back and watch the sparks fly.

However, in today's networking world, the term *workstation* has a more general, more relaxed meaning. For our purposes, a workstation is any full-fledged computer attached to a local area network. That is, a workstation is any computer that has client and application software, advanced storage facilities, and essential extras such as a hard disk, a CD-ROM drive, a floppy drive, a monitor, a mouse, and a keyboard.

Another way to classify a workstation is this: any computer that can operate effectively as a standalone, without network connectivity. In other words, while workstations are often wired to networks, they needn't be, because they already contain all the hardware and software they need to do serious computing.

Workstations come in every size and flavor, and run a wide variety of operating systems. In any given network, you might find workstations running any (or even all) of the following operating systems:

➤ BeOS

➤ DOS

➤ Linux

➤ MacOS

➤ NetWare

➤ OS/2

➤ Plan 9 from Bell Labs

➤ UNIX

➤ Windows 95 or 98

➤ Windows for Workgroups

➤ Windows NT

Advantages of Workstations

Workstations offer many advantages. First, by using workstations as network nodes, you empower your users. At any time (whether connected to the network or not), your users will be able to get serious work done.

Second, workstations aren't dependent on servers for processor power. Therefore, if one of your users starts crunching serious numbers, network performance doesn't suffer. All calculations and data processing is kept local to that particular workstation.

Perhaps most importantly, however, workstations are versatile. They can be adjusted to do almost anything, and that's a powerful advantage. To understand why, consider this: Suppose you installed 30 network computers and, for the first year, these machines served your purposes. However, now suppose that you've decided that client/server networking isn't required for all departments. Instead, you want to convert from client/server to peer-to-peer. If you had workstations, that would probably take 20 minutes and no additional hardware or software. If you had network computers, you'd have to purchase 30 new machines (NCs don't do peer-to-peer).

In this respect, workstation versatility is well worth the extra money. After all, a network is a long-term investment. You don't want to be tied to any particular architecture or network design.

Disadvantages of Workstations

The principal disadvantage of workstations is the cost. Even relatively inexpensive workstations (such as PCs) cost a minimum of $1,000. If you're building a 20-node network, that's twenty grand right there. Moreover, workstations have a high TCO (as previously noted, almost $10,000).

Additionally, workstations can give your users too much power. For example, they have the choice of installing any software they like. They also have the choice of configuring their own machine, tweaking it to their particular tastes. These operations allow more latitude for human error. Frankly, you may encounter high-tech support costs. Each time a user mangles his machine's configuration, someone (maybe you) will have to fix it (and as we all know, time really is money).

Servers

Servers are powerful computers or processes that manage disk drives, printer services, network traffic, and other network resources.

There are many different server types, including

➤ Application servers
➤ Communications servers
➤ Directory services servers
➤ Fax servers
➤ File servers
➤ Internet servers
➤ Mail servers
➤ Print servers

Let's examine each in turn.

Application Servers

Application servers house applications such as ledgers, databases, and office-oriented programs. In an application server-based network, clients rarely store information locally. Instead, clients make inquiries and send updates to the server.

A typical application server environment is where the server houses a contact database and its accompanying application. In contrast, clients run a scaled-down version of the application. This scaled down version allows users to view records from (or transmit new information to) the server.

Many mainstream software firms have developed complex packages for application server environments. Good examples are Lotus Notes and Microsoft Access.

The principal advantage of application servers is centralized management of data. Also, application servers obviate the need to install full-blown applications on client workstations. This saves space and money.

Communications Servers

Communications servers control traffic between LANs, WANs, mainframes, the Internet, and other communication transmission media. Typically, communications servers function as entrances or gateways into private networks, using a wide range of networking devices (for example, modems, routers, or dedicated lines).

Communications servers provide users with quick, secure network connections. There are many such communications servers, and their functionality and cost vary considerably.

Directory Services Servers

Directory services servers contain indexes of users, nodes, and network servers. Their chief function is to enable easy administration of large networks. Often, directory service servers provide an index of absolutely everything on the network.

Fax Servers

Fax servers manage network fax traffic though one or more fax/modem cards. Users request faxes that have been sent or received with software on their client or workstation. In turn, the server reports (and can deliver) those faxes to the user.

Though fax servers are a relatively new phenomenon, many manufacturers have created fax server software. For more information, check out http://www.3com.com or http://www.panasonic.com.

File Servers

File servers centralize data storage. The server stores files, and the client requests them. Commonly used for development in software design, file servers are excellent for use in collaborative work environments.

Learn more about Internet servers in Chapter 17, "Intranets, Extranets, and the Internet."

Internet Servers

Internet servers manage Internet or intranet traffic. They allow you to create and publish Web pages, sell products over the World Wide Web, and gather contacts and feedback. These servers can come in all shapes and sizes using a multitude of different software.

Internet servers are used for many things, including

➤ Company promotional programs

➤ General information dissemination

➤ Online commerce

➤ Remote computing

However, Internet servers are now being used in even more creative ways. For example, you can now run a microcosmic version of the Internet in your company's offices. These new networks (called *intranets*) run common Internet protocols. Many firms are now using intranets to offer World Wide Web–like capabilities to their local documentation and databases.

Mail Servers

Mail servers manage email and messaging for clients. Software on the client workstation can send messages through the server to both the local network and the Internet.

Print Servers

Print servers manage networked printer peripherals, and allow anyone to print from their workstation. Today, folks use print servers less than they used to. Many software companies have integrated printer management into their software, eliminating the need of a dedicated server. Furthermore, certain printers now even have print management firmware, so print servers are rarely used except in large networks.

As you can see, client/server computing is complex. There are servers for nearly everything. Indeed, some network operating systems (most notably UNIX) ship with all the aforementioned servers. The question is, do you really need all that power? The next section will help you answer that question.

A Comparison of Peer-to-Peer and Client/Server Networks

Before closing this chapter, we thought it was a good idea to compare the two network types side-by-side. This might help you to decide which type best suits your needs. In Table 3.1, we list the most important characteristics of both network types.

Table 3.1   Peer-to-Peer and Client/Server Networks Contrasted

Issue	Peer-to-Peer	Client/Server
Cost	Inexpensive	Can be expensive
File Sharing	Yes	Yes
Geek Factor	Low	High
Growth	Very limited	Potentially unlimited
Logging	Virtually none	Advanced logging
Maintenance	Moderate	Significant
Management	Little or none	Advanced management
Remote Printing	Yes	Yes
Remote sessions	Not generally	Yes
Scalability	So-so	Excellent
Security	Little or none	Advanced security
Setup	Quick and painless	Complex
Shared peripherals	Yes	Yes

The Least You Need to Know

The two most common network types are peer-to-peer and client/server. To determine which is best for you, consider the following:

➤ *Peer-to-peer networks* are superb for small businesses. They're fast, cheap, simple, and easy to establish. Among other things, peer-to-peer networks offer file and peripheral sharing. However, peer-to-peer networks don't scale well and have serious limitations on distance and size.

➤ *Client/server networks* are excellent for large enterprises. They provide completely centralized management and security, remote services, mail, Internet connectivity, and a wide range of specialized server applications. Moreover, client/server networks scale well and have potential for unlimited growth. On the other hand, however, client/server networks are difficult to establish, complex, and expensive.

## Chapter 4

Network Topologies

> ➤ Learn about topology
>
> ➤ Learn about different topologies and their purposes
>
> ➤ Choosing a topology for your network

Once you choose your network type, you must next choose a topology. *Topology* refers to the manner in which your network is wired. The paths of your network wire (and the connections they create) form your network's topology.

There are many different topology types, including

➤ Bus

➤ Star

➤ Ring

➤ ARCnet

➤ Switched

➤ Daisy chain

➤ Mesh

In this chapter, you'll learn the advantages and disadvantages of each topology type and which one is best for you.

Topology Generally

Much like different network types, different topology types have many advantages and disadvantages. These qualities in many instances run parallel to the advantages and disadvantages of networks. For example, various topologies will render you varying performance in the following areas:

➤ Centralization

➤ Cost

➤ Maintenance and troubleshooting

➤ Scalability

➤ Security

➤ Speed

➤ Stability

Your choice of network topology will be also influenced by other considerations, including distance. Network cable types (and other transport hardware such as hubs, routers, switches, and bridges) have widely varying limitations on distance. Some can transmit only a few hundred feet, while others can transmit well over a thousand. To learn more about wire, hardware, and distance, see Chapter 6, "Network Hardware."

In addition to these factors, you'll also need to consider a special issue called the *single point of failure* (SPF). This is a physical or logical location (a server, hub, wire, or router) where one or more network device connects. When this connection fails, one or more workstations will be unable to transmit data.

Every network has at least one single point of failure. In networks that perform mission-critical tasks, the trick is to minimize the damage that occurs when that single point finally fails. As you'll see, different topologies pose different limitations in this regard.

Let's start with the simple topologies:

➤ Bus

➤ Star

➤ Ring

The Magic Bus: Bus Topology

Bus topology (sometimes called *linear bus topology*) is simple and works like this: The network is supported by a long, uninterrupted cable called a *backbone*. This backbone is the root of all connectivity. Network devices (workstations, terminals, and peripherals) draw their network feed from the backbone, as shown in the following figure.

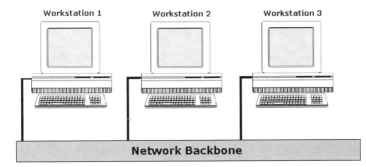

All workstations tap their connectivity from the backbone. In this respect, a backbone is much like a river. It flows through the valley (your network), supporting life on its banks.

Bus topology is typically used in smaller networks. A common scenario is where 10 users (or fewer) need to share data and peripherals. In such environments, not only are workstations usually within close proximity of each other, but users rarely send data very far.

Advantages of Bus Topology

For many years, bus topology was exceedingly popular, due largely to its simplicity. Implementing bus topology is very straightforward: You simply string a backbone and plug in your workstations. Moreover, bus topology is inexpensive because it requires neither hubs nor routers.

Hubs and Routers

Hubs are hardware devices that centralize network activity. Network cables run from workstations to the hub. The hub then repeats the signals it receives, and these are routed out again to other network devices. *Routers*, on the other hand, are more complex, and route packets in and out of networks. Read more about these devices in Chapter 6, "Network Hardware."

Additionally, with effort, you can implement a bus topology in a small office environment. It's not necessary, for example, to house all workstations in the same space. You can still achieve a widespread office LAN by winding your backbone through the building. (So long as the wire is continuous, it doesn't matter how many twists and turns it takes.)

T2: The Terminator

The backbone cable must be *terminated* at both ends. This is accomplished with a T (sometimes called a T-pin), a device that terminates the signal at either end. T-pins are so named because they're shaped like a letter T with 3 connectors. Two of these connectors ensure a continued signal, and one is used to splice in a workstation. When T-pins are used for termination, a small plastic or metal cap is placed on the end. This terminates the signal. (Note that if you establish a bus-based network and fail to terminate the backbone on either end, the workstations probably won't recognize one another.) More on termination in Chapter 6.

Disadvantages of Bus Topology

There are three chief disadvantages to bus topology:

➤ *Bus topology–based networks are difficult to troubleshoot*   If you experience problems at the network level, you may find it difficult to isolate the source. (Problems of this nature include traffic jams, where, for a variety of reasons, packet delivery may slow to a crawl.)

➤ *Bus topology lacks central administration*   Because most bus topology–based networks have no hubs, routers, switches, or bridges, they're difficult to manage. For example, you can't perform network segmentation. (*Network segmentation* is where hardware devices segregate some workstations from others. Such segmentation increases your security and ease of management.)

➤ *Bus topology is subject to speed and performance constraints*   In bus topology, only one workstation at a time can send data. Thus, each additional workstation eats substantial network resources. Bus topology is therefore undesirable for use in client-server networks because clients often make multiple requests. A large population of clients attached via bus topology will slow your network considerably.

Additionally, bus topology–based networks have a high-profile single point of failure. That is, if your network backbone fails, the entire network is effectively knocked out.

Finally, bus topology is undesirable from a security standpoint. Data sent from one workstation is transmitted to all remaining workstations. Under normal conditions, only the intended recipient captures that transmission. However, with simple modification, any connected workstation could capture all transmissions (even though that workstation is not "entitled" to the information). This is a minor point, though. Bus topology is rarely used in secure network environments.

Thank Your Lucky Stars: Star Topology

Star topology is significantly more structured than bus topology, and focuses on centralization. In a typical star network, each computer or peripheral is connected to a central point, as shown in the following figure. Thus, the failure of one connection will not usually affect the others.

This is not always true. Certainly, if the main connection houses a mail server and it fails, other workstations will not be able to retrieve mail. However, in star networks, if one cable connection goes down, the others remain unaffected.

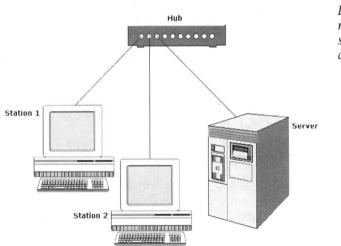

In star networks, each network device attaches separately to a centralized hub.

Advantages of Star Topology

The chief advantages of star topology are

➤ *Star topology offers centralization* Thus, star networks are more easily managed and secured.

➤ *Star networks are usually faster* Because each workstation is independently wired directly to the hub, data is transmitted directly, allowing greater speed and organization.

➤ *Star networks are stable* If one workstation fails, the rest continue to operate unhindered. Damage control is therefore much easier. (Compare this to the total single point of failure in bus topology.)

Another major advantage of star topology is that reconfiguration is a snap. For example, you can instantly add or subtract workstations and peripherals simply by plugging them into the hub.

Additionally, star networks free you from many limitations common to bus-based networks. For example, star topology allows you to break your network into segments. (These are small groups of workstations in close physical proximity to one another.) You needn't necessarily house all workstations in close physical proximity. Instead, you can create departmental islands and later connect these to other LANs or LAN segments of varying topologies.

Disadvantages of Star Networks

The chief disadvantage of star networks is that they have a single point of failure at the hub level. Hence, if a hub cable breaks (or the hub fails for other reasons), all workstations on that segment will lose connectivity.

Finally, star networks represent a greater initial investment because hubs are expensive. Additionally, the average hub has between 8 and 20 ports (*ports* are what your workstations get plugged into). If the number of workstations you have exceed the number of available ports, you'll need to buy another hub. (Frankly, if your network is of any size, you may end up stringing several stars together.)

Ring Topology

Ring topology features a single cable to which all workstations and peripherals are connected. In this respect, ring topology marginally resembles bus topology. The difference is that a ring network's backbone is a closed loop (hence the term *ring*), as shown in the following figure.

In a ring configuration, data travels around the ring from one workstation to the next. Each workstation or network device acts as a repeater, regenerating the signal and passing it on. Each workstation also has two neighbors, forming a closed ring or circuit system as illustrated in the following figure.

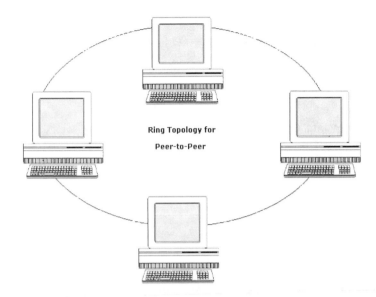

Ring Topology for
Peer-to-Peer

Ring networks rely on a single backbone, much like bus-based networks

Advantages of Ring Topology

Ring topology has the same basic advantages as bus topology:

➤ Ring networks are easy to establish

➤ Ring networks represent low initial overhead

Disadvantages of Ring Topology

The chief disadvantage of ring networks is that they have not just one point of failure, but many. (That number is equal to the number of connected network devices.) This is a pretty critical issue.

Ring networks are rarely used today (classic ring topology is an antiquated technology). However, when used, such networks are almost always peer-to-peer.

To appreciate the difference, imagine this: Suppose you had a star network with six workstations and one file server. If the file server died, all six workstations would be unable to download files. However, all six workstations could still function and communicate with one another. In a ring setting, that simply isn't true. If even one network device fails, the entire network is temporarily incapacitated.

Other Network Topologies

In addition to those previously mentioned, other interesting topologies exist, including

➤ ARCnet

➤ Compound topologies

Let's briefly run through those now.

ARCnet Topology

One very popular (though antiquated) topology is ARCnet. ARCnet topology is a hybrid of both token and bus topologies.

What's an ARCnet?

ARCnet (Attached Resource Computer Network) is LAN system developed by Datapoint Corporation that supports 255 workstations in a star topology at speeds of 2.5Mbps. To learn more about ARCnet (and Datapoint's contributions to early LAN development), visit Datapoint's Web site at http://www.datapoint.com.

ARCnet's defining characteristic is the way it transmits data. ARCnet servers continuously circulate empty message frames throughout the network. When a workstation needs to send a message, it grabs an empty frame and inserts a *token* and the message data into it. The frame is then carried to its destination.

When the message reaches its destination, the receiving workstation reads the message and then resets the token to 0 (an empty state). At that point, the frame is ready to be used again by any workstation or network device. This token scheme is quite efficient even when traffic increases because all devices have the same opportunity to use the shared network.

ARCnet can use coaxial cable or fiber-optic lines. Cable lengths can be 2,000 feet per segment with a total network span of 20,000 feet (that's quite a bit). Additionally, ARCnet systems can operate over those distances with no appreciable loss of speed.

Of the four major LAN technologies (which also include Ethernet, Token Ring, and FDDI), ARCnet is said to be the least expensive to install.

Compound Topologies

Up until now, I've discussed simple network topologies and how they relate to small LANs or even LAN segments. In most cases, these networks interconnect using a single, consistent topology.

In larger networks, however, you may combine several topology types to interconnect LAN segments of varying design and size. These large systems are themselves classified as topologies—hybrids that can be aptly referred to as *compound topologies*.

Compound topologies are typically more complex (and perhaps, by translation, more difficult to manage) than those previously mentioned. However, compound topologies offer you many advantages, including greater scalability, size, efficiency, and control.

In this section, you'll examine three major compound topologies:

➤ Daisy chain topology

➤ Mesh topology

➤ Switched topology

Daisy Chain Topology

Daisy chaining is a basic compound topology and works like this: Hubs (which could feasibly contain star network segments) are chained together, one after the other, as shown in the following figure. This topology is also sometimes called a *star-bus*.

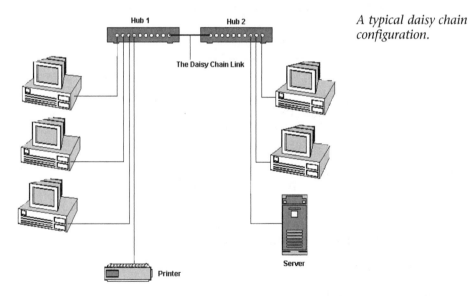

A typical daisy chain configuration.

Daisy chaining is an intermediate compound topology, typically used to inexpensively transform small LANs into medium-sized ones. (Using daisy chain topology, you can avoid purchasing more expensive routing and segmentation hardware such as routers, bridges, and switches.)

I recommend using daisy chain topology only when stringing two small network segments together. Exceeding that is probably unwise and here's why: Daisy chain configurations can heavily tax your network's backbone. In other words, don't daisy chain six hubs—and some 48 workstations—to a single backbone. If you do, your network performance will fall considerably.

Mesh Topology

Mesh topology is highly advanced and typically used in wide area networks. Its purpose is to interconnect two or more sizable LANs, as shown in the following figure.

Mesh topology offers multiple transmission paths between networks. Notice that each router can directly reach all its peers.

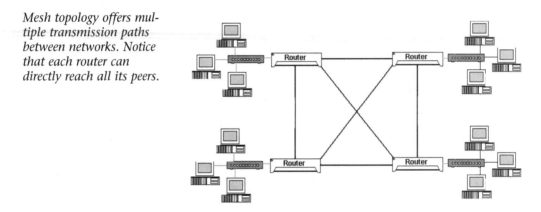

You may remember that in Chapter 1, "What Is a Network," I discussed the Internet's origins as a military project. Its purpose was to establish a communication system immune to nuclear attack. In this system, if one, 10, or 100 workstations were incapacitated, the remaining workstations would continue to function.

This was accomplished with a *net* or *mesh* approach. In mesh topology, isolated networks have multiple paths to their counterparts. This way, total system failure is unlikely. If one network goes down, you can still reach others through an alternate route.

Mesh topology is used in mission-critical systems essential to business, academic, military, and government institutions that cannot afford system failures. (Many universities now use mesh topology to network different departments.)

How the Mesh System Works

In a mesh setting, a router is placed between your network and the outside world. Hence, when connecting six isolated LANs, you'd need six routers. These routers handle the process of intelligent data transport, which works like this:

1. Data is sent from your network to the router
2. The router polls the network to determine the best path
3. The data is then sent along that path

If systems along the original path fail while the data is still moving, other routers step in and find a new path. As a result, to incapacitate such a network, you'd need to destroy all but one LAN. (As long as two LANs remain, data can still be routed from one to the other.) The chief advantage of mesh topology, therefore, is stability. You are almost guaranteed that your data will arrive safely.

The chief disadvantage of mesh topology is its expense, and not simply for hardware and software. There's the added expense of training. Certified engineers with considerable experience usually implement mesh topology.

Switched Topology

Switched networks closely resemble star networks—at least from a physical viewpoint. Network devices are attached to a central hub, as shown in the following figure. However, while overtly similar to star networks, switched LANs work very differently. In switched networks, bandwidth is dedicated on a device-by-device basis. Each device is allocated the full bandwidth and, therefore, each enjoys the maximum available transfer rate.

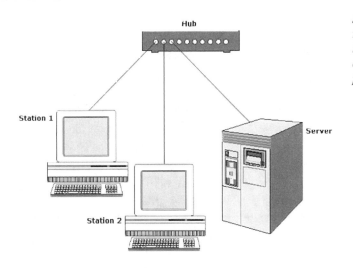

Switch topology physically resembles star topology because devices are attached at a centralized point.

Contrast this with bus and ring topologies. In bus and ring configurations, your network slows considerably as you add more workstations. This is because each workstation's bandwidth and speed is dependent on other network devices. (In such networks, bandwidth is shared between all devices.) This drastically limits your speed and growth, particularly in client/server networks.

Switched networks are far superior in this respect. Network devices do not share the wire and, therefore, switched networks yield better and faster performance. Moreover, switched networks make diagnostic tasks a snap.

As usual, though, nothing is perfect. There's an old adage often quoted in the networking world: Fast, cheap, efficient. Pick any two. Thus, while switched networks are extremely fast and efficient, they are not cheap. Switches are quite expensive. (So is the training you'll need to construct a switched LAN.)

A Comparison of Bus, Star, and Switched Topologies

Chances are you'll be erecting a Local Area Network supported by bus, star, or switched topology. In Table 4.1 below, I've contrasted the advantages and disadvantages of these topologies side by side.

Table 4.1 Comparison of Bus, Star, and Switched Networks

Issue	Bus	Star	Switched
Bandwidth	Shared	Shared	Dedicated
Cost	Inexpensive	Moderate	Expensive
SPF*	Critical	Less Severe	Less Severe
Growth	Limited	Good	Good
Management	Little or none	Considerable	Advanced
Scalability	Poor	Good	Excellent
Setup	Easy	More difficult	Complex
Speed	Variable	Can be variable	Static
Stability	Low	Moderate	High
Suitable for...	Peer-to-peer	LAN/Client/server	LAN/Client/server
Troubleshooting	Difficult	Manageable	Easy

* This represents single point of failure factor (or, how devastating an actual failure is)

The Least You Need to Know

Your choice of topology will be based on many factors, including

➤ What you're using the network for

➤ Your network type

➤ The layout of your office or home

When building a Local Area Network, choose your topology carefully. Try to factor in cost, bandwidth, scalability, growth, stability, and management (remember, too, that your network topology has great bearing on your network's security). The following checklist is a good yardstick:

➤ If you're building a very small peer-to-peer network (10 nodes or fewer), bus topology might suffice. Such networks are easy to configure, expand on, and connect to. Typically, you can establish a bus topology–based network with little more than your workstations, some cable, and a few network interface cards (NICs). This makes your installation and administration costs quite low. Bus networks are cheap, quick, painless, and suitable for home or small business environments.

➤ If you're building a medium-sized LAN for more serious business settings, choose star topology. It offers speed, increased security, reliability, and a less critical single point of failure. It also allows you to more incisively segment your network. Star networks are relatively easy to establish, only moderately expensive, and exceptionally versatile. Star topology is most often employed in Ethernet LANs.

➤ Ring networks are easily established, inexpensive, and suitable for close-quarters. However, I don't recommend ring networks for mission-critical tasks.

➤ If you're building a large LAN and need dedicated bandwidth, choose a switched topology. It offers high-speed transmission, exceptional reliability, and easy troubleshooting.

## Chapter 5

System Architectures and Protocols

The first computers didn't play well with others. They consisted of proprietary hardware and software and connected—if they connected at all—only to computers like themselves on proprietary networks. In other words, each computer vendor did things its own way.

Before long, an outcry came from organizations that wanted to be capable of sharing information among different types of computers. As a result, industry groups began creating rules to allow all computers, regardless of the size or type, to effectively communicate on networks. Rules took the form of *architectures*, whole frameworks for interoperating on networks, and *protocols*, which are specific implementations of services within those frameworks.

This chapter describes three major network architectures: OSI, TCP/IP, and SNA. It also describes some of the protocols for networking that fit within those frameworks.

Understanding Network Architectures

Most people think of networks as the wires that connect computers together and the software that sends messages across those wires. Network architectures can, however, be much broader, describing not only the wires and transmission service but also the services provided to network applications—and how they can be put together.

The *Open Systems Interconnection (OSI)* Reference model is the network architecture most often used to illustrate networking theory. This is because its architecture not only encompasses how to interconnect diverse physical networks (such as Ethernet, X.25, and so on), but it also defines the network services that must be offered on diverse computer systems (such as UNIX, OS/2, and Windows). Also, OSI is a good way to learn about which networks strictly follow OSI standards—and about those that don't.

Open System Interconnection (OSI)

The OSI Reference model is a seven-layer model that illustrates how networking protocols and services work together to form a computer network. The seven layers represent everything from the physical electrical transmission of bits on a wire (level 1) to the distributed network services available to user application programs (level 7).

OSI was designed to provide a framework that would coordinate development of networking standards but still allow existing protocols to fit into that framework. The *International Organization for Standardization (ISO)* developed this model and, along with organizations representing governments around the world, continues to develop and issue related standards.

Not every network needs to implement every standard, or even every layer, for the network to function. For example, network applications on similar computer systems might communicate directly to the transport layer. Even when all seven layers are represented on communication-end systems, there are usually communications nodes in between that only implement some of the lower layers.

OSI Illustrations

The OSI reference model is easier to understand if you look at a few representations. The following figure illustrates how the seven layers of the OSI Reference model are organized. It shows two end systems, with the communication passing through a network-level node.

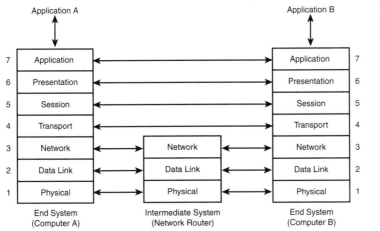

The OSI Reference model divides networking services into seven layers.

The preceding figure shows communications taking place between application A and application B on two different computers. In this illustration, the communication crosses two different types of networks, with a network router managing the communication between the two networks. (If a single LAN connects the two computers, only the two end systems are shown.)

Following are some details about the illustration in the preceding figure that will help you understand the OSI Reference model:

➤ The applications shown here are communicating over a full OSI protocol stack. This means each application can make requests for services, such as a file copy request or database query, without knowing anything about the location of that resource on the network.

➤ The applications request services from the application layer, which requests services from the presentation layer, which requests services from the session layer, and so on, all the way down to the physical layer before leaving end system A.

➤ Each layer negotiates with its *peer layer*—the layer of the same name on the next adjacent system that implements that layer—to obtain the requested service.

➤ There are different protocols that can be used to represent each of the layers. This is particularly true from the network layer and those below it, which can consist of a variety of wide area and local area networks.

➤ To be capable of plugging different protocols into an OSI protocol stack, extra software can be added to support the *service provider interface* at a particular level. For example, a transport level interface can be created to access an X.25 network.

➤ When it comes to real OSI networking products, a service provider interface only needs to be created when a product expects to have another product plugged into it at that level. For example, an X.25 network might not expose a data link service provider interface because it expects networking products to use the full X.25 stack rather than to connect into the middle.

65

What the Heck is X.25?

X.25 is a packet-switched network standard created by the CCITT (an international telecommunications standards committee). In particular, the X.25 standard focuses on managing connections between DTE entities (such as computer end systems) and DCE entities (such as modems that provide connections to the packet-switched network).

The protocols associated with the X.25 protocol provide services for OSI-RM layers 1 (physical), 2 (data link), and most of 3 (up to the subnetwork portion of the network layer). Although it is not as popular in the United States, X.25 is commonly used in Europe—especially in telephone systems.

The reason X.25 comes up a lot in OSI examples is that it was designed to fit that model. This is in opposition to other network products that came about because of market needs and therefore don't fit cleanly into the OSI model.

To further illustrate OSI layers, the following figure shows how data flows through end systems and intermediate systems on a network.

Information can flow through intermediate systems.

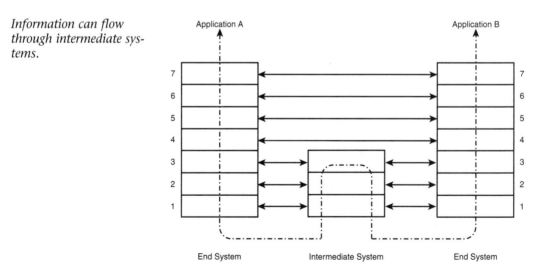

In the preceding figure, the network router is connected to two different networks: one connecting to end system A and one connecting to end system B. Following is some pertinent information about the preceding figure:

➤ The transport layer on end system A requests to communicate to end system B. Because, in this case, the two computers are on different physical networks, the communication must go through an intermediate system (a network router).

➤ On end system A, layers 1, 2, and 3 communicate with peer layers on the network router. The same layers communicate together between the router and end system B.

➤ From the transport layer up, peer processes communicate together on end systems A and B.

Theory is nice, but sometimes it helps to put real components in place to understand how something works. The following figure shows examples of actual protocols that can be used to carry out the features of the different levels.

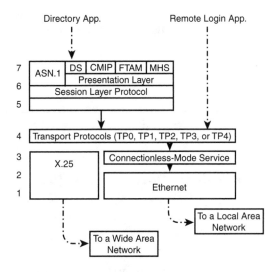

OSI layers can be represented by different protocols.

The illustration in the preceding figure shows an end system with both a directory application and a remote login application running. The directory is requesting services from a full OSI protocol stack; the remote login program communicates directly to the transport provider. Following are some details about the illustration:

➤ The directory application requests some information from software that implements the three upper layer protocols. (Application, presentation, and session layer services are described later in this chapter.)

➤ The remote login application communicates directly with a transport provider, asking to connect to a particular end system.

➤ There are two different types of networks available for the applications to use to connect to remote end systems. Using connection-oriented transport protocols (TP0, TP1, TP2, or TP3), either application can connect to an X.25 wide area network. Using a connectionless transport (TP4), either can utilize a connectionless network (such as an Ethernet LAN).

Although all this information might look complicated, it is actually designed to simplify life for the end user. Programmers create the protocols. Administrators connect the wires, install the protocols, and configure the protocol stacks so that they can be used by end users.

A user of this kind of network configuration simply runs the necessary programs. For example, the directory application might be a form filled out by a user to look up a telephone number that's stored in a database somewhere on the network. The login application might be as simple as someone running the command

```
rlogin compxyz
```

where compxyz is a computer end system on the network that is known to the transport provider. In any case, most of the details relating to the complexity of the networking configuration are hidden from the end user.

Features of OSI

The seven-layer model might give you some idea of what OSI does, but it doesn't tell you much about how it works. The following sections describe some of the details of how OSI layers and protocols carry out their business.

Service Access Points (SAPs) and Protocol Data Units (PDUs)

The point at which services are requested by a layer to the layer below it is called a *service access point* (*SAP*). A SAP must not only allow the services it represents to be available from this point, it must also represent those services in a very particular way. There is a separate SAP for each connection between two layers.

Information is passed to the adjacent layer in the form of *protocol data units* (*PDUs*). A PDU contains both header information and data. For example, the following types of PDUs are supported at the transport layer:

➤ Connection request (CR)

➤ Disconnect request (DR)

➤ Connection confirmation (CC)

➤ Disconnect confirmation (DC)

➤ Data (DT)

➤ Expedited data (ED)

➤ Acknowledgement (EA)

➤ Rejection (RJ)

➤ TPDU error (ER)

Normal data that is being passed on is contained in a DT protocol data unit. Data consists of the information sent down from the application in addition to header information added by layers above the current layer. Any header information from higher layer protocols is not interpreted until it reaches the peer layer process on the remote computer.

Peer-to-Peer Communications

The arrows shown between layers in the first two figures are meant to illustrate peer-to-peer communication. This means that although the layer hands requests for services to the layer below it, it is up to the peer layer on the end system or intermediate system to fulfill those requests.

For example, suppose the transport layer receives a request to connect to another computer. The transport layer packages up that request and sends it to the adjacent network layer (the layer below the transport layer). The request continues down the stack and out to the network, until it arrives at the peer transport layer on the requested computer. That transport layer then responds by sending back a connection confirmation or rejection.

Here is an analogy: When you make a telephone call to a friend, you make a request to the communications layer below you (the telephone) to connect to a particular address (a telephone number). After your peer accepts the connection (your friend picks up the phone), you talk directly to your friend and tell your friend what you want. The fact that the communication between you two runs over a series of wires or bounces off of satellites doesn't matter to you. You merely start the connection, and then communicate with your friend. The network handles the rest.

Connectionless and Connection-Oriented Networks

There are two different types of networks that can be used to communicate between peer layers: connectionless and connection-oriented networks. These two types of networks are appropriate for different kinds of communications.

Communications to peers on connection-oriented networks begin with the establishment of a connection between two systems at the same layer. After a connection is established, data is transmitted across that connection. When the communication is complete, the communication is disconnected. With a connection-oriented communication, there is no need for each packet of data to contain address information.

Connectionless networks, on the other hand, do not establish a connection before transmitting data. Each data unit must contain address information to get it to the proper layer on the remote system. In this situation, data can be carried over a variety of routes, and then be reassembled at the destination.

It is possible that different types of networks can be used to carry out a communication. For example, you might call a friend using telephony software from your PC. You establish a connection to your friend at the application level (audio from your PC and from your friend's PC). For your words to reach your friend, however, they might first pass from your PC to your own LAN (a connectionless network), and then to an X.25 network (a connection-oriented network), and then to your friend's LAN (another connectionless network) before reaching your friend.

The Seven OSI Layers

Each of the seven layers has specific services it must offer to layers above it, and each layer has the means of requesting services from layers below it. The following sections describe the characteristics of each of the seven layers.

The Physical Layer

The physical layer defines how bits of information are physically passed from one communication device to the next. Characteristics defined at this layer include functional, electrical, mechanical, and procedural characteristics.

An example of a physical layer standard is RS-232C. The COM1 and COM2 ports on the back of your PC are RS-232C ports. This standard defines the number of pins on the connector, the size of the connector, and the type and meaning of electrical signals that go across the pins. Modems are the networking equipment most commonly attached to an RS-232C port.

Data Link Layer

The job of the data link layer is to start the link between two communications devices, manage the link, and then make the link inactive. Some amount of error correction is done by this layer to ensure that the raw stream of bits being passed by the physical layer is reliable.

Besides providing error checking, the data link layer must handle flow control to prevent more information flowing to the next device than the device can handle. A simple point-to-point link consists of managing data on a single wire between two devices, whereas multi-point links might consist of many peer stations broadcasting on the same line.

Network Layer

The network layer is by far the most complex of the seven layers. This layer must understand the underlying transmission technologies that connect network entities (end systems and routers). The network layer is designed to shield the transport layer from these complexities so that the transport layer can simply request communication with an end system.

Because OSI encompasses entities that are sometimes referred to networks on their own, OSI refers to those entities as *subnetworks*. To manage the different types of subnetworks, the network layer implements internetworking features that allow data to be routed over the different subnetworks.

The network layer supports both connectionless and connection-oriented subnetworks.

Transport Layer

The transport layer is responsible for providing end-to-end communication between communications end systems. This layer must be capable of accepting transport addresses, establishing and terminating connections, and managing flow control of data.

The transport layer supports both connectionless and connection-oriented networks. There are five different transport protocols:

➤ *TP0*   Connection-oriented protocol that segments and reassembles transport layer data. This is the most basic transport protocol.

➤ *TP1*   Connection-oriented protocol that, on top of segmenting and reassembling data, can resend unacknowledged data units. When many errors occur, this protocol can restart the connection.

➤ *TP2*   Connection-oriented protocol that can segment and reassemble data. In addition, it can handle multiplexing over a single virtual circuit.

What the Heck is Multiplexing?

Multiplexing occurs when several streams of data can be sent simultaneously over the same communications channel. This can allow several protocols or several sessions to work on the same line simultaneously. For example, there are some telephone companies that offer a service that enables you to use one telephone line to connect to the Internet, but still allows telephone calls to come in and out on that line. Multiplexing allows this to happen.

➤ *TP3*   Connection-oriented protocol that does segmentation, reassembly, and error recovery (like TP1). However, it also can multiplex data (like TP2).

➤ *TP4*   Can function as a connection-oriented or a connectionless protocol. This protocol can provide reliable transport, assuming that the underlying network does not perform error detection.

The transport layer can be thought of as the top of the subnetwork services. All layers above the transport layer provide services to applications, as opposed to managing the transmission of data between systems or devices.

Session Layer

The session layer allows applications to control the interactions that occur during a communications session. For example, this layer can control which entity can send data, and at what times. The session layer is particularly useful when data entered during a session needs to be kept in sync.

During the course of a session transaction, a user might be capable of going back to a major or minor sync point. For example, with a grocery checkout application, a clerk might type in the wrong price. The session layer might enable the clerk to back up to the previous item entered (minor sync point), or possibly to back out all the items for that customer (major sync point).

Presentation Layer

The presentation layer manages the presentation of data between application entities. Different computer systems can represent data in different ways. The presentation layer can, therefore, allow the two entities to agree on the type of data representation they will use and implement exchanges using the chosen data representation.

You might use a presentation protocol, for example, to encrypt data or to present data in a generic way that can then be translated into a form that can be used by a specific type of terminal.

The *Abstract Syntax Notation (ISO ASN.1)* is a way of representing different types of data in much the same way that programming languages do. A tag represents each data type, identifying the class of data as universal, application-wide, context-specific, or private. The tag also identifies the particular item of data within that class.

Application Layer

The application layer offers a variety of services to the application programs. This layer communicates directly with the user process that is engaging in the communication. Following are some of the application service elements that are supported at the application layer:

➤ *File Transfer, Access, and Management (FTAM)*   Defines a means of transferring files and how remote files are accessed.

➤ *Common Management Information Protocol (CMIP)*   Defines a *management information base (MIB)* and objects for managing data.

➤ *Message Handling System (MHS)*   Defines methods for delivering email among hosts. MHS is based on the CCITT X.400 protocol.

➤ *Virtual Terminal (VT)*   Defines how terminals can be emulated across networks.

➤ *Directory Services (DS)*   Defines methods for naming services, hosts and other network items. DS is based on CCITT X.500 protocol.

TCP/IP Architecture

Transmission Control Protocol/Internet Protocol (TCP/IP) is the network architecture of the Internet. Unlike OSI, which was primarily created by committee, TCP/IP was created by engineers. Of the two architectures, OSI is a more structured architecture—more beautiful in theory—whereas TCP/IP is a more flexible architecture—more beautiful in reality.

For a standard to be created for TCP/IP, an organization must submit a *Request for Comments (RFC)* document detailing the component. The RFC can describe all kinds of things—it can specify a full-blown protocol, or it can just describe how to use a particular facility. For the most part, an engineer simply has to convince those who oversee the RFCs that the approach is feasible, and the RFC will be accepted.

The TCP/IP architecture is much simpler than OSI. Instead of seven fairly structured layers, TCP/IP is loosely structured around the following layers:

➤ Application Layer

➤ Transport Layer

➤ Internetwork Layer

➤ Network Interface and Hardware Layer

Unlike OSI, TCP/IP does not have many shared application services. Most applications communicate directly with the transport layer, without homogenizing application services to be used by lots of applications.

The following figure illustrates the TCP/IP architecture layers, as well as showing some of the protocols that represent each layer.

Note

This chapter describes the organization of the TCP/IP architecture and the protocols that implement the different layers. If you want information about TCP/IP addressing and details about the types of networks built on TCP/IP, see Chapter 17, "The Internet, Intranets, and Extranets."

In TCP/IP, applications communicate to the transport layer.

TCP/IP Layers
Application
Transport
Internetwork
Network Interface and Hardware

TCP/IP
Layers

Examples of TCP/IP Protocols			
File Transfer (FTP), Web Pages (HTTP), Remote Login (Telnet), File Sharing (NFS)...			
TCP		UDP	
Internet Protocol (IP)	ICMP	ARP	RARP
Local Area Networks (Ethernet, Token Ring), Wide Area Networks (X.25), many others...			

Examples of TCP/IP
Protocols

Application Layer

TCP/IP relies on the client/server model at the application layer. Typically, a user from one end system is requesting a service and another end system is providing that service. Following are a few application layer services that are available between TCP/IP systems:

Check This Out

Although some of the names of TCP/IP's layers are the same (or similar to) those of OSI's, the layers are only generally the same. Layers for the two architectures reflect different services and different interfaces between services.

➤ *File Transfer Protocol* (*FTP*)   Used for browsing directories of documents and copying files to—and possibly from—those directories. On the client side, an `ftp` command enables the user to request a connection to an FTP server system. The user logs in (often with the user name anonymous) and browses the directory structure for software, images, documents, or other types of files.

On the server side, the administrator is responsible for setting up who is allowed access to the FTP server and what areas of the server's file system they can access.

➤ *Web pages* (*HTTP*)   A Web server is set up to allow Web pages (HTML) and other Web content to be published to the network. The client accesses Web content using a Web browser (such as Netscape Communicator or Microsoft Internet Explorer). The Web server organizes and sets up security for Web content. The protocol used to manage distribution of Web pages is *Hypertext Transfer Protocol* (*HTTP*).

➤ *Telnet*   The Telnet service enables remote clients to log in to the server. When logged in, the client can run any applications or access any files that are accessible to the user.

➤ *Network File System* (*NFS*)   NFS is a service that allows one computer to connect part of a remote computer's file system to its local file system. The result is that the local system can browse and use the remote file system as though the files and directories existed locally.

On the server side, the remote computer offers a point in its file system to be shared (either generally or to specific other computers). On the client side, the remote file system is mounted at a convenient point in the local file system. For example, the /usr/files directory from a remote system can be mounted on the /usr/files directory locally. By listing the contents of that directory locally, the user sees (and has the capability to access) the files contained on the remote directory.

The location of each server application is usually associated with a port number on the server. Because these port numbers are well known, a user can typically just run an application or type a command to access the service on the remote computer. For example, the user makes an FTP request to connect to an FTP server. The FTP server has a listener process running to handle incoming FTP requests, so it responds by enabling the user to log in, and then have access to the server.

Transport Layer

Within the transport layer, two major protocols are supported:

➤ *Transmission Control Protocol* (*TCP*)   TCP is a connection-oriented protocol that establishes connections between end systems before transferring data.

➤ *User Datagram Protocol* (*UDP*)   UDP is a connectionless protocol that simply broadcasts packets of addressed data to the network. UDP is best for applications that need fast data transport, without requiring flow control or other connection-oriented services.

Internetwork Layer

This is the layer responsible for routing packets of data across multiple networks to make sure that data reaches the end system. This layer hides the details of the physical networks from the transport layer. Whereas the transport layer can just ask to connect to an end system, the internetwork layer must know how to reach that end system.

Internet Protocol (*IP*) is the main protocol at this layer. IP is a connectionless protocol, assuming no end-to-end reliability of its data transfer. TCP, above IP, is responsible for making sure that the data is exchanged reliably between the end systems. Other protocols at the internetwork layer include

➤ *Internet Control Message Protocol* (*ICMP*)   This protocol manages error recovery, control data, and information data among IP hosts. For example, ICMP returns a failure message when a host computer can't be reached.

➤ *Address Resolution Protocol* (*ARP*)   This protocol translates IP addresses into addresses that can be used by the underlying network drivers (typically media access and control drivers).

➤ *Reverse Address Resolution Protocol (RARP)*   This protocol resolves the physical addresses of a network device into its IP address. RARP is useful when a device, such as a diskless workstation, doesn't know its own IP address and must ask the RARP server that manages the device for that information.

Network Interface and Hardware Layer

This layer is roughly the same as the data link and physical layers of the OSI model. TCP/IP can use almost any network medium available to carry messages between IP systems. Because TCP/IP is so popular, there are few network media that don't offer a means of interfacing with the TCP/IP protocol stack. Supported media include Ethernet, Token Ring, X.25, and a variety of other network media.

Systems Network Architecture (SNA)

Systems Network Architecture (SNA) is IBM's own network architecture. When IBM ruled the computing world in the 1960s and 1970s, it created a lot of ground-breaking technology: mainframes, terminals, mini-computers, and so on. SNA was IBM's way of getting many of these devices that were not designed to communicate together to do just that.

Like OSI and TCP/IP, SNA instituted a layered approach to networking. At the top is the *Virtual Telecommunications Access Method (VTAM)* application interface. For data transmission, SNA primarily relied on *Synchronous Data Link Control (SDLC)*. Computers, terminals, and other nodes on the network are represented as *physical units (PUs)* and *logical units (LUs)*.

With the dominance of TCP/IP, IBM has been changing the focus of SNA. White papers and other documentation related to SNA (and being produced by IBM) focus on how to integrate SNA with TCP/IP. SNA was originally designed as an enterprise computing architecture. The new approach makes an attempt to integrate SNA components into public, as well as private, networks.

In IBM's newer architecture for computing and networking called Open Blueprint (http://www.software.ibm.com/openblue), SNA is referred to as a transport service. So, instead of being touted as a way of creating computing products, SNA is being looked at as a means of getting information from here to there.

Where To From Here?

After reading some of the theories of networking in this chapter, you understand many of the services that are contained within the structure of computer networks. In particular, this chapter covered the OSI reference model and the TCP/IP architecture, as well as giving a brief mention to IBM's once-popular SNA model.

From here, you might want to check out detailed descriptions of features in today's popular TCP/IP networks in Chapter 17. Furthermore, you might want to start looking at real networking components such as those described in Chapter 6, "Network Hardware," or Chapter 7, "Network Operating Systems (NOSes)."

The Least You Need to Know

Right now, the least you need to know about network architectures is this:

➤ Open Systems Interconnection (OSI) reference model divides networking features into seven layers, each of which can be represented by a variety of protocols.

➤ OSI layers communicate with peer layers on other intermediate and end systems.

➤ OSI provides three layers of application services (application, presentation, and session layers), which seek to shield user applications from needing to know anything about the underlying networks.

➤ Transmission Control Protocol/Internet Protocol (TCP/IP) is the most commonly used architecture today, acting as the basis for providing networking services to the Internet.

➤ TCP/IP applications tend to communicate directly with the transport layer and generally behave in the client/server model.

➤ A wide variety of network media (LANs and WANs) can be incorporated into a TCP/IP network to carry the messages between network nodes.

➤ TCP and UDP are the predominant protocols for managing transport of data between end systems. IP, in the layer below TCP and UDP, manages the details of routing messages across a variety of subnetworks.

➤ IBM's System Network Architecture (SNA) was once the primary architecture of enterprise computing, particularly for companies using mostly IBM equipment. Today, SNA has taken a back seat to the more popular TCP/IP networks.

## Chapter 6

Network Hardware

In This Chapter

➤ Choose computers that meet your network needs.

➤ Select cables and connectors.

➤ Understand communications hardware (Hubs, Bridges, Routers, Switches, and Gateways).

To most computer users, information magically comes and goes from their computers. They don't think about *network interface cards* (*NICs*), cables, or *routers*. To the uninitiated network administrator, that "magic" can look like a puzzle of wires and black boxes.

To help you unravel the puzzle of computer networks, this chapter describes the kinds of hardware you can use to connect your network, as well as the types of computers and other devices you can connect to it. If you are nervous, you can start with something as simple as a wire connecting two personal computers. If you are adventurous, you'll want to know about equipment used to connect LANs and to route messages to other networks.

Choosing Types of Computers

If you are creating your first network, you will probably be connecting the existing computers in your organization. That usually means connecting Windows PCs, Macs, and possibly UNIX workstations, so the job of choosing computers might already be done for you.

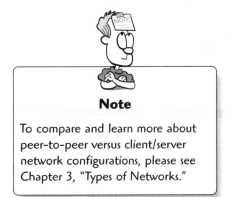

Note

To compare and learn more about peer-to-peer versus client/server network configurations, please see Chapter 3, "Types of Networks."

If you are starting from scratch, however, there are a variety of hybrid computers that are specifically designed for use on a network. Remember that with a network, every computer doesn't need to have every piece of hardware directly connected to it. Instead of all the computers being the same, you can have a few very powerful computers and many that are less powerful.

The more powerful computers typically act as *servers*. This simply means that the computer offers a service to *client* computers on the network. There are a few different types of servers:

➤ Print servers manage document printing.

➤ File servers centrally store files.

➤ Application servers launch applications that appear on the clients.

➤ Management servers manage a group of personal computers.

For the purposes of discussing the different types of computers you can have on your network, the next sections divide computers into three categories:

➤ *Standalone computers* Those computers that can work without being connected to a network (although, of course, they can be connected).

➤ *Network computers* Network computers might lack key hardware or software components, allowing them to work only when connected to a network.

➤ *Servers* Servers are computers that offer services (such as printing or applications) to other computers on the network.

Standalone Computers

Personal computers were not originally designed to connect to a computer network. In fact, the first homes and even many small offices that owned computers rarely had more than one computer, making the idea of a network rather silly.

Today, with many multi-computer locations, most computers either come network-ready (with a NIC installed) or enable you to add a card later. The following are some of the most common types of computers you might encounter when you connect your first network:

➤ Personal computers (PCs)

➤ Laptop computers

➤ Macintosh computers

➤ UNIX workstations

Personal Computers (PCs)

PCs are by far the most common type of computer around today. Typical configurations have everything needed to run applications and save data locally. Hardware usually includes a hard disk (for permanent storage), CD-ROM, and floppy disk, as well as a monitor, keyboard, and mouse. The CPU is usually from the Intel Pentium family (or is compatible). Built-in modems are included in most new PCs, and NICs (usually Ethernet) are almost always available.

Laptop Computers

It's convenient to have the capability to go on the road and take your computer with you. It's even more convenient if you can connect that laptop into a network so you have access to the information you need. Most laptop PCs come with a PCMCIA card slot that is about the size of a credit card and enable you to add NICs (or other types of cards) so you can connect to the network while you are at the office. From the road, you typically use the laptop's built-in modem to dial in to the network.

Macintosh Computers

Apple Macintosh computers have been popular for multimedia applications such as graphic arts and audio/video applications. Some Apple Macintosh computers have built-in Ethernet ports, including the Macintosh Centris 650, Power Macintosh, and most Quadra computers. The new iMac computer includes a 10/100BaseTx Ethernet card. Apple Workgroup Servers also contain Ethernet cards. If your Macintosh doesn't have an Ethernet port, you can purchase several different Ethernet cards from Apple.

UNIX Workstations

For CPU-intensive applications, UNIX workstations have always been popular. For example, UNIX workstations are often used by scientists, special-effects artists, architects (using CAD/CAM), and stock brokers. Imaging and modeling are excellent applications for UNIX workstations.

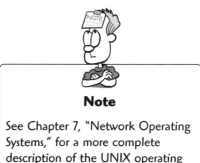

Note

See Chapter 7, "Network Operating Systems," for a more complete description of the UNIX operating system.

While it's true that some of the most popular versions of UNIX, such as Solaris, SCO Open Desktop, and Linux, do run on PCs, UNIX can also run on many other types of hardware. UNIX workstations tend to mean higher-priced computers with large disk capacities, a powerful processor (or possibly several), lots of RAM, and probably built-in Ethernet hardware. Sparc processors are very popular for use on UNIX workstations.

Although typical UNIX workstations operate just fine on their own, they almost always include NICs. This is because UNIX workstations are most often used in businesses where people need to work together on projects.

Network Computers

When huge mainframe computers ruled the world, many people used the same computer from multiple dumb terminals. Using simple text and function keys, users performed repetitive tasks such as data entry, reservations, or telemarketing.

These days, network computers are available to replace dumb terminals with hardware that can run today's more sophisticated applications. Network computers are actually scaled-down PCs or workstations that offer a few advantages over dumb terminals:

➤ Applications can be graphical instead of text oriented.

➤ Much of the processing can take place on the network computer, avoiding bottlenecks from slow networks or overburdened servers.

Network computers also are intended to offer the following advantages over full-blown PCs or workstations:

➤ By including less hardware, the initial cost of the network computer can be lower.

➤ Maintenance costs can be lower because each network computer can be managed from a server. Therefore, users are not responsible for maintaining their own computers.

➤ By centrally distributing software, a company makes sure each client runs the latest applications.

➤ Because these computers might have no floppy disks, CD-ROM, expansion slots, or even a hard disk in some cases, the risk of corruption or computer viruses is greatly reduced.

The client network computer might be a mere shell of a computer. In fact, the popular term used to describe one of these computers is *thin client*. In essence, the use of thin clients offers a way for an organization to more tightly control computer costs and usage but still offer sophisticated applications.

Although the concept of distributing computing in this way isn't new, there are some new ways to go about it. Each method requires slightly different computer hardware on the thin client and different ways of creating and distributing software. The choices described here include

➤ JavaStations

➤ Net PCs

➤ X Window Terminals

JavaStation

The *JavaStation* is Sun Microsystems' answer to thin clients. As the name implies, JavaStation systems are intended to run Java-based applications. However, with additional software, the JavaStation can also run existing PC applications and X Window System applications.

Check This Out

Because network computers often lack either hard disks or full operating systems, users might not have the capability to run certain high-end applications that expect a full PC operating environment.

JavaStations have no hard disks, so all applications must be downloaded from a Sun server.

What the JavaStation does provide is a high-performance processor (100MHz microSPARC-IIep), a NIC (10/100BaseT Ethernet), and graphics (1280×1024 by 8-bit color). It can also hold up to 64MB or memory.

What Is Java?

Java is a programming language from Sun Microsystems that is used to create applications that work securely over the Internet. All major Internet browsers and operating systems support the Java environment (called the *Java virtual machine*) so Java applets and applications can run on them.

Net PCs

Net PCs are the Microsoft/Intel entry into the network computer arena. Several vendors have signed on to produce Net PCs based on a published Net PC standard. Like other thin client computers, Net PCs aim to offer a platform for repetitive task applications once handled by dumb terminals.

Unlike JavaStations, Net PCs do include a hard disk. However, to prevent users from having to mess with the insides of the computer, there is no floppy drive or CD-ROM, and the Net PC's case is either locked or sealed. As you might guess, this can severely limit the Net PC from being used for anything but its appointed tasks.

To connect to the network, the Net PC offers a Fast Ethernet controller that can be configured to operate on 10BaseT or 100BaseTX wiring when the system is installed. Software can be installed and the computer can be configured remotely.

To manage a Net PC, you need a dedicated management server, which maintains each client configuration and offers tools to manage each client.

Here are some examples of Net PCs that are available from several different vendors:

➤ Optiplex Net PC N/NX (from Dell Computer)
http://www.dell.com/products/optiplex/nnx

➤ Network PC (from Intel)
http://www.intel.com/businesscomputing/netpc/what.htm

➤ Deskpro 4000N (from Compaq Computer)
http://www.compaq.com/products/desktops/dp4000n/index.html

Note

Besides the fact that the box is sealed, it's hard to understand what advantage a Net PC has over a regular PC with an Ethernet card. The cost savings on the hardware are negligible.

X Window Terminals

One of the first ways to have graphical applications available on low-cost displays over the network was with *X Window* terminals. An X Window terminal enables you to work with applications created for the X Window system.

An X Window application runs on an application server (typically a UNIX server) but is displayed on the X terminal. The X terminal consists of a display monitor, keyboard, and mouse, along with a connection to the network and enough processing power to drive the display.

X Window terminals are different from Net PCs and JavaStations because they don't include the capability to run applications locally. Processing is done on the server, whereas the results are displayed and manipulated on the X terminal.

Server Computers

From a hardware standpoint, a server computer doesn't need to be much different from a client computer. Servers often run on the same computer architectures—PCs and Sparc workstations—as client computers. However, because many users rely on servers, servers usually are much more loaded with hardware than the typical client.

A server computer generally has more RAM, larger hard disks, and a higher-speed processor (or multiple processors) than a client computer. For example, it's not unusual for a file server to have 64 or 128MB of RAM, whereas client processors might have only 16 or 32MB. A client might have a 1GB hard disk, whereas a server might have three 2GB hard disks.

Larger server systems, such as the Dell PowerEdge 6100, can carry up to four processors and 4GB of RAM. That server can also hold up to 54GB of internal disk drive storage capacity. As for its capacity to handle traffic from the network, this server can manage several NICs at the same time.

Server computers do tend to run different operating systems and management software than clients. For example, file servers tend to run on NetWare, Windows NT, or UNIX operating systems.

Software such as Compaq's Intelligent Manageability can be used to manage PCs, provide fault management (to minimize downtime), and handle security management to prevent unauthorized access. To deploy and maintain JavaStations, a Sun server must run Netra software.

Note

For more information on network operating systems and server management software, see Chapter 7.

Computer Networking Components

To connect to a network, most computers rely on either a modem (for phone line or other serial connections) or a NIC (for a LAN connection). Modems come with nearly every computer made these days. NICs are most often used to communicate on Ethernet local area networks (LANs).

In the scramble to control what is expected to become a huge market for home and small business networks, a variety of new methods for connecting networks has begun to appear. These include network hardware that enables you to connect computers using existing telephone or electrical wiring in the home.

Modems

Modems enable you to connect your computer to a computer network over standard telephone lines. Although the first modems were painfully slow, improvements in technology have made them viable even for applications—such as Web browsing—that are graphics-intensive.

Contributing to the popularity of modems is the fact that most modems adhere to a common set of standards. Protocols used in modems are defined by agreed-upon standards (with the exception of the newer high-speed protocols). Hardware standards dictate that modems be connected to RS-232C ports (COM ports on PCs), and a standard control language is used (modems using said language are referred to as Hayes-compatible).

Modem Features

Though most modems sold today sport similar features, performance can vary greatly—especially among those modems that are rated at higher speeds. Here are a few things to know about the modems you use:

➤ *Speed* The speed at which modems transmit and receive data is rated in bits per second (bps). When communicating over telephone lines, speeds can range from 300bps to 57,600bps. Achieving higher speeds not only requires clean phone lines but also requires that both sides of the communication support the transmissions rate (also called the *baud rate*).

➤ *Compatibility* Not only do both sides communicating by modem need to *support* higher speeds in order for data to be transported at those speeds, there are different standards supported by modem manufacturers to achieve those speeds. For example, U.S. Robotics (now part of 3Com) supports the x2 technology, whereas most other manufacturers use the k53flex technology for speeds of 57,600bps.

Check This Out

Don't always believe the numbers on the box when it comes to how fast a modem really performs. Significantly different speeds are realized depending on line conditions, the type of data being sent, and whether or not compression is used. Read some modem reviews before you make a purchase. Visit the C|Net computers.com site, and then select Modems for modem reviews.

➤ *Fax/voice support* Most modems today can support fax transmissions and voice communications, as well as data transmissions. If you have an older modem, make sure those features are included if they are important to you.

➤ *Flash memory* Some modems today come with flash memory for storing supported protocols. This means that if the manufacturer corrects or updates the software that runs the modem, you can install those changes. If you have a modem from 3Com, you can visit 3Com's Web site (http://www.3Com.com) to download the latest software to your modem.

Using Modems with Your Network

Although most of the traffic in networks used by small businesses probably occurs on the LAN in the office, modems can serve an important role in your network. Modems connected to your network can be used to

➤ Provide a method for employees on the road to dial in to the network to check email, download documents, or run applications. For users who work at home or in another location, this might be their only way to reach your network.

➤ Offer access to outside networks (such as the Internet or other wide area networks, or *WANs*) for your network's users.

If there is a lot of traffic between your network and outside networks, you might want to consider getting a higher speed communications line. Special modems are available to handle higher-speed lines. For example, ISDN modems can communicate on ISDN lines at transmission rates exceeding 120,000bps.

NICs

A NIC fits into the expansion slot on your computer to provide an access point to the network. A cable plugs into the back of the NIC to connect to your local area network.

The type of NIC you use depends on several issues:

➤ The type of network you are connecting to. Ethernet is the most popular type of LAN, followed by token-ring networks. With Ethernet, you can connect up to 1,024 nodes and communicate at speeds of 10Mbps. Token ring can connect up to 255 nodes at 4–16Mbps.

➤ The type of bus used in your computer. The bus consists of the wiring inside the computer that connects the internal parts (CPU, memory, and so on). The expansion bus allows expansion boards (such as NICs) to be added to the computer. Most bus types are ISA (for 8- and 16-bit cards), EISA (for faster 32-bit cards), PCMCIA (for notebook computers), or PCI (for 32- and 64-bit cards).

➤ The type of connectors used on the NIC. Popular types of connectors include BNC and RJ-45. (See the descriptions of cables and connectors later in this chapter.)

All the NICs used on your network must support the same network protocol (that is, Ethernet or token ring). However, the computers can have different bus types and connectors (if you use adapters or hubs).

Techno Talk

Instead of buying NICs, hubs, and cables separately, you can buy LAN connection kits that include everything you need. Typically these kits enable you to start with two PCs and add hardware for additional PCs. Examples of these kits include 3Com OfficeConnect Networking Kit (`http://www.3Com.com`) and D-Link DE-905 Network Kit for Small Workgroups (`http://www.dlink.com`).

New Networking Hardware

Studies on home and small-office computer use have determined that users are ready for the power that can be gained by networking their computers. However, many people shy away from the idea of running new cables through their house. Several relatively new network technologies have been developed to deal with that issue.

Some of the new technologies aimed at small networks enable people to create computer networks without adding new wiring to their homes. Although not yet widely used, many of these technologies are available today:

➤ *Phone lines* HomeRun from Tut Systems enables you to connect computers in your home or business through the standard copper wires and phone jacks already in the building. These wires can be shared simultaneously without disturbing telephone traffic. Standard Ethernet protocol is used at speeds of 1Mbps.

➤ *Power outlets* Products for connecting computers over the power lines that run through a house are being developed by Intelogis, Inc. One feature that makes this approach attractive is that there are usually many more power outlets than phone outlets in a house. This makes it more convenient to connect computers almost anywhere in the house.

➤ *Radio frequency* RadioLAN, WebGear, and Proxim are products that use radio wave technology to create LANs. Although this type of technology has been around for a while, it is still prohibitively expensive for most small networks.

➤ *Infrared* Another type of wireless networking relies on infrared technology. Add an infrared adapter card to a computer at one end of the room. Connect an infrared sensor to the hub or daisy chain network, and point it toward the computer. The computer can then log on to the network.

In the coming years, some network technology will probably arise as the leader in the home and small business market. As of today, however, the jury is still out.

Hardware for Joining Computers

Even though there is a wide range of networking hardware available today, relatively few components are needed by an administrator of a small network.

If you are connecting a LAN (with no connections to outside networks), you probably only need cables to connect each computer's NIC and optionally a hub to connect the computers. Other networking hardware described in this section will help you if your network routes data to other networks or must extend beyond the physical limits of a LAN (for example, to extend a LAN to another building).

Cabling and Connectors

Each of the different types of cabling you can use with your LAN has different characteristics. In particular, cabling affects how far apart the computers can be and how quickly data can travel between them. (Of course, distances can be extended using repeaters and bridges.) Popular types of cable are

➤ Coaxial

➤ Twisted pair

➤ Fiber optic

Coaxial

A coaxial cable is similar to the type of cable that is probably already in your home, connecting your cable television. A center wire is inside the coaxial cable and is wrapped in insulation and a grounded shield of braided wire. Coaxial cable can carry more data than telephone wires and protects better against interference.

Standard coaxial cables used with Ethernet LANs are often referred to as *thicknet* and *thinnet*. Each type has different characteristics:

➤ *Thicknet*   This was the original type of cable specified for Ethernet. Because the cable is thick (about 1 cm), it is fairly difficult to install. Supported cables include Belden numbers 9880 (PVC) and 89880 (plenum rated). Thicknet uses male N type connectors.

With thicknet, an AUI cable is also needed to connect the NIC to an external transceiver before connecting to the thicknet cable. On one end of the AUI is a female 15-pin connector (with a sliding latch). The other end of the AUI has a male 15-pin connector.

➤ *Thinnet*   This type of cable is more flexible than thicknet cable. The cable is about .5 cm thick. Coax thinnet cables can be of type RG 58 A/U or RG 58 C/U. Each end of the cable must have a male BNC connector.

Coaxial cable is more difficult to string through a building than twisted pair (telephone-style). Often, workstations are connected together using twisted pair, whereas coaxial might be used to connect Ethernet hubs.

Twisted Pair

Twisted pair cables consist of two pairs of wires that are connected on each end to an eight-pin connector (RJ-45). The name is derived from the fact that the two wires in each pair are twisted together from one end to the other. (Wires are twisted to help reduce interference.)

Unshielded twisted pair (UTP) and shielded twisted pair (STP) are the two basic cable designs that are available. In STP cables, the wires that carry the signals are covered in a conducting shield. In UTP cables, balancing and filtering techniques are used instead of shielding.

Although the designs of UTP and STP are different, it is not clear that either provides superior performance.

Fiber Optic

A fiber-optic cable consists of a bundle of glass or plastic threads that transmit data in the form of modulated light waves. Bandwidth (that is, the amount of data that can pass through) is much higher with fiber-optic cables than with traditional metal cables.

Although fiber optic is more expensive and more difficult to install than metal cables, it has become more popular in recent years. The tremendous performance gains can outweigh the initial setup costs in a short time.

Ethernet Connection Standards

A variety of standards can be used to connect computers in an Ethernet network. Each standard defines the types of cable and connectors to be used, which in turn defines the distances between computers that can be supported. Your options include 10Base2, 10Base5, 10BaseT, and 100BaseT. (See later sections for descriptions of each type of cable and connector used.)

Ethernet 10Base2

This connection type uses thinnet coaxial cables. With thinnet, you can string your computers together in a *daisy chain*.

To create a daisy chain, you use a T connector on each NIC to connect the computer from one neighbor to the next. A BNC 50-ohm terminator is used at both ends of the chain.

The following figure shows the hardware used in connecting a 10Base2 Ethernet network.

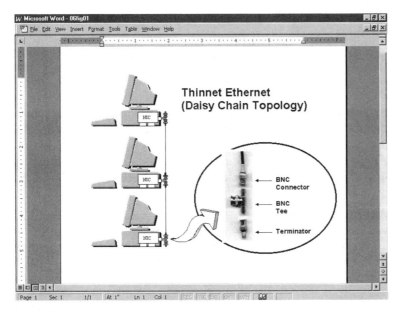

10Base2 thinnet Ethernet networks enable you to daisy-chain computers.

Thinnet wires carry signals at 10Mbps. Each segment can be up to 185 meters. Up to 30 connections can be supported (each workstation and repeater connection point represents a connection).

Ethernet 10Base5

The 10Base5 standard is older than the 10Base2 method, and uses different cabling (referred to as *thicknet*). Though the cabling is thicker and more difficult to handle, it does support greater distances between computers and more computers on each segment.

Extra cabling is required with 10Base5 because the transceiver is external to the NIC. Here, an AUI connector on the NIC is connected by an AUI cable to an external transceiver. The transceiver then connects to the thicknet coaxial cable via an AMP tap. The thicknet cable itself is terminated with type N connectors. A thicknet cable tap is also called a *vampire tap*.

Thicknet wires carry signals at 10Mbps. The AUI cable can be up to 50 meters long, whereas the thicknet cable can be up to 500 meters. Up to 100 connections can be supported.

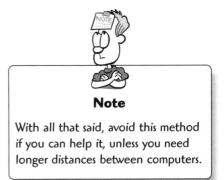

Note

With all that said, avoid this method if you can help it, unless you need longer distances between computers.

Ethernet 10BaseT

The 10BaseT method relies on twisted pair wiring (either shielded or unshielded) to connect computers. This wiring is similar to the wire you use to plug in your telephone, except that it uses 8-pin RJ-45 jacks instead of the smaller 4-pin RJ-11 jacks. This is the most popular method of connecting computers in a LAN.

Most often, wires are plugged into the NIC on one end and a hub on the other. You can purchase hubs with different numbers of ports, depending on how many computers you need to connect together.

The following figure shows an example of hardware used in connecting a 10BaseT Ethernet network.

Simple jacks and hubs connect computers on a 10BaseT LAN.

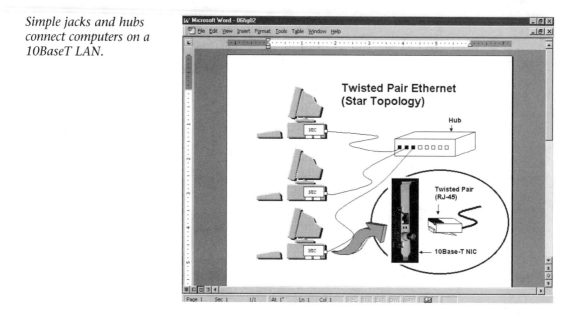

RJ-45 twisted-pair wires carry signals at 10Mbps. Distance from the NIC to the hub should not be more than 100 meters.

Check This Out

You can connect two computers together using twisted pair cable. However, that cable must be what they call a *crossover cable*. On this cable, the pins are crossed over (pin 1 to pin 3; pin 2 to pin 6) so that both sides transmit and receive on different wires.

Ethernet 100BaseT

To support the new Fast Ethernet, new cabling standards have been developed. These new transmission and cabling schemes can support data transfer rates of 100Mbps.

There are several different cabling methods associated with Fast Ethernet:

➤ *100BaseTX*   This type of cabling consists of two pairs of twisted pair wiring (high quality).

➤ *100BaseT4*   This type of cabling consists of four pairs of twisted pair wiring (normal quality).

➤ *100BaseFX*   This type of cabling consists of fiber-optic cables.

Other Network Equipment

Networks that consist of more than a few computers around the office usually require more equipment than NIC cards and cables. The following sections define some of the other networking equipment you might encounter in a computer network.

Hubs

Hubs are used to connect multiple Ethernet segments. These segments can be of different media types (thinnet, thicknet, twisted pair, and so on). The hub acts as a repeater by taking incoming signals and repeating them out of all the ports. Hubs also amplify the signals to improve signals that can be weakened from traveling great distances. Most 10BaseT networks use hubs to connect computers together on a LAN.

When computers in a network are connected to a hub, this is referred to as a *star topology*. This is in contrast to a *bus topology*, where computers are daisy-chained together.

Routers

Routers are used to route messages among subnetworks on a computer network. For example, a router might be connected to a company's LAN that contains a Web server. That router is also connected to a line to the Internet backbone. Both incoming and outgoing messages between the company's LAN and the Internet pass through the router.

There are dedicated routers designed to route messages as their main job. Some computers have routing protocols built in, so instead of purchasing a separate router, you can use that computer to do routing between various networks. The UNIX operating system is an example of a system that has built-in routing capabilities.

Bridges

A *bridge* connects one LAN to another LAN of the same type. Bridges are a way to extend the boundary of a LAN when you need connections to more local computers than the LAN can handle.

Techno Talk

When you plan your network, you must take into account bandwidth and other limitations that determine how many computers you can connect on a LAN. For a discussion of network planning issues, please see Chapter 8, "Planning Your Network."

Bridges are implemented at the data link layer (level 2). This means that the network layer above it sees the LANs that are connected by bridges as the same network.

You might purchase bridge hardware if, for example, you need to connect hundreds of computers in the same building. They can't all be on the same LAN, but they can be on the same Class B or C Internet network address.

Switches

Like bridges, *switches* are used to connect several LANs together. Ports on a LAN switch can be connected to end computers or to other LANs. The switch can act to divide LANs into separate segments to improve performance and reduce the number of collisions.

Techno Talk

Collisions occur on an Ethernet network because of its design. Ethernet is a CSMA-CD (Carrier Sense Multiple Access with Collision Detection) type of network. Because all computers on an Ethernet LAN broadcast on the network without waiting for a turn, messages sometimes run into each other. Ethernet is designed to correct for that, but if there are too many computers on the network, collisions can slow down network performance.

Gateways

A *gateway* is similar to a router, except that a gateway routes messages from one type of network to a completely different type of network. For example, a gateway might route messages between the Internet (a TCP/IP network) and an IBM SNA network. In this case, the two networks are different all the way to the top of the seven-layer OSI reference model.

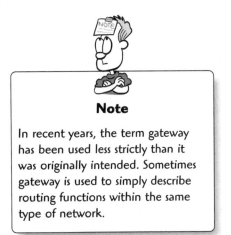

Note

In recent years, the term gateway has been used less strictly than it was originally intended. Sometimes gateway is used to simply describe routing functions within the same type of network.

Where To From Here?

This chapter described the different networking hardware items you can use to put together your network. Managing the networking hardware (and software, for that matter) requires an understanding of the operating systems running on the network. To learn next about these systems, see Chapter 7.

The Least You Need to Know

Right now, the least you need to know about networking hardware is this:

➤ A variety of computer workstations and servers can be connected to your network. These can include network computers, such as JavaStations and Net PCs that rely on the network to function correctly.

➤ NICs and modems can be used to connect to a network. Modems are used to dial remote networks whereas NICs are used on local area networks.

➤ Most LANs communicate over coaxial or twisted pair cables. However, some newer technologies allow computer LANs to connect using a building's electrical wiring, telephone lines in the building, or wireless radio frequencies.

➤ Bridges and switches are used to connect LANs to improve overall performance of the network. Routers deliver messages across network boundaries, among networks of the same type.

## Chapter 7

Network Operating Systems (NOSes)

In This Chapter

➤ Find out what a network operating system does.

➤ Understand basic networking features in Microsoft Windows 95 and 98.

➤ Learn about more advanced networking features in Windows NT, NetWare, UNIX, and Linux systems.

The *operating system* is the combination of software programs that work together to manage your computer. It stands between the application programs (such as word processors and spreadsheets) and the hardware. In essence, it allows your programs to use the hard disk, CPU, CD-ROM, printer, and so on.

A *network operating system* (*NOS*) is one that is dedicated to managing network resources. It can be a server—handling file storage, printer sharing, application sharing, or Web publishing—or it can act as a central place for managing network traffic, users, or computers.

With the exception of NetWare (which is a pure network operating system), most of the operating systems described in this chapter can act as regular workstations. However, each system contains enough networking features to allow it to be configured to provide dedicated network services.

Network Operating System Features

Though most operating systems provide many of the same services, they often do so with different levels of complexity and power. You can expect to find some or all of the following features in the systems described in this chapter:

➤ *Network hardware support*   With most systems you can connect modems (for dial up networks) and Ethernet cards (for local area networks) to your computer. Some systems support hardware that allows connections to wide area networks as well.

➤ *File sharing*   Most systems enable you to share file folders or whole disk drives with clients on the network.

➤ *Printer sharing*   Most systems enable you to share printers with client computers over the network.

➤ *Web services*   Most systems enable you to add software that allows the computer to act as a Web server (to publish Web pages on the Internet).

➤ *Network administration*   Most systems include features for monitoring the network and managing other computers on the network. Advanced systems might offer directory services, which enable you to store and disseminate information about computer resources on the network.

➤ *Security services*   Most systems provide some level of network security. This can be as simple as providing passwords for users to protect their files or as complex as a firewall for screening traffic between multiple networks.

This chapter describes several network operating systems that are available.

Microsoft Windows Operating Systems

All the Microsoft Windows operating systems contain some level of networking support. Although Windows 95/98 systems are primarily desktop computers, they offer most basic client networking features. Windows NT, however, was designed for working in networked environments.

Microsoft Windows 95/98

If you have Windows 95 or 98 computers connected to your network, you might already have all the support you need for basic networking. To expand the networking capabilities of Windows, you can add a variety of software enhancements (such as NetWare client support).

Here are some of the networking features built into Windows 95/98:

➤ *Dial-up and LAN connections* Most popular modems and network interface cards (NICs) are supported by Windows 95/98. Modems enable you to dial up remote computer networks, whereas with NICs you can connect to higher-speed local area networks.

A variety of software programs can use these devices, including those that enable you to work with bulletin boards, faxes, electronic mail, and the Internet. Likewise, various protocols can work with each device to provide you with access to TCP/IP, NetWare (IPX/SPX), and other types of networks.

➤ *Network administration* Windows 95 and 98 come with utilities for administering and monitoring the network. These include Net Watcher (to monitor clients and shared resources), System Monitor (to allow remote monitoring of a system), and Remote Registry Service (to enable a remote administrator to change a computer's registry).

If you add NetWare servers or Windows NT systems to your network, there are many more services available for managing your workstations.

➤ *Remote user profiles* With user accounts set up properly, you can log in from another computer on a network and have access to the user's desktop and applications.

➤ *Sharing of printers and files* The printer and file sharing features in Windows 95/98 allow networked computers to share each other's printers and files. With file sharing, you can share individual folders or entire drives.

➤ *Connect to the Internet* Using dial-up networking or built-in LAN support, you can use Windows 95/98 protocols to connect to the Internet. With the addition of the Internet Explorer Web browser (described later in this chapter), you have all the most important Internet applications in one package.

Note

Internet Explorer comes built into Windows 98. If you have Windows 95, but do not have Internet Explorer, you can download Internet Explorer free from Microsoft. Go to `http://www.microsoft.com/ie` and select to Download IE.

Surfing with Internet Explorer

Microsoft Internet Explorer is not just a Web browser. Rather, it is a bundle of software applications that enable Internet clients to manage email, have conferences, play audio and video, and publish Web pages.

In only a couple of years, IE has nearly surpassed the popularity of Netscape Communicator, which once completely dominated the browser market. Here's what IE includes:

➤ *Browser* Enables you to browse Web pages on the Internet and play a variety of graphical, audio, video, and other content.

➤ *NetMeeting* Enables you to connect to audio, video, and typed (chat) conferences on the Internet.

➤ *Outlook Express* Enables you to compose, send, receive, and manage electronic mail and newsgroup messages.

➤ *Media Player* Plays live audio and video broadcasts.

➤ *FrontPage Express* Can be used to create basic Web pages that can be put on the Internet.

➤ *Web Publishing wizard* Enables you to manage the Web content you create and publish it to the Internet.

The following figure shows an example of an Internet Explorer window.

Microsoft Windows NT

Microsoft offers its Windows NT operating system as a more powerful alternative to its Windows 95/98 desktop systems. Unlike those desktop systems, Windows NT was created with networking in mind. This allows it to compete with UNIX and NetWare in the server market.

The Windows NT Server offers the following networking services:

➤ *File server* Windows NT can be used as a file server, offering file services to Windows 3.1, MS-DOS, UNIX, Macintosh, Windows 95, Windows 98, and Windows NT workstations.

➤ *Print server* Can support more than 1,000 printer models. Features include priority printing and remote administration.

➤ *Applications server*   Offers application services, including those based on Microsoft's Component Object Model (COM) and the Distributed Component Object Model (DCOM).

➤ *Web server*   Provides Web services for the Internet and corporate intranets using Internet Information Server (IIS) 4.0 software. The Web server also supports Web-based application services.

➤ *Management services*   Provides administration tools for centrally administering network resources.

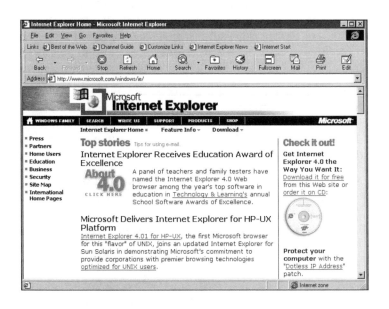

Internet Explorer provides a popular way to access the Internet.

An advantage of Windows NT over other network operating systems is that it offers an easy migration path from Windows 95/98 systems. Many of the same applications can be run on both platforms. A disadvantage of Windows NT is that it has not been battle-tested as long as NetWare and UNIX systems have. Windows NT also tends to be more Microsoft-centric than more standards-based operating systems such as UNIX and Linux.

Novell NetWare

A decade ago, NetWare was the leading product for providing file and print services to networked PCs. Although the rise of the Internet has shifted the focus of networking, NetWare and other Novell products are still used by millions of network users all over the world.

NetWare is, by all definitions, a network operating system. Its main job is to act as a server for file and print services. Along with those features, NetWare offers a complex set of security and management features to determine who has access to which services from the network.

Novell Directory Services and Z.E.N.works

Novell Directory Services (NDS) sets NetWare apart from other operating systems that are less dedicated to networking. With NDS, administrators can manage network resources from a central directory of information.

To enhance the value of NDS, Novell has added some fairly sophisticated network management features. Z.E.N.works, which stands for Zero Effort Networks, sets a new direction for network management with NDS from Novell.

Advantages of the zero effort part of Z.E.N.works are felt mostly by the end users. Instead of being tied to a particular workstation, users can get their desktop and applications from the network. For the network administrator, some time spent creating NDS entries can result in efficient software distribution, user setups, and workstation support.

The Novell Application Launcher (NAL) feature of Z.E.N.works enables administrators to gather and distribute even the most complex applications. Using a utility called SnAppShot, NAL captures applications by scanning the workstation before and after an application is installed. The resulting files, folders, configuration files, and Registry entries are gathered and distributed automatically to user workstations with NDS.

The following figure shows the NAL SnAppShot utility scanning a Windows 95 workstation for the files to include with an application.

Novell's SnAppShot gathers applications for distribution.

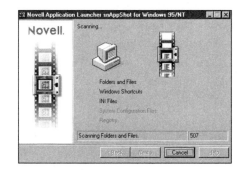

UNIX

Networking features were being built into the UNIX operating system before PCs even existed. From the beginning of the Internet, UNIX has been the predominant Internet operating system. Today's UNIX systems are rich in networking features and are still the systems most often used to develop cutting-edge networking technology.

Strictly speaking, UNIX is not a network operating system in the same way that NetWare is. Whereas NetWare is dedicated to managing network resources, UNIX offers a full range of features that allow it to act as a workstation, a peer, a server, or a client. By design, UNIX is also not limited by PC hardware. There are versions of UNIX running on everything from PCs to super computers.

Although UNIX was once used primarily from dumb character terminals, *graphical user interfaces* (*GUIs*) are now available on every version of UNIX. In fact, even the GUIs are network ready (see the description of the X Window system later in this chapter).

Advantages of UNIX

Powerful features and the capability to grow are perhaps the greatest assets of UNIX. Other advantages include the following:

➤ *Rich set of networking features*   Not only are more networking features implemented on UNIX, but many advanced features are included with the basic system. Programs for using networks (email, browsers, ftp, and so on) and tools for administering the network (routing, logging, and management tools) are available when you install the system. Some advanced features (such as firewalls and Web servers) are often available at additional cost.

➤ *Scalability*   You're not stuck with a certain computer size or architecture when you use UNIX. In fact, UNIX runs on PCs (Intel X86 and up), workstations (SPARC), and a variety of high-end processors. If your organization grows, you can easily trade up to a bigger machine.

Another way that scalability is built into UNIX is in its capability to take advantage of upgraded hardware. You can often keep your same computer and install additional hard disks, massive amounts of memory, and extra central processing units. UNIX can typically take on those additions without the users even knowing that anything has changed (except that the computer probably performs better).

➤ *Multiuser cost economies*   Besides being built to network, UNIX was also built to be multiuser and multitasking. This means that many users can be using the computer at the same time and that each user can be running many programs at once.

By having many users working from the same computer, you can save money in various ways. If your applications are character-based (as some form-driven programs still are today), users can run dumb terminals instead of everyone having their own PCs. For graphical applications, users can have less expensive X terminals.

➤ *Centralized administration*   From a central UNIX system, an administrator can manage many users, workstations, and even multiple networks. Applications, disk space, printers, and a variety of devices can be shared in a way that makes life easier for end users.

Disadvantages of UNIX

Incompatibilities among UNIX systems and the fact that higher skill levels are required are drawbacks to using UNIX. Other disadvantages follow:

➤ *Made for geeks*   Though UNIX was designed for networking from the ground up it was not designed for ease of use. It's nearly impossible to do everything required to manage a network without an understanding of the UNIX shell, editing system files, and compiling programs.

Many of the most powerful UNIX tools (especially those for managing networks) still require you to run text-based commands. With menus or icons for some tools, you need to remember command names and options to do your job. The bottom line is that you probably won't want to take on UNIX to manage your network without some training first.

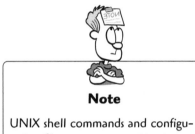

Note

UNIX shell commands and configuration files are more consistent among different UNIX versions than GUI-based tools are. So if you learn how to use UNIX from the shell, your knowledge will transfer better to other UNIX systems.

➤ *UNIX systems are different*   Even though most UNIX systems began from source code originally delivered from AT&T, the UNIX systems that have made it to market all contain some subtle— and some not so subtle—differences. In particular, many vendors have added their own simplified methods for administering the systems.

As a result, even if you learn how to set up one type of UNIX system, chances are you can't use the exact same sequence of commands, options, or configuration files to do it on another UNIX version. That's why administering a UNIX system doesn't mean learning an exact set of procedures—it means fiddling with it until it works.

For users, the same issues apply. Although underlying networking protocols can be the same between different UNIX systems, the graphical programs for launching remote applications, using email, or transferring files can be quite different. In fact, the entire look and feel can be different from one UNIX system to another.

➤ *Difficult to find applications*   Many application developers build programs for Microsoft Windows systems. They might or might not ever create a version that runs on UNIX. If they do, it might not run on the particular version of UNIX that you have.

In other words, it's not easy to go into your local computer store and find a pile of UNIX applications that you can pop into your CD-ROM drive and install in five minutes. Also, because many packaged applications are geared to a particular UNIX version, they might not run on your UNIX system at all. Often you need to get an application in source code form and compile it yourself for it to work on your UNIX version.

UNIX Networking Features

Just about any feature you can think of for using, configuring, and managing networks (especially TCP/IP networks) is available in the UNIX system. These features might not be as simple as similar ones in Microsoft Windows, but with some patience you can make UNIX do almost anything you want.

Although the first UNIX networking features were centered around a set of tools that were generically labeled UUCP (UNIX-to-UNIX copy), current UNIX networking features focus on TCP/IP (the protocols that drive the Internet). Most of the features described here can be used with TCP/IP networks.

User Programs

On a TCP/IP network, there are a variety of tools you can use to communicate with other users and computers. Some of the most common programs are

➤ *Web browser*   For browsing the World Wide Web, Web browsers have become an indispensable tool. Some UNIX systems include Netscape Communicator. Besides browser features, users also get graphical email, conferencing, calendar, Web page composition, and other Web features.

➤ *Remote login* (`rlogin` or `telnet`)   The `rlogin` command enables the user to log in to a remote computer over TCP/IP networks. The `telnet` command is a more generic tool for logging in to a remote computer that works on a variety of network types.

➤ *Remote copy* (`rcp`)   The `rcp` command enables a user to copy a file from one computer system to another. Files can be copied to and from any directory on any computer to which the user has permissions.

➤ *File Transfer Protocol* (`ftp`)   FTP is both a command and protocol (set of rules) for browsing through an area of files and directories on a remote system and copying files to or from that system.

➤ *Remote shell* (`rsh`)   Using the `rsh` command, you can request that a command be run on a remote system and that the output be returned to your screen.

SLIP and PPP

To communicate with remote computers on the Internet over serial lines (such as modems), most UNIX systems support both *Serial Line Interface Protocol* (*SLIP*) and *Point-to-Point Protocol* (*PPP*). These are the common protocols used by personal computers to connect to the Internet over telephone lines. PPP is more versatile and reliable than SLIP. Therefore, PPP is by far the more popular of the two protocols.

File Sharing

UNIX systems enable you to share files on a peer-to-peer basis. That means that any computer on the network can offer parts of its file systems for other computers to use (read or write files).

The most popular method of sharing files among UNIX systems is called Network File System (NFS). With NFS, one computer offers a directory by sharing files to the network. Another computer uses the directory (and all subdirectories to that directory) by mounting that directory on its local file system.

Printer Sharing

UNIX systems can allow access by other computers to their printers using the lpsystem command. Usually there is also a graphical interface available (depending in which version of UNIX you are using) that allows you to make a printer available to the network. A user on another computer can simply direct printing output to the shared printer (using the lp command or through an application).

Many UNIX systems, especially those based on UNIX System V, offer strong support for NetWare printing as well. Graphical tools enable you to browse accessible NetWare servers to choose a NetWare printer.

X Window System

Most, if not all, graphical user interfaces available on UNIX systems are built on top of the X Window system (also referred to as *X*). X provides the framework in which graphical applications can run—you start an application and X handles the communication between the application and your display, mouse, and keyboard.

One of the most powerful features of X (and the reason X is described here) is that it is designed to be used on networks. So, when you use X, you can run applications from anywhere on the network and have them appear on your display.

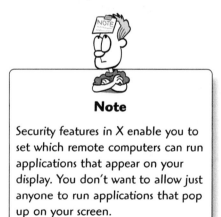

Note

Security features in X enable you to set which remote computers can run applications that appear on your display. You don't want to allow just anyone to run applications that pop up on your screen.

The reason GUIs can look so different from one computer to the next is that X must be used with a window manager to manage the applications on your desktop. The window manager defines the borders and menus on each window, how mouse and keyboard controls work, and style issues (such as colors and fonts used). Motif is the most popular window manager for commercial UNIX systems.

Because X applications can be run on remote computers, it's possible to have your workstation only be running the X display, while all applications you use come from application servers on the network. X terminals were designed to meet the need for inexpensive workstations that run the X display, but run applications from other computers that appear on the screen.

Network Management

The UNIX system contains features that enable you to manage multiple computers from one computer, monitor network activities, and route data across multiple networks. The following are some of the more powerful network management features available on UNIX systems:

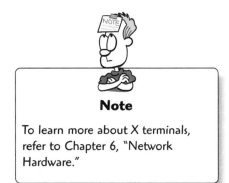

Note

To learn more about X terminals, refer to Chapter 6, "Network Hardware."

➤ *Domain Name System (DNS) servers*   When an application (such as a Web browser) requests an Internet address (for example, `http://www.mcp.com`), that address needs to be translated into an IP address (such as `111.11.11.1`). A UNIX system can be identified as a DNS server to do the actual name to address translations.

➤ *Routing*   Instead of using a dedicated router on your network, you can have your UNIX system handle your routing functions. Using standard TCP/IP protocols, UNIX can monitor your local network and route messages to other networks. Likewise, the system can forward messages from remote networks to the recipient on the local network.

To handle routing, the UNIX host is what is referred to as *multihomed*. Typically this means that one wire connects the host to your LAN and another connects the host to another network (such as one that provides a high-speed connection to the Internet). Daemon processes (such as `routed` or `gated`) gather routing information from other routers on the network, so the computer knows where to route messages.

What the Heck is a Daemon?

A *daemon* process is a program that is running in the background of a UNIX system. Usually, the daemon waits for a request for a service, then responds by either handling the request or passing the request to another program.

For example, a printer daemon listens for requests to print a document. When you try to print a document, the print daemon forwards that request to the appropriate printer.

Although routing from a UNIX system might not be as efficient as using dedicated routers, it can save money by taking advantage of the hardware that you already have running on the network.

➤ *Simple Network Management Protocol (SNMP)*   With SNMP, you can monitor computers on the network and analyze how well they are performing. After SNMP identifies a problem, you can troubleshoot and fix the problem on the network without leaving your own computer.

SNMP can, for example, enable you to change routing tables if network traffic is not flowing efficiently. You can see right where the network bottlenecks are and make a case for changing or increasing your network capacity.

➤ *Network Information System (NIS)*   With NIS you can gather information needed to manage computers on a network. It then enables you to disseminate that information to those computers. For example, you can gather information about your TCP/IP domain (`/etc/hosts file`), computer users (`/etc/password file`), and network services (`/etc/services file`). That information can then be automatically distributed to the computers on your network, so they don't have to be updated one at a time.

➤ *Bootp*   A network administrator can manage a set of diskless workstations using the Bootp protocol. Such a workstation can start up with minimal support for TCP/IP. It contacts the Bootp server (on a UNIX system) which in turn provides the workstation with the information it needs to start up. This might include the workstation's IP address, name servers, gateway lists, and boot files.

Linux

Linux is a free, UNIX-like operating system that was created in 1991 by Linus Torvalds when he was a student at the University of Helsinki. He posted it to the Internet and soon received code fixes and new programs. Today, nearly 10,000 programmers contribute to the coding, testing, and discussion groups that continuously improve the Linux operating system.

Although Linux code was written from scratch, the operating system didn't exactly come from thin air. Published standards that drove the development of the UNIX system, POSIX in particular, made Linux about as much like UNIX as possible without actually owning the trademark. In many ways, however, Linux has developed beyond UNIX because there are so many people contributing to its features and improvements.

There is no shortage of networking standards for Linux to adhere to. Linux contains a full complement of networking features, particularly related to the Internet. Linux programmers tend to be especially savvy about the Internet—they used the Internet as the primary tool for communicating and distributing information about Linux.

Linux networking features are very similar to those networking features described earlier for UNIX. There are Linux implementations of Bootp, FTP, NIS, NFS, UUCP, PPP, and many other abbreviations. There is software for managing news servers, Web servers, and IP firewalls. Most standards-based UNIX networking features are in Linux.

Distributions of Linux

Currently, there are Linux versions that run on Intel compatible PCs, Digital Alpha computers, and Sun SPARC computers. Although the source code of Linux is available for free on the Internet, there are ready-to-run (binary) versions of Linux available from commercial vendors for a fee. These include

- ➤ Red Hat Linux (`http://www.redhat.com`)
- ➤ Caldera Open Linux (`http://www.caldera.com`)
- ➤ Debian Linux (`http://www.linuxpress.com`)
- ➤ S.u.S.E. Linux (`http://www.suse.com`)
- ➤ Slackware (`ftp://ftp.cdrom.com/pub/linux/slackware`)

These commercial versions of Linux tend to be fairly inexpensive (starting under $30). With the addition of installation procedures and often some form of technical support, many users find the benefits of a commercial distribution worth the small price.

Advantages of Linux

Using Linux offers many advantages, including the following:

- ➤ Linux is free to anyone who wants to download it and is inexpensive in packaged CD-ROM forms.
- ➤ Corrections and enhancements are continuously being made by thousands of developers around the world. (Some say Linux developers outnumber the developers on any other operating system 10 to 1.)
- ➤ Because the source code is readily available, those who are so inclined can modify it to suit their own needs.
- ➤ There are thousands of free or inexpensive add-on packages available to run on Linux.

Disadvantages of Linux

Of course, using Linux has its disadvantages, too:

- ➤ Some people feel that Linux has not yet proven itself as being reliable enough for a company's mission-critical applications.
- ➤ Some organizations that once provided the direction followed by Linux are either no longer around or are beginning to charge for their services. Eventually, this might cause Linux to have to create more of its own specifications.

For example, the X Consortium, which formerly distributed the X Window System for free, has been replaced by the Open Group (which now charges for future X Window System releases). Companies such as AT&T, which originally owned the UNIX trademark, no longer take a strong lead in setting the course for UNIX.

Where To From Here?

Some of the more popular network operating systems were described in this chapter. To understand how to put together your network operating systems, computers, application programs, and peripheral hardware to form a network, go to Part III, "Putting Your Network Together."

The Least You Need to Know

Right now, the least you need to know about network operating systems is this:

➤ Basic networking, such as file and printer sharing, can be done from even the least sophisticated network operating systems (such as Windows 95).

➤ With the addition of Internet Explorer and dial-up networking, Microsoft Windows operating systems have become more powerful tools for connecting to the Internet.

➤ NetWare offers advanced networking features, including Novell Directory Services (NDS). By using Z.E.N.works with NDS, administrators can centrally administer user configurations, software distribution, and computer hardware setups.

➤ The UNIX operating system has the richest set of networking features. UNIX can be difficult for non-technical people to administer and work with, however.

➤ Linux contains a full set of UNIX-like features, rivaling commercial UNIX systems in networking support. Along with its excellent set of features, Linux has the advantage of being available for free.

Part 3

Putting Your Network Together

Ready to jump into your first computer network? First, a little bit of planning is in order. What do you need to do with your network? What kind of budget do you have? How sophisticated are your network users?

Once you answer a few questions, you will be better prepared to design your network and purchase the necessary hardware and software. Chapters in this part help you do that planning in addition to providing an example of a small office/home office network that might help as a model for your network.

## Chapter 8

Planning Your Network

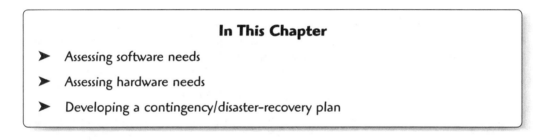

In This Chapter

➤ Assessing software needs

➤ Assessing hardware needs

➤ Developing a contingency/disaster-recovery plan

Establishing your first network is quite a task—and one that always needs to be done right the first time around. So before actually going out and buying all the equipment, you need to engage in at least minimal planning. This chapter covers basic points of network planning as well as ways to save some money.

In the Beginning

Your first step is to develop a basic framework—a baseline strategy that answers the following questions:

➤ What do you want to accomplish with your network?

➤ What applications do you need?

➤ What services does each user require?

➤ What type of network (client/server or peer-to-peer) do you need?

By answering these four questions, you'll also answer perhaps a dozen more. For example, in determining which applications you need you'll also be determining what hardware you need. Certainly, if you intend to do much computer aided design, you'll need hard-hitting processors and gobs of memory. If, on the other hand, you're establishing a network for an accounting department, you might not need much horsepower at all.

Similarly, by determining what you want to accomplish with your network you can determine not only the type of network you need, but also the type of support and development you'll require. For example, suppose you're establishing a network where collaboration and document distribution are both major factors. You'll probably choose a client/server network. Knowing this, you'll need staff (support and developers) with experience in TCP/IP.

Note

To learn more about TCP/IP, see Chapter 5, "System Architectures and Protocols."

NOS Considerations

Start by trying to answer the most important question first: What do you intend to accomplish with this network? The answer will help you determine which network operating system is for you.

When deciding on a NOS, consider the following factors:

➤ *Availability of supporting applications*   Does your NOS support many applications? In particular, does it support applications critical to your business?

➤ *Compatibility*   Can your NOS seamlessly interface with other systems?

➤ *Cost*   Is your NOS cost-efficient and within your means?

➤ *Scalability*   Does your NOS scale well? Will you be able to easily expand your operation?

For example, in a legal or medical office the appropriate choice might well be Novell NetWare. It has security (see Chapter 13, "Security"), it scales nicely, it can support other operating systems (DOS and Windows), and hundreds of critical third party applications have been written specifically for it. NetWare can also run on meager hardware—or at least cheaper hardware than it takes to run other operating systems.

On the other hand, perhaps your network will be used chiefly for editing digital media (text, graphics, sound, and video). If so, you'd be better off with IRIX, BeOS, Amiga, or MacOS (if not for the entire network, at least for much of it).

What the Heck is BeOS?

BeOS is a new cutting-edge operating system designed expressly for editing and manipulating digital media—particularly very large files that demand heavy number crunching. Check out BeOS at `http://www.be.com`.

Finally, consider whether your system will be entirely homogeneous. If not, then you'll need to choose a primary NOS that has at least minimal compatibility with other systems. This is becoming less of a problem, as integration is no longer the exception but the rule. There are even Windows NT NFS clients available to seamlessly import UNIX file systems.

Isn't NFS What It's Called When You Write Bad Checks?

NFS is short for *Network File System*, a Sun Microsystems technology that enables you to share directories across networks. With NFS, local users see remote directories as though they are local. (For example, you can see files on a UNIX system in Windows Explorer or File Manager.) NFS is primarily used in UNIX environments. Here's a typical example: centralizing management of all Web sites by placing them on a single RAID server and then using NFS to get these directories out to individual machines where other developers can access them.

Sophistication of Users

Another important issue is your users' level of sophistication. (As much as it might pain you, you must accommodate your users.) Therefore, even if UNIX is your best choice for cost and scalability you might end up with Windows anyway (at least, on most workstations).

The truth is, most users don't have years of computer experience; instead, the typical user has about 2–3 years worth, if that. Furthermore, it's almost certain that their experience is with Windows or MacOS only. Be sure to account for that when purchasing your system.

Remember that the less user-friendly your network is, the more user support you'll have to provide—and user support is truly a resource hog. (Think about your last telephone call to technical support; how long did it last?) For these reasons, it makes sense to design an easy-to-use network where users require little assistance.

Text Support: A Knowledge Base

One good way to reduce support costs is to establish a Web-oriented knowledge base. This is a Web server with support documents that answer every question a user might possibly ever ask—including how to use the knowledge base. Add a search capability to this and you'll save thousands of dollars. (It's true, however, that no matter how extensive your knowledge base is, users still need some human interaction.)

Finally, it's worth choosing a system that's easily managed. After all, you're the one responsible for running the system. You don't really want to spend your days with your nose in a book like this one, do you?

Standardizing Your System with an Application Set

Whatever NOS you decide on, make sure it supports an office suite, a groupware suite, or both. This will help your users tremendously, even if they don't currently have much computer experience. This is because these software suites introduce a climate of standardization.

For example, consider Microsoft Office. All Office applications have a standard look and feel. The menu bar invariably has choices such as File, Edit, View, Help, and so on. These characteristics make Office applications exceptionally easy to learn; many people have remarked that if you know one Office application, you know them all.

Some good choices in office and groupware suites are

➤ ApplixWare (distributed by RedHat Software)
➤ Corel Office Professional

➤ Lotus Notes and Lotus Office Suite

➤ Microsoft Office

➤ Novell GroupWise

➤ StarOffice by Star Division

However, even if you don't choose groupware or an office suite, always strive for standardization. The single savviest move you can make is to establish and enforce the use of a consistent application set. This will save you thousands of dollars a year.

Licensing Requirements

Not only does a consistent application set save you support money (you only need someone who can troubleshoot a limited application set with a finite number of problems), it also allows you to opt for special licensing arrangements.

Licensing can dramatically influence cost, and this is a very real concern. True, religiously licensing each and every application is cumbersome and expensive. (Many of my clients knowingly violate licensing agreements by installing the same unlicensed application on 30 machines or more.) However, there can be repercussions from failing to adhere to licensing schemes.

Techno Talk

An *application set* consists of the applications installed on your workstations. Maintaining a *consistent application set* means that you have the same applications installed on all workstations, and you establish a policy approving only those applications. That means that if you designate Microsoft Word as the word processor, that's what users must use. No exceptions!

Crime Doesn't Pay

Your friends might persuade you that only large companies get raided for software license violations. That's no longer true. A recent case told of a small publishing company with eight unlicensed copies of PageMaker. They were raided, brought to justice, and fined. Such cases are becoming more common. In particular, authorities target network consultants and resellers that haphazardly load unlicensed software onto their clients' drives. To learn more about anti-piracy efforts, check out the Software Publisher's Association at `http://www.spa.org`.

If you can avoid violating licensing agreements, do it; but abiding by the law doesn't necessarily mean you need to bankrupt yourself. There are smart alternatives, a few of which are revealed in the next sections.

The Microsoft Open License Program

One solution to licensing costs is the *Microsoft Open License Program* (*MOLP*). MOLP offers your organization volume discounts by allowing you to purchase a single license for multiple users. For example, the one-time fee for a two-year, 100-user Windows 95 upgrade license is approximately $86. You simply buy one CD-ROM and pay a nominal premium to license that software on your other PCs.

Check This Out

Corel recently implemented a similar program that covers many of its products (including WordPerfect). For more information, check Corel's Web page at
`http://www.corel.com`.

Check This Out

Sun Microsystems has instituted a similar program with its popular Solaris operating system. Sun is offering Solaris 7 for $10 plus shipping and handling. This works out to approximately $30–45, depending on where you're located. Check Solaris 7 out at
`http://www.sun.com`.

As of this writing, many (but not all) Microsoft software packages are being offered through MOLP, including Access, Back Office, Exchange, FrontPage, SQL Client, Visual J++ Pro, Windows NT, Word, Excel, and Works.

Non-Commercial Licenses

If your primary goal is merely to learn networking, you might consider obtaining a non-commercial, educational license. For example, SCO will send you a full distribution of UNIXWare/OpenServer for about $19 (or current shipping and handling costs). This is an especially good deal because the distribution includes development tools (C/C++, Java SDK), networking (TCP/IP, UUCP, Netscape FastTrack Server, and so on), and even real Motif. You can obtain SCO OpenServer from SCO's Web site (`http://www.sco.com`).

Non-commercial, educational licenses allow you to use the software for any non-commercial purpose. This means that you can run your own network or Web site with it, or you can even develop your own software for it. You just can't sell the software you develop, and you can't use the software to make money.

Linux and GNU Software

A still more inexpensive approach—especially if you're building an intranet—is to choose Linux and GNU software. You can download this software from the Internet free of charge. More importantly, however, this software is free in another sense of the word; Richard Stallman, head of the Free Software Foundation, says in the preamble to the GNU Public License Agreement:

> When we speak of free software, we are referring to freedom, not price. Our General Public Licenses are designed to make sure that you have the freedom to distribute copies of free software (and charge for this service if you wish), that you receive source code or can get it if you want it, that you can change the software or use pieces of it in new free programs; and that you know you can do these things.

Stallman's concept of free software was born of necessity. He recognized, for example, that most folks like to share software with their friends. Because this is generally unlawful—and breaks licensing agreements—people are forced to choose between their friends and the law. Naturally, most people choose their friends. As an alternative, Stallman founded the Free Software Foundation and began the world's largest and most successful free software project. (Check out the FSF at `http://www.fsf.org`.)

Linux was released as free software and, therefore, Linux and GNU software were a marriage made in heaven. Hence, the average Linux distribution contains dozens of popular GNU applications and utilities, all of which are legally transferable to third parties. However, not everything on your Linux CD-ROM is necessarily free. Whereas nearly all stock Linux applications and utilities come under the GNU public license, many third-party extras don't. If you purchase a commercial Linux distribution, read the fine print. You might be forbidden from using more than one copy of certain proprietary programs.

As an example, Caldera's OpenLinux includes an excellent desktop suite called *Looking Glass*. Looking Glass provides more than simple window management; it offers a comprehensive file manager, search capabilities, customization tools, and visualization packages. These do not fall under the GNU license; technically, therefore, if you redistribute these or run them on more than one station, you break the license agreement. (Red Hat Linux has similar tools that are also covered by a separate license). So beware of third party applications on Linux. If you intend to redistribute Linux, even around your own office, be sure to strip proprietary third-party tools from it before installation.

Hardware Needs

After you've figured out which NOS is for you, determine what hardware you need to use to support that NOS. To a certain degree, this is influenced by the aforementioned factors. For example, you'll want to preserve the high-end, power-packed machines for either servers or graphics/development workstations. In contrast, you'll want to save money where clients or low-level nodes are concerned. To see this concept in action, check out the following figure.

A well-planned network.

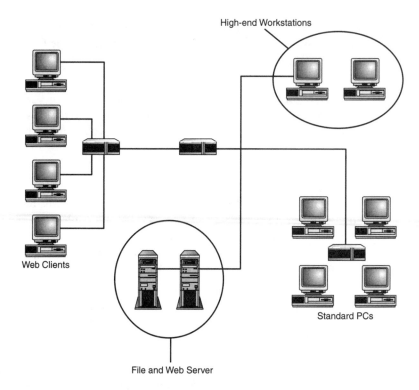

High-end Workstations

Web Clients

File and Web Server

Standard PCs

Surfing with DOS

You can actually establish Web clients for next to nothing. Caldera currently markets.a DOS version (dubbed DR-DOS) that sports a JavaScript-compliant Web browser and full TCP/IP support. The DR-DOS operating system will run on 386s and up, enabling you to take salvage machines and turn them into cheap and efficient clients. Check it out at `http://www.caldera.com`.

In the preceding figure the power is concentrated between two workstations, one file server, and one Web server. These machines would likely be faster than 300Mhz and they'd have at least 128MB of RAM each. (The servers need this horsepower to cope with data requests from 10 clients, whereas the workstations need it to perform extensive calculations.)

In contrast, the standard PCs (suitable for, say, accounting) could be old Pentiums (133–166Mhz) with 32MB of RAM because those machines request files only and perform very basic calculations.

Finally, the four Web clients can be anything you like. They can even be old 486 boxes, because they're nothing but cheap clients. They make requests only to the Web server and do hardly any number crunching.

Here are some other tips that will save you money in the long run:

➤ *Build your own workstations*   Whenever possible, avoid buying canned, ready-to-rock, proprietary systems. These boxes initially seem inviting but they're often error prone, poorly engineered, and built with inferior components—they'll cost you a bundle later in support and repair. Instead, purchase each component separately. Moreover, avoid hybrid components such as motherboards with on-board sound and video.

➤ *Standardize*   Wherever possible, purchase identical equipment networkwide. For example, purchase all modems, all hard disks, all motherboards, and so on from the same manufacturer. (I even prefer buying precisely the same models.) This way you can establish a consistent, easily managed device set that will allow you to implement repairs or upgrades on a wide scale without fear of unexpected results.

➤ *Spend the money*   You've heard it a thousand times before about everything from cars to stereo systems: You get what you pay for. Nowhere is that saying more true than in computing. Don't skimp on important components, especially hard disk drives, backup systems, network adapters, and routing hardware. Always place your main focus on reliability, longevity, and performance. Moreover, it's worth going with established manufacturers. Sure, that super-duper, plug-and-play, multimedia CD-ROM/sound/video capture-plus-modem card from Screaming Silicon Emporium might seem like a great deal for $29.95, but the truth is far more sinister. The card is probably cyberjunk, one step up from salvage material. (Your local neighborhood outlet has probably been trying to get rid of it for months.)

When building a server, focus primarily on scalability, functionality, and compatibility. Of these, scalability is exceedingly important. These days, you want

➤ Support for multiple processors

➤ Support for 1GB of RAM or more

➤ Multiple drive bays

➤ High throughput for fast Ethernet

➤ Standard (non-proprietary) components

Without these options you're buying a dead-end system. That is, if you can't expand it concurrently with user and network demand, you might ultimately have to shelve it. This represents a significant financial loss. Instead, always purchase upgradeable systems.

121

When the Chips Are Finally Down

Sadly, even upgradeable systems eventually run out of upgrade life. There are several reasons for this, but the most influential is that hardware architectures change. For example, no matter how wisely you chose to purchase upgradeable 486 servers, you'd eventually reach their processor power apex because most motherboards designed to take DX chips do not accommodate Pentium chips. Hence, most 486 motherboard/chip pairs can only yield you 120MHz. However, the period during which an upgradeable 486 did have a valid upgrade life was about four years (and if you can get four years out of the same box, you're smoking!)

Putting It All Together

Express your network plan in writing. I've found that mapping out the network on paper, especially in graphic form, can help tremendously. This way you visualize how the network will meet your organization's needs, and you don't miss anything. For example, you can anticipate often-unseen expenses by identifying each workstation's location, hardware, and software.

Other Types of Network Planning: Contingency Plans

Although you can use a network at home, most networks are employed in a business environment where computer resources are critical. In such environments, take every possible precaution to establish contingency plans—plans you'll put into action if and when the network fails.

At a minimum, make plans for temporary outages by employing network appliances, a RAID, and an *Uninterruptable Power Supply (UPS)*.

At a minimum, your plan should include

➤ An assessment of risks and threats, as well as their impacts. Order these in priority for each network component. For example, what might conceivably bring down this or that network segment or this or that server? In other words: *What events or forces can incapacitate your network?*

Earthquake!

How often do networks fail? That depends on many factors. In many cases, networks run for years without event and then, suddenly, fate steps in. One client of mine had a network that stayed up continuously for five years. During that time, there were absolutely no problems. Unfortunately, however, my client had never done any disaster studies and had no contingency plans. Too bad, too, because on January 17, 1994, at 4:30 a.m. in Northridge, California, a 6.7 magnitude earthquake hit.

The quake lasted only 15 seconds, but that was quite enough. (Actually, that's an incredibly long time in earthquake land.) My client's network was destroyed. Servers were hurled against walls, monitors were thrown to the ground, and things were generally a mess.

The following day, damages were assessed—and they were considerable. There were few backup tapes (the last backup had been done one month before) and most of the original software no longer existed. These folks were actually using WordStar—an ancient word processor—and a proprietary database written some 10 years before by a programmer who had since passed on. Because the hard disk drives were physically damaged, my client was out of luck. That's when I got called in to create a disaster plan.

➤ For each network component, calculate the maximum acceptable downtime. This is the length of time that a component can be down before a major disaster ensues. In other words: *If your network is incapacitated, how much time do engineers and technicians have to fix it?*

➤ Establish alternative, manual procedures that personnel can undertake if a total failure occurs. In other words: *What can employees do while the system comes back online?*

➤ Collect a checklist of all hardware and software that is critical to operations and what steps must be taken to secure these.

Techno Talk

RAID stands for *Redundant Array of Inexpensive Disks*. These are hard drives strung together that act as one unit. Data is spread out across several disks and one drive continuously verifies that data. If something goes wrong (such as one drive failing), the data is rebuilt from the RAID's duplicate, archived storage facilities.

123

Clearly identify the measures to take if and when failure occurs (including RAIDs, UPS systems, and the like). In other words: *What automated systems can you employ in recovery?*

You'll also need to develop a plan to prioritize recovery. That is, you'll need to identify what services must be recovered first in a minor, partial, or complete system failure. Every phase of your contingency/disaster plan is aimed at one thing: Getting business back online as quickly and efficiently as possible.

If you have the cash to do it, I recommend total redundancy the old-fashioned way. I usually build servers that are identical to my critical servers, or, at worst, hard disk drives that contain precisely the same software. This way, when something goes drastically wrong I simply disconnect the affected system and drop my duplicate right into place. (This is for those rare times when even your RAID system dies on you.)

Finally, in drafting your contingency plan, pay careful attention to details. Sometimes it's the small things that get you. For example, although RAID systems are important in preserving server availability, smaller subsystems and tools also need attention. Two good examples are communication and peripheral devices; few small businesses have recovery plans for either device type.

About Backups

Another key element of your disaster recovery plan is the system backup. There's one immutable rule in computing: Eventually, your data *will* get corrupted. There's no sense in denying it, and it makes no difference how much experience you have. Eventually, something terrible will happen.

Often, these disasters can have serious consequences. For example, suppose you've created an entire intranet site with hundreds of Web pages. Suddenly, your disk drive dies. If you don't have backups, forget it. You must redo every shred of work that took you months to accomplish. Don't let this happen to you!

You're probably wondering how often you need to back up; that depends. If yours is a business network, back up every day, archiving at least the following resources:

➤ User directories and files

➤ Any changes to your business documents and databases

➤ All your logs

I recommend having several copies: one for the office, one for the safe, and one for safekeeping. (Fire safes are not secure. In a fire, your backup tapes will melt even when deposited in a fire safe.)

Check This Out

There are companies that are in the business of store-housing backups. There are similar *vaults* in the film industry; for a price, they'll keep your reels—or in this case, your tapes—nice and cozy. If your information is valuable, confidential, proprietary, or just plain critical, you might consider securing the services of such a firm. This way, if the office burns down and your house is destroyed in an earthquake (God forbid), your backups will still be available.

Where To From Here

Now that you know a little about planning your network, your next step to go out and buy your components. This is addressed in Chapter 9, "Where to Shop for Equipment and Supplies."

The Least You Need to Know

Right now, the least you need to know is as follows:

➤ Determine your network's intended purpose and your users' needs, expectations, and level of expertise.

➤ Determine your required applications.

➤ The result of the preceding two steps determines what hardware you need.

➤ Be sure to address licensing.

➤ Purchase your hardware wisely, avoiding proprietary solutions.

➤ As you plan your network, concurrently develop your disaster recovery plan.

➤ Always strive for reliability, recoverability, and longevity. These are key factors and without them your network will be more troublesome than helpful.

## Chapter 9

Where to Shop for Equipment and Supplies

In This Chapter

➤ Learn about resources that can help you choose the best networking equipment and supplies.

➤ Find where you can get free, inexpensive, or trial software for network operating systems and tools.

➤ Learn who are the best computer networking vendors and where to find them.

When it comes to purchasing your networking hardware and software, you have a lot of choices. You can buy them from computer retailers, office supply stores, Internet sites, department stores, auctions, or from the manufacturers themselves.

Because of the Internet and the way the computer industry works, there are many ways you can avoid paying top dollar—or even any dollars—for your networking supplies. This chapter describes how to research what networking software and hardware to buy, how to find free networking software on the Web, how to comparison shop, and how to choose a vendor.

Choosing Networking Hardware and Software

Note

Chapters 6, "Network Hardware," and 7, "Network Operating Systems (NOSes)," describe the kinds of hardware and software you need for networking. Specific products and pricing, however, change daily. For that reason, we strongly recommend checking the latest reviews and costs before you make networking equipment purchases.

There are so many ways to obtain networking supplies, and so much to choose from, that a novice network administrator might feel overwhelmed. Fortunately, there are many resources available to help you figure out what hardware and software you need, and to help you find the best prices. For example, computer magazines offer equipment and software reviews as well as ads that list prices for computing equipment. Your greatest resource for shopping for networking supplies, however, is the Internet. Not only can you find all the information you need, but you can also make your purchases online when you are ready.

Researching Networking Equipment

Are all Ethernet cards the same? Which computers perform best as network servers? Should a networking cable cost $2 or $200? Fortunately, many people have walked down this road before and are willing to share information about choosing networking equipment. The next few sections describe where you can find reviews of networking equipment, newsgroups where you can have specific questions answered, and specifications of networking equipment.

Networking Equipment Reviews

Most computer-oriented magazines publish reviews of different kinds of equipment and software. Often, these magazines also have Web sites that republish parts or all of their reviews. In some cases, hard-copy magazines have been abandoned and only electronic magazines are supported. Here are a few magazines (some hard copy and some online-only) that have network equipment reviews, along with a listing of each magazine's Web site:

➤ *PC World* (http://www.pcworld.com)   This magazine has many articles on different types of computer technology. In particular, you can click the Top 400 area on the *PC World* Web site, and then select Networking to see a rather extensive group of networking reviews and articles. The following figure shows the networking hardware reviews available from *PC World Online*.

Networking reviews from PC World help you learn before you buy.

➤ *Computer Shopper* (http://www.computershopper.com)   This magazine is a huge resource (tabloid size) for computer equipment prices. Hardware reviews are available to help you make some buying decisions as well. The Web site enables you to search for products by category (such as Networking). Alternatively, you can select the Top 100 Products area for information on the top-rated products in a category.

➤ *LAN Times* (http://www.planetit.com/prodreviews)   Although this magazine has recently stopped publication, there are some excellent *LAN Times* networking product reviews still available from the *PlanetIT* Web site. In particular, there are reviews and recommendations for servers, switches, wide area networks (WANs), and storage devices.

➤ *PC Magazine* (http://www.zdnet.com/pcmag)   The PC Labs Review section covers a variety of computer-related reviews. From the home page, click on Networking under PC Labs Review. From there you'll find articles on servers, hardware and peripherals, and software for networking.

➤ *PC Week* (http://www.pcweek.com)   Select Labs from this home page and you see links to a variety of technology reviews.

➤ *Network Magazine* (http://www.networkmagazine.com)   Articles tend to be more general to networking than specific to networking products. However, from this home page, you can click the Products link to bring you to a product guide that is currently under construction.

➤ *Network Manager* (http://www.zdnet.com/products/networkmanager)   This Web site offers links to a wide range of networking products. Categories include Net Hardware, Servers, Network Software, Peripherals, Infrastructure, and Network OS.

Networking Newsgroups

Several newsgroups are dedicated to a variety of networking topics, ranging from networking hardware to server systems. One newsgroup that might be particularly helpful is a group that focuses on networking hardware for the PC:

```
comp.sys.ibm.pc.hardware.networking
```

Although you might find that some of the discussion in this group is fairly technical, you'll also find that the people who participate in this group patiently answer basic questions. In fact, participants in the group gave some excellent answers to questions, including

➤ What hardware do I need to connect together three computers in my home?

➤ What is the maximum length for thin Ethernet cable?

Another newsgroup is used by people who sell network hardware:

```
misc.forsale.computers.net-hardware
```

If you are looking for a particular piece of networking hardware, this is the place to enter that message.

Check This Out

You can participate in newsgroups using most popular mail readers. For example, with Microsoft Outlook Express you can select newsgroups, read messages, and respond to messages using basically the same program you use for mail.

Networking Specifications

If you want to read the technical details of networking products before you buy, you can get spec sheets either by calling the manufacturers of the products that interest you or by visiting their Web sites. In addition, the Catalogs NOW Web site (`http://www.catalogsnow.com`) can help you obtain product catalogs for many different computer products including network hardware, computer hardware, hardware add-ons, and supplies/accessories. From the Catalogs NOW site, you can search for catalogs containing the products you are interested in by entering catalog ID, product or company name, or keywords and phrases about the product. Alternatively, you can click on a category, such as Network Hardware, to see a list of product categories under that heading.

Shopping Resource Guides

Because online shopping has become such an integral part of the Internet, there are shopping resource guides associated with all the major Internet search engines. Besides offering links to online shopping sites (by categories such as computers and networking equipment), these sites also contain links to supporting information, such as tips and reviews:

Techno Talk

Catalogs are stored in PDF format. To read the catalogs, you need to have an Adobe Acrobat PDF viewer installed on your computer. With this viewer, you can view the catalog exactly as the printed catalog for the product appears.

➤ *Yahoo!* (`http://shopguide.yahoo.com`) From the Yahoo! shopping site, select the Computer Hardware link. Click the link to the research area, and you find connections to helpful sites, pricing guides, and computer hardware merchants.

➤ *Excite* (`http://www.excite.com/shopping`)   On the Excite Shopping page you choose a category (such as computer hardware), and then search for hardware reviews, products, and prices based on your selections.

➤ *Lycos* (`http://www.lycos.com/shopnet/computers`)   When shopping for computer hardware, the Lycos shopping site enables you to do a search of the Buycomp.com site. After the site finds what you are looking for, you can purchase the product online.

➤ *Hotbot* (`http://shop.hotbot.com/comp_hard`)   This site offers a search tool for finding the computer hardware products you want. It also contains links to online computer retailers and auctions.

Comparison Shopping

One thing that the Internet is particularly good for is gathering information from many locations and putting it together in a helpful form. Comparison shopping sites are even more efficient than letting your fingers do the walking through the Yellow Pages.

With a comparison-shopping site, you enter information about the kind of product you want. The service then finds the product (or products) that meets your criteria and shows you the prices offered by several vendors on that product. Several of these services are outlined as follows:

➤ *Tech Shopper* (`http://www.planetit.com/shopper`)   This Web site helps you research and buy computer equipment. Select the Networking Hardware link to view 30 categories of networking hardware. Select one of the categories to see product names and reviews, reader comments, specifications, and prices. To view side-by-side comparisons of the products, select several items, and then select Click to Compare.

➤ *Excite Computer Hardware Shopping* (http://www.excite.com/shopping/ computer_hardware)   Type the name of any product or manufacturer, and a search displays a list of computer hardware reviews that meet your criteria. You can also choose Editor's Picks to see reviews and tips related to a particular topic.

➤ *PC Today & Processor* (http://www.pctoday.com)   Find a variety of computer systems and networking products from this site. After you register for the site, you can select from nearly 100 product categories. The resulting search shows products in that category, listed by vendors who sell each product. You can select the best prices for the items you want.

Risks of Shopping Online

If the idea of shopping online gives you the jitters, don't worry. There are things you can do to greatly reduce the risks, at the same time taking advantage of the great cost savings and convenience of purchasing online.

➤ *Patronize credible businesses*   Anyone can create a Web page and call them-selves a business. To lessen your chances of being ripped off, check into the credibility of a company before you buy. Companies listed on a major stock exchange or that have known physical retail outlets are pretty safe bets. Sites that offer unrealistically low prices or that list no physical address on their Web site might be suspect.

➤ *Use credit cards*   If you aren't satisfied with the products you get, you have some recourse with the credit card company. Also, you can use a card with a low limit, so there is a lid on what a fraudulent company can charge you.

➤ *Use secure sites*   Major online retailers will offer you a secure method for entering your credit card number and other personal information. The latest releases of Netscape and Microsoft browsers support the encryption features needed to support secure transactions.

➤ *Know all the costs*   Just as with any mail-order transaction, be aware of ship-ping, handling, and other charges associated with your order. The last page displayed before your order is placed usually shows all your costs. Print this page and keep it for reference, in case there is a dispute in the future.

Finding Free and Trial Software

Getting networking software is much less of a risk than it was only a few years ago. Software used to be extremely expensive, and usually had to be purchased before you used it. Today, however, you can get a tremendous amount of software free—at least on a trial basis. Many software vendors give away light versions of their products or offer many extra software utilities for free if you buy their main product. Obtaining these products is as easy as downloading them from the Internet. Free or cheap networking software includes network operating system software, browsers, application sharing software, and many network drivers.

General Software Download Sites

There are some very large software repositories on the Internet, where you can download software of all kinds:

➤ Freeware, which costs nothing to use

➤ Shareware, which costs a small, on-your-honor fee

➤ Trialware, which is free for a set period, then costs something

➤ Commercial, which you must pay for before you use

Download.com (`http://www.download.com`) contains hundreds of software titles. This site, shown in the following figure, is also associated with BuyDirect.com, which enables you to purchase the software you download (when there is a cost). Select Internet from this site to see a list of Internet networking categories that you can choose from.

Download networking software from Download.com.

For Microsoft Windows and Macintosh computers, the Tucows site (http://www.tucows.com) has a large selection of networking software. Not only does this site enable you to download software, it also includes descriptions and ratings of each program. (A rating of one cow means the program is lousy; five cows means the program is exceptional.)

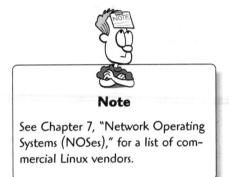

Note

See Chapter 7, "Network Operating Systems (NOSes)," for a list of commercial Linux vendors.

Free Operating System Software

The Linux operating system is the mother of all free software. Not only is the operating system itself free, but so are literally thousands of applications that work with Linux. You can purchase packaged versions of Linux for a small fee and install from CD-ROM. Alternatively, you can download free versions of Linux from the Web.

To download free copies of Linux software, you can visit the following Internet sites:

➤ ftp://ftp.funet.fi/pub/Linux   You can download Linux from this site. The Readme and Index files describe the directory structure of the FTP site and contain a complete listing of files at the site.

➤ http://sunsite.unc.edu/pub/Linux   This is another site for downloading Linux. Select the welcome.html page to find links to descriptions of the contents of Linux software at this site.

For information about how to use the different features of Linux, go to the Linux How-tos (/pub/Linux/docs/HOWTO). The distribution has become quite large, so some sort of roadmap is preferable.

Check This Out

If you have never compiled programs or used Linux (or UNIX) before, downloading and installing Linux from the Internet can be difficult. We strongly recommend you use a packaged distribution of Linux on CD-ROM for your first time. The CD-ROM will contain a simplified installation and start-up procedure.

Sometimes other operating systems are available inexpensively or for a free trial. Recently, Sun Microsystems offered a special promotion for its Solaris operating system. (Solaris is one of the most popular commercial versions of UNIX that runs on a PC.) For only the cost of shipping and handling, Sun sends CD-ROMs and documentation on Solaris to registered Sun developers. They can then install and use Solaris non-commercially. To see if the promotion is still going on, check out the Free Solaris Promotion site at `http://www.sun.com/developers/solarispromo.html`.

Free Software from Manufacturers

Every commercial networking software manufacturer offers some free software. Free software often includes device drivers (to make different kinds of hardware work) or utilities that enhance the company's main product lines. For example, to make its NetWare operating system more attractive to potential customers, Novell offers a bunch of free software programs that work in conjunction with NetWare. You can download the free software from the Novell Software Downloads page, located at `http://www.novell.com/download`. Downloadable software includes Z.E.N.Works client software, Groupwise client software, Novell Directory Services administration tools, and Netscape Server software.

Many of Microsoft's networking software products also have trial versions or supporting software that can be downloaded. The Microsoft Free Downloads site is located at `http://www.microsoft.com/msdownload`. There are large selections of server software, Internet development tools and SDKs, and hardware drivers.

In addition, you can obtain a free trial copy of Artisoft's LANtastic 8—a popular product for sharing files, applications, printers, and drives—from the LANtastic download site at `http://www.artisoft.com/download`.

Where to Buy Networking Equipment

Some people like to search for products on the Internet and purchase them with a credit card. Others prefer to actually speak to a warm body and put their hands on a physical product before they buy. Each of these options is available to you for purchasing networking equipment. When Computer Retailer Week ranked the 1997 Top 100 U.S. Computer Retailers, the list included computer centers, direct mail, office supply stores, and department stores. The top ten from that list, shown in order in the following list, represent the types of retailers you have to choose from:

1. CompUSA (`http://www.compusa.com`)
2. Best Buy (`http://www.bestbuy.com`)
3. Office Depot (`http://www.officedepot.com`)
4. Micro Warehouse (`http://www.microwarehouse.com`)
5. Computer City SuperCenters (`http://www.computercity.com`)

6. Circuit City Stores (`http://www.circuitcity.com`)

7. Staples (`http://www.staples.com`)

8. Computer Discount Warehouse (CDW) Computer Center (`http://www.cdw.com`)

9. Micro Center (`http://www.microcenter.com`)

10. OfficeMax (`http://www.officemax.com`)

Of those top ten computer retailers, only Micro Warehouse has no retail outlets, and CDW Computer Center only has two showrooms (both in Illinois). Each retailer's Web site has a store locator that gives you the addresses, and possibly directions, to each store.

When you need a piece of equipment right away (sometimes overnight isn't fast enough), it's good to know the retailers in your area. Office centers and department stores tend to have more generic equipment. If you need that special terminator or cable, your local Radio Shack (number 20 of the top 100) might be your best bet.

Online Retailers

It's so much easier to open a Web site than it is to open a physical store, which is why many companies have done just that. Although there are disadvantages—such as not seeing the product or a sales person—there are also many advantages:

➤ *Price* Like other mail-order businesses, online retailers usually have lower overhead because they don't have to maintain and staff stores. Even with mailing costs, prices are typically lower than can be found in stores.

➤ *Information* There are often more complete descriptions of the products online than you can find on a box in a store. Full product specifications are often only a click away.

➤ *Convenience* You can probably check the price of a product at about a dozen online retailers in the time it takes to drive your car to one store. This can save you a lot of time and energy.

The online retailers described in this chapter are those that include a good selection of computer networking products. It's easy to find and use these vendors, but before you buy make sure you understand the vendor's return policy and support. If something goes wrong, you want to make sure that help is there.

Micro Warehouse

All sorts of networking cables, connectors, converters, cards, hubs, and modems are available from this online computer store. To look for products you can select from one of the networking categories, select the manufacturer of the product, or run a keyword search. Associated with Micro Warehouse are

➤ Webauction.com, which enables you to bid on computing equipment

➤ Download Warehouse, where you can select from thousands of software titles to download

➤ USA Flex, which sells upgradeable and expandable PCs

Computer Discount Warehouse (CDW) Computer Center

Computer Discount Warehouse (`http://www.cdw.com`) offers an extensive stock of computer networking equipment. Select Networking from the CDW home page, and then you can choose from nearly 100 categories of networking equipment.

When you select a product category, CDW lists the products by manufacturer. Click the product name to see a description of the product. The listing also shows you the current price and whether or not the item is in stock.

Insight.com

Besides sponsoring a college football bowl game, Insight.com (`http://www.insight.com`) offers a full range of computer networking products. From the home page, select Products then Networking. On the Networking products page, Insight.com offers a couple of specials, shows the best selling networking products, and enables you to search the networking subcategories for the products you want.

PC Connection

Browse for networking hardware by category from the PC Connection site (`http://www.pcconnection.com`). You can get some good deals on clearance items by selecting the Clearance link from the home page. A quick search box on the home page also enables you to search the site for the product you want.

Egghead.com

This company, which once operated software retail locations, has moved its expertise to the Internet (`http://www.egghead.com`). The result is a large software and hardware inventory, along with specialty Surplus Direct and Surplus Auction sites. There is also a Liquidation link for special deals. As you might expect from a former software retail operation, the software selection is more extensive than the hardware. It also seems that more software than hardware is in stock.

Equipment Vendors

If you know the manufacturer of the product you want, you can often go to that company's Web site to find the product. Besides offering a path to buying their equipment, the manufacturer also has the latest white papers and technical specifications to describe and compare products. There are tons of networking equipment vendors who enable you to shop online; here are a few vendors you can check out:

➤ *3Com Corporation* (http://www.3com.com) This company is a leading supplier of LAN and modem products. From the 3Com Shopping site (http://www.3com.com/3sn), you can browse the company products and add them to your shopping list. When you are finished shopping, click the Where to Buy link. You can then choose an online site, local retail store, mail order company, or sales and consulting firm to help you make your purchase.

➤ *IBM* (http://www.ibm.com/Shop) The IBM Shopping site helps you find and purchase IBM computing products. Select Products A-Z, and then choose from networking products for the home or for various IBM workstations.

➤ *Compaq Computer* (http://www.compaq.com/products) Along with the computers they sell, most PC vendors will also sell you networking hardware to go with the computers. From the Compaq Products page, select Networking and Communications Products. Next, select the Solutions and Innovations page and choose products based on the size of your business.

Check This Out

If you are new to networking, view the Networking Demo from the Compaq Networking Products page (http://www.compaq.com/products/networking). It illustrates the most basic form of networking between two computers.

Online Auctions

Computing products are popular fare for online auctions. Several of the major online computer stores have related auction and surplus Web sites. There are general auction Web sites that regularly feature computer-related items.

Because the rules vary greatly between the different auction sites, read the auction guidelines before you participate. Different styles of auctions maintain anonymity at different levels. Also, you need to clearly understand the terms of the transaction (product information, shipping terms, addresses, and so on) to avoid misunderstandings. Here are a few online auctions you can check out for computer networking and other equipment:

➤ *eBay* (http://www.ebay.com) Although eBay offers dozens of categories of items, there is always a substantial listing of computer networking products available (see the following figure). From the home page, click on Computers, then select Networking. For information on how eBay operates its auctions, click the Buyers or Sellers link on the top of the home page. You see several documents including guidelines and frequently asked questions.

Bid for networking hardware at the eBay Web site.

➤ *Yahoo! Auctions* (http://auctions.yahoo.com)   This is another large auction site that offers computer equipment along with other stuff. Select Computer, Hardware, PC, and Components. From there you can find some adapters, converters, terminators, cables, and connectors to bid on.

➤ *uBid Online Auction* (http://www.ubid.com)   This site is an online auction that is associated with the PC Mall computer vendor (http://www.pcmall.com). Look under the Components category for networking equipment.

Where To From Here?

By now you understand why you want to network computers, the kinds of networks there are, the kinds of systems and hardware available, and (from this chapter) how you can get the equipment you need. Basically, you now have a pretty good network foundation.

To tie everything together, proceed to Chapter 10, "Case Study: Building a Windows SOHO System." That chapter steps you through the planning and installing of a simple small office/home office network.

The Least You Need to Know

Right now, the least you need to know about shopping for networking equipment and supplies is this:

➤ Use computer magazines, online product reviews, and newsgroups to research your networking equipment before you buy.

➤ Most Internet search engines (such as Lycos, Yahoo!, and Excite) offer online shopping guides. From those sites you can find computer shopping sites, as well as guidelines for online shopping.

➤ There are online comparison shopping sites to help you find the best prices and do side-by-side product comparisons.

➤ Even for advanced networking features, there is lots of free and cheap software available. Check sites such as Download.com and Tucows.com to find software to download.

➤ The top computer retailers include computer specialists, office supply houses, and a variety of direct mail companies. Even those with physical stores usually also have Internet sites from which you can order.

➤ Online computer equipment vendors can offer low prices, easy access to information, and convenience. Popular vendors include MicroWarehouse.com, Insight.com, and CDW.com.

➤ Computer auctions, many of which are online, can offer some good deals. However, you need to feel secure, both about the people you are dealing with and about the particulars of how the transactions are handled.

## Chapter 10

Case Study:
Building a Windows
SOHO System

In This Chapter

➤ Planning your SOHO network

➤ Installing hardware and software

➤ Sharing out network resources

1999 is the year of the *Small Office/Home Office (SOHO)* network—at least, that's what Madison Avenue is saying. Is it true? You bet. It's estimated that some 20 million Americans own more than one PC, and some ten percent of those users take work home from the office or run a bona fide home-based business.

Knowing this, you might think that home-based networking had taken the computing world by storm. Until now, though, it hasn't. There are some good reasons for slow SOHO network growth; one of these reasons is cost. Until recently, networking was an expensive proposition, and one that casual or even semi-serious users weren't likely to undertake. Why spend that kind of money if you really don't have to?

Another reason for slow SOHO network growth is lack of technical knowledge. Until recently, most consumers were not very computer savvy. For many users, just installing and running games was difficult enough. Networking was another ball of wax—and intimidating.

Well, times have changed. Today networking hardware is cheap, and today's networking environments are more feature-rich than ever. Microwave oven manufacturers, for example, make oven doors that double as touch-screen activated Web browsers. These enable you to download recipes from the Internet any time, day or night.

So, prices have dropped and networking is the rage. Are you ready to take the plunge? If so, this chapter is for you. It focuses on planning and installing a small, Windows-based SOHO network.

Planning Your SOHO Network

Your first step involves planning your SOHO network's parameters and design. To erect a three-station SOHO network, you'll need

➤ One Ethernet hub

➤ Three or more Ethernet cables

➤ Three or more computers running a network operating system

➤ Three or more network interface cards

Each component presents you with multiple options, and the choices you make influence your network as a whole. Following are some examples of your options:

➤ *Cabling—RJ45, BNC, or thicknet?*   Your cabling choice might place limits on distance and bandwidth. For instance, if you're planning on having one workstation in your garage, 1000BaseCX cable—with a maximum range of 75 feet—just isn't going to cut it.

➤ *Ethernet hub—10 Mbps or 100?*   Your hub choice, and your choice of network speed, influence your choice of OS and NIC. For example, if you compose your network of Intel-based workstations running Windows 95 on basic IDE disk drives, 10 Mbps is more than sufficient. After all, your system can't transfer data much quicker than that.

In most cases, you'll have little need for exotic configurations; simple 10 Mbps RJ45 and a 10 Mbps hub are probably sufficient. However, there are some anomalies you might encounter along the way; these are covered in the next section.

Disparate Connectors

Older computers and components often sport strange connectors. For example, antiquated workstations (particularly Sun and SGI models) have on-board Ethernet via thicknet (see the following figure).

Thicknet connectors are 10Base5-style 15-pin cable connections. To integrate thicknet

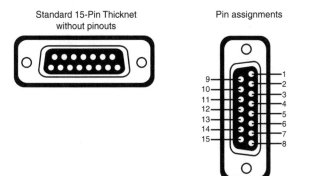

Standard 15-Pin Thicknet without pinouts

Pin assignments

Thicknet connectors have 15 pins.

systems into your SOHO network—which will probably be 10BaseT/RJ45-based—you'll need a transceiver.

A *transceiver* is a device with two connectors, one for thicknet and the other for RJ45. These connectors are usually female, but not always; much depends on whether the transceiver is box- or cable-based. Box-based transceivers have a junction box with male thicknet and female RJ45 on either side, whereas cable-based transceivers are uninterrupted cables (without a junction box) on which both thicknet and RJ45 connectors are male.

Either way, if you're stringing a thicknet-based workstation to your SOHO and don't yet have a transceiver, prepare to exercise diligence and patience. Neighborhood computer outlets (such as CompUSA) rarely keep transceivers in stock. In fact, you might have to special order this item. (To learn more about thicknet, check out Chapter 6, "Network Hardware.")

Need a Wire? Get Wired!

If you need a transceiver, check out the USENET newsgroup misc.forsale. computers.workstation. Folks in that group can often get you transceivers—or other network-related hardware—quicker and cheaper than big vendors can.

Old NICs

Did you inherit an obsolete machine from the office? If so, you might encounter problems. Older systems usually have legacy NICs and this can spell configuration trouble. There are two likely scenarios:

➤ You need the original installation software to configure the card because configuration is entirely software-driven, but, unfortunately, the vendor no longer exists.

➤ The card provides no software-based means for configuration, and although you can see the jumpers you cannot reliably determine what they do.

The easiest solution is to purchase a new NIC. However, if you're bent on keeping the old one, turn to the Net. There you can find folks that have the necessary software, or you can get jumper pinouts and other schematics from the vendor.

About Jumpers

The jumpers on many older NICs are clearly marked, so examine the card carefully before you search the entire WWW for further information. Chances are, the information you need is right on the card. For example, old Western Digital cards have the IRQ jumpers individually marked for clarity. This enables you to painlessly change the IRQ settings.

Distances and Cable Layouts

Distance and cable layout are important issues because they strongly influence your network's design.

In general, almost any cabling scheme offers ample straight-away distance—especially if you're establishing this network at home. Table 10.1 lists some common cabling schemes and their maximum distances.

Table 10.1 Approximate Distances for Various Cabling Schemes

Network Cable	Distance
10Base2	600 feet
10Base5	1640 feet
10BaseT	328 feet
1000Base-CX	75 feet
1000Base-LX	9000 feet
1000Base-SX	1500 feet
1000Base-TX	330 feet
100Base-FX	1300 feet
100BaseT	328 feet

However, Ethernet cable is expensive; therefore, exploit every opportunity to reduce cost and increase efficiency. (For example, go through walls and not around them.)

If you're planning on workstations being in different rooms or on different floors, you might consider a professional cabling job. In the short run, this seems expensive—but looks are deceiving. The cable can be run through the wall, and permanent socket plates can be established in each room (see the following figure).

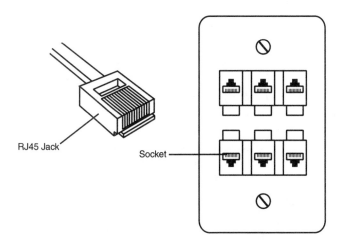

RJ45 Jack

Socket

Socket connections can be embedded in the wall.

From there, you can run patch cables from your workstations to the wall. This saves you the substantial costs of running individual straight-ahead RJ45 cables throughout the house or office—patch cables run between three and six dollars each. This is just one area of many in which you'll benefit from taking an industrial-strength approach to your SOHO network.

Installing Your NIC

After you've physically installed your NIC, you must take two additional steps:

➤ Installing your NIC software

➤ Configuring your NIC software

Installing Your NIC Software

To install your NIC software

1. Double-click My Computer. This brings up the My Computer window (see the following figure).

The My Computer window.

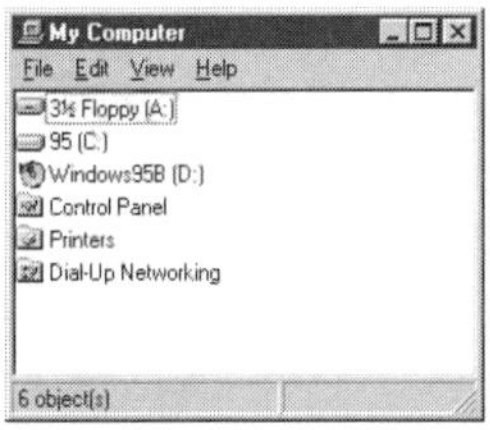

2. Next, choose Control Panel | Add New Hardware. This initiates the Add New Hardware Wizard (see the following figure).

To add a new NIC, choose the Add New Hardware icon.

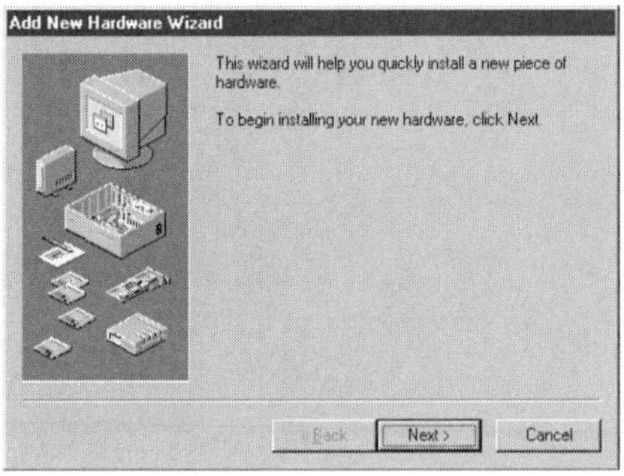

146

3. Choose Next. At this point, you'll be confronted with a choice: Do you want Windows to detect your new hardware? To avoid complications, you can stick to these simple rules:

➤ If you're using Windows 98 and your motherboard or NIC is three years old or older, choose No.

➤ If you're using Windows 95 and your motherboard or NIC is brand spanking new, choose No.

➤ If neither of the aforementioned scenarios is true, choose Yes.

You're probably wondering how I arrived at these crazy rules. Here's how: Windows 98 performs superbly with newer hardware but has difficulty with more antiquated gear. Conversely, Windows 95 is excellent for older hardware but lacks drivers for many new models.

Pulling the Ripcord on Automatic NIC Detection

Alas, plug-and-play is too often play-and-pray. Don't feel rejected—or dejected—if Windows fails to auto-detect your NIC. This isn't indicative of anything, really; the card was probably manufactured before plug-and-play was popular. If so, install the driver manually.

If you chose Yes and Windows successfully identified your NIC, please skip ahead to the section titled "Configuring Your NIC Software." Otherwise

1. Choose Network Adapters. In response, Windows provides you with a vendor list (see the following figure).

The NIC vendor list.

Pulling the Ripcord on Identifying Your NIC Adapter

What if your card isn't listed? Is this fatal? Hardly. It simply means that your current Windows version doesn't have a driver for your NIC. If this is the case, choose Have Disk and provide Windows with a floppy disk or CD-ROM that has the manufacturer's driver. Or, if you don't even have the manufacturer's installation disks, turn to the Net. There you'll find help. (Your best bet is the manufacturer's WWW page because their technical support section will offer drivers and installation notes.)

2. Next, scroll down the NIC list to find your card's manufacturer. Choose your model, click Next, and wait.

3. Windows will try to communicate with your network adapter. This process might take several moments or, on older systems, as long as five minutes.

4. When it's finished, Windows displays several important values, including your network adapter's memory range, IRQ, and so on (see the following figure).

Your NIC's current settings.

```
Add New Hardware Wizard

       Windows can install your hardware, using the following settings.

       WARNING: Your hardware may not be set to use the resources listed. If you
       need to, you can adjust these settings by using the Device Manager in the
       System control panel before restarting your computer. To change your
       hardware settings, see the documentation that came with your hardware.

       To continue installing the software needed by your hardware, click Next.

       Resource type        Setting
       Input/Output Range   0200 - 021F
       Interrupt Request    05
       Memory Range         000D0000 - 000D3FFF          [ Print... ]

                                      [ < Back ]  [ Next > ]  [ Cancel ]
```

5. Choose Next. Windows notifies you that your new hardware has been installed, and you are asked to reboot.

Congratulations—your NIC drivers have been installed.

Pulling the Ripcord on Card Settings

If Windows can't communicate with your network card, there can be several reasons. For example, perhaps you've run out of IRQs. This is a problem that is both common and easily fixed: Disconnect one or more devices, or check for an IRQ conflict. (Devices that eat IRQs include scanners, modems, NICs, and such.) If that fails, check the card's integrity. For example, are you sure that the card works properly? Try it in another machine to verify that it does. Also, is the card completely proprietary? Such cards do exist. A good example is any NIC that doubles as a modem; such cards are integrated packages. (In other words, the manufacturer tried to cut some corners by lumping two components together on the same card). For these cards you might need special drivers. Finally, if the card seems fine (it works in another box), it's possible that your current Windows version has a bad driver. Try using the manufacturer's latest driver or reinstalling the Windows driver.

Configuring Your NIC Software

Now that you've installed your card you need to configure its software. Doing this will tell the card what protocols to use, how to transfer data, and what drives and resources are available. To configure your card's software, use the following steps:

1. Double-click My Computer, and then choose Control Panel | Network. This brings you to the network settings window. You'll notice that your NIC's name and model are present (see the following figure).

The network settings store your NIC's name and model.

149

2. Highlight the card's entry and choose Add. This initiates the Select Network Component Type window (see the following figure).

The Select Network Component Type window.

3. Choose Client | Client for Microsoft Networks. This installs Microsoft's networking software, which enables you to connect to other Microsoft machines. When this has been marked for installation, it will be visible in the network settings (see the following figure).

Your client settings are visible in the network settings box.

4. Choose Add | Protocol | NetBEUI.

This returns you to the network settings window. At this point, both the Microsoft Client for Windows and NetBEUI are visible in the settings list (see the preceding figure).

You're nearly home free!

Net Whooey?

NetBEUI stands for NetBIOS Extended User Interface. (When discussing NetBEUI, pronounce it *net-booey*). NetBEUI is a protocol used to transfer data on several IBM-based network systems, including all Microsoft operating systems.

About TCP/IP

Depending on the type of network you're constructing, you might need additional protocols and clients. For example, if you intend to use your SOHO network as an intranet you'll need Microsoft's implementation of TCP/IP. If so, choose Add | Protocol | Microsoft | TCP/IP to add standard TCP/IP.

Techno Talk

If you install TCP/IP, be mindful that you don't accidentally install a second TCP/IP Dialup Adapter with identical settings. If you do, not only will your network not work but your machine will spontaneously reboot each time it loads Windows. (This is a reboot loop that never ends). On the off chance that you already goofed in this regard, it's easy to backtrack. Simply wait for the machine to reboot, hold down the F8 key, wait for the menu, and choose Safe Mode. This enables you to safely load Windows with the bare minimum in drivers. While there, you can delete the second TCP/IP Dialup Adapter.

Introducing Intranets

Intranets are internal networks that run Web servers. You can think of an intranet as a miniature version of the Internet, housed right in your very own office. Intranets are becoming increasingly popular because they enable companies to distribute dynamic documents and data without incurring substantial overhead. Additionally, intranets enable you to completely customize your operating environment. By enforcing a consistent application set, you can ensure total compatibility across the board. Therefore, you can employ more exotic technologies, such as Java or ActiveX. Finally, intranets enable companies to share proprietary data without exposing that data to the world at large.

Windows automatically binds TCP/IP to your NIC. However, you'll need to manually set each workstation's IP address. The quickest and most headache-free way of structuring your address scheme is to use reserved IP addresses starting with 172.16.0.1. Hence, if your network consists of one intranet server and two workstations, assign 172.16.0.1 to the server, 172.16.0.2 to your first workstation, and 172.16.0.3 to your second workstation.

Initially, to enjoy Web access on your intranet server you'll need to specify the server's full address:

```
http://172.16.0.1:80
```

To remedy that, create a hosts file. hosts files store IP address-to-hostname translations. In Windows 95 and 98, a sample host file is provided in c:\windows:

```
# This is a sample HOSTS file used by Microsoft TCP/IP for Chicago
#
# This file contains the mappings of IP addresses to host names. Each
# entry should be kept on an individual line. The IP address should
# be placed in the first column followed by the corresponding host
➥name.
# The IP address and the host name should be separated by at least one
# space.
#
# Additionally, comments (such as these) may be inserted on individual
# lines or following the machine name denoted by a '#' symbol.
#
# For example:
#
#      102.54.94.97     rhino.acme.com          # source server
#       38.25.63.10     x.acme.com              # x client host

127.0.0.1 localhost
```

For example, suppose your intranet server's hostname was www2.mycompany.com. You can educate all your workstations to this fact by adding the following entry to your hosts file:

```
172.16.0.1 www2.mycompany.com
```

From that point forward, you can reach 172.16.0.1's Web server through the following URL:

```
http://www2.mycompany.com
```

Check This Out

Microsoft's sample hosts file is `c:\windows\hosts.sam`. If you decide to use `c:\windows\hosts.sam` as a template, note that you must rename or copy the file to `c:\windows\hosts` before you can use it. Also, note that if you intend to access workstations by name (instead of IP address) you must provide a `hosts` entry for each host. However, if you do intend to use IP addresses exclusively, the `hosts` entries are not necessary.

For further information about intranets, check out Chapter 17, "The Internet, Intranets, and Extranets."

Identifying Your Machine

After you install the networking software, Windows asks you to name your machine (see the following figure).

Windows requests some identification information.

153

What's in a Name?

When naming your workstations you might want to adhere to a theme. This technique not only makes names easy to remember but can actually assist you in visualizing your network's topology. For example, suppose you created a network segment of *island machines*—machines that can access shared print resources but do not otherwise share their drives, files, or directories with their peers. You might name those machines after islands, such as Maui, Kawai, Fiji, and so on. Also, note that NETBIOS names are limited to 15 characters.

This name differentiates your current box from other network nodes.

Additionally, you'll need to specify your machine's workgroup. *Workgroups* are small clusters of machines that share common network resources. By assigning machines a common group identity (a workgroup), you ensure that simple changes can be made en masse. Changes can be applied to the workgroup and all members inherit those changes.

Note that it's not necessary to include every machine in this or that workgroup. Non-workgroup member machines can still access local network resources if you allow them to. The difference is that non-member machines remain unaffected by work-group-wide changes.

When you specify your machine's name and work-group, you'll need to reboot. Upon reboot you'll be logged to the network for the first time. You'll notice that a new icon (Network neighborhood) was added to your desktop. Double-click Network Neighborhood to view your machine and other hosts on the network (see the following figure).

If you can see other machines in the Network neighborhood window, your network has been established.

Use Network Neighborhood to view available computers on your network.

Setting up Your Shared Resources

Your next step is to share out resources. You might remember that when configuring the NIC software you specified that you wanted to share files and printers; now, it's time to set that up.

Before allocating shared resources, consider just exactly what you need to share out. To prevent shared resources from becoming a headache, always share the least resources possible. (In many cases an isolated directory will do the trick.) After all, you don't want folks rummaging through your files and altering important data.

To share out your C: drive (or any portion of it)

1. Double-click My Computer and right-click the C: drive. This produces a tool menu.

2. Choose Sharing (see the following figure).

Choose the Sharing option to begin your shares configuration.

3. In response, Windows launches the C: Properties window with the Sharing tab active (see the following figure).

The Sharing window.

Here you can share drives and designate user access levels. There are two chief levels:

➤ *Read-only*   Read-only is exactly what it sounds like. Users can read directories and files but not change them.

➤ *Full*   Full access is where users have essentially the same privileges as you do: They can read, write, or execute any file.

As you have probably surmised, sharing is best used among trusted personnel. When it's not, sharing opens your network to considerable security risks. For this reason, you need to create special isolated share directories, or even partitions. This allows others to have access to important files but bars them from accessing truly sensitive data.

Completing Your Network

After successfully configuring one machine as previously described, you can duplicate the procedure for each workstation. So long as each machine has a similar hardware and software base, you'll have no problems at all.

Check This Out

When implementing a full-scale TCP/IP network, be sure to enable TCP/IP over NETBIOS. (You'll be offered a chance to do just that when you first install Microsoft TCP/IP).

Connecting machines that run other operating systems is a different matter; much depends on the system. Certainly, when connecting UNIX systems TCP/IP is the preferred protocol. You can quickly establish a UNIX workstation by adhering to the intranet address scheme described earlier in this chapter. Immediately upon reboot, all traditional UNIX network services will be available, including Telnet, FTP, HTTP, and so on.

Where To From Here

This chapter discussed implementing a SOHO network. The next chapter, "Networking VIP: The System Administrator," covers the responsibilities of a system administrator.

The Least You Need to Know

➤ SOHO networks are probably the easiest to install and configure.

➤ Given the right equipment, you can establish a SOHO network in less than an hour and for just a few hundred dollars.

➤ Implementing a SOHO network enables you to increase efficiency and convenience.

Part 4

Maintaining and Administering Your Network

Even the best-planned networks often go astray. When they do, the person wearing the big "S" isn't Superman—it's the system administrator. While troubleshooting problems is an important job, even more important are the maintenance and security taken to prevent problems.

Chapters in this part describe the system administrator's role. They also discuss administrative duties such as issuing passwords, backing up data, troubleshooting, and preventing break-ins. The last chapter in this part describes how to enable telecommuting.

Networking VIP: The System Administrator

In This Chapter

➤ Learn about managing your network.

➤ Learn about permissions.

➤ Learn about assigning permissions.

➤ Learn about adding and removing users.

As system administrator you're responsible for adding and removing users, maintaining system security, and basically running the entire show. That's a lot of responsibility. This chapter offers essential tips on system administration in both Windows NT and UNIX.

General System Administration Concepts

Network operating systems are unique because they support many users at once, often on the same machine. To preserve order in such environments there must be a central authority, a big cheese, or a Supreme Being. If you're running the network, you are that Supreme Being.

Each network operating system has a special name for its Supreme Being. In Windows NT, for example, that being is called *administrator*; in UNIX, it's *root*, and in NetWare, it's *supervisor*. This being is represented on the system by a special user account of the same name. Whoever has the password to this account has complete control of the local machine—and perhaps of the entire network.

To perform the tasks described in this chapter, you must have access to this special, privileged account. Therefore

➤ If you're using Windows NT, log in as administrator.

➤ If you're using UNIX, log in as root.

Check This Out

While logged in as administrator or root, take care not to roam around needlessly. Moreover, carefully consider each step you take and each command you issue. Why? While you're logged in as the Supreme Being you can accidentally or inadvertently cause irreparable damage to your system.

NT System Administration: User Manager

The most common system administration task—besides answering users' questions—is to add or remove user accounts. During this process you establish user access policies, initial privileges, user groups, and so on. In Windows NT, you perform these tasks with an application called User Manager.

Starting User Manager: Creating a New Account

To create a new account, start User Manager and choose User | New User. This opens the New User screen, shown in the following figure.

Creating a new user with User Manager.

The New User screen presents you with several fields and check boxes; each represents an option. Those options are as follows:

➤ *User name*   This field must be filled in. For the sake of convenience, try to choose user names that reflect either the user's real name or their job function. For example, suppose the user was Bill Wagner, an account executive. You might give him a user name of bwagner or accountexec. This way, when you receive email from Mr. Wagner, you can make a split-second educated guess as to who he is.

➤ *Full Name*   Filling out this field is optional; it is used for identification purposes. Often, a user name is unique but not very descriptive. By providing the user's full name, you ensure that you—or any manager—can identify the specified user. This is especially useful when you are trying to discern between two users with similar user names.

➤ *Description*   Filling out this field is also optional; it is reserved for any comments you might have.

➤ *Password*   This field is where you enter the user's password. Typically, you provide only a temporary password and the user sets his or her own later. The user's password can be up to 14 characters long.

➤ *Confirm Password*   You must re-enter the password in this field to verify that it was entered correctly. This is to ensure that you didn't mistype the password.

➤ *User Must Change Password at Next Logon*   This is a security feature. As administrator, you're responsible for setting each account's initial password. However, it's not necessary—and in fact, it's quite risky—for you to know every user's password. Force users to change their password on their first login; this way, only they know their own password.

➤ *User Cannot Change Password*   This is a seldom-enabled option that prohibits a user from changing his or her own password. Is there ever a reason to use this option? Maybe, and here's an example: You might someday create an account that's accessible to more than one user, sometimes called a *shared account*. If so, you want to ensure that users cannot change the password. By enabling this option, you prevent renegade users from locking out legitimate folks.

➤ *Password Never Expires*   There are some accounts that sponsor services or other shared resources that are permanently available to all users. On these accounts you probably don't want the password to expire, so check this option.

➤ *Account Disabled*   This option momentarily freezes the account. You might have several reasons for enabling this option; for example, you might be creating an account for a new employee that hasn't yet transferred over, or perhaps you need to clear their access with other co-workers first.

After you've established the user's initial settings, you need to specify additional values including

➤ User group membership

➤ User profile

➤ User access time

➤ User logon access control

➤ User dial-in permissions

➤ User rights

The following sections run through each step.

The Groups Button: Setting User Group Membership

Windows NT supports *user groups*, entities composed of users with similar permissions and rights. The group system streamlines your job as a system administrator in several ways. For example, NT enables you to apply permission changes to a group and have all users within that group inherit the changes. This obviates the need to set these options for individual users.

Perhaps more importantly, however, the group system enables you to build network security and trust relationships that mirror your company's organizational structure. For example, everyone in the accounting department will naturally have access to accounting files, whereas most folks in other departments won't. Therefore, it makes sense to create an accounting group that only accounting personnel can access. This keeps accounting folks grouped together—and keeps everyone else out.

To set a user's group membership, click the Groups button. This opens the Groups Membership window, shown in the following figure.

Managing the user's group membership with User Manager.

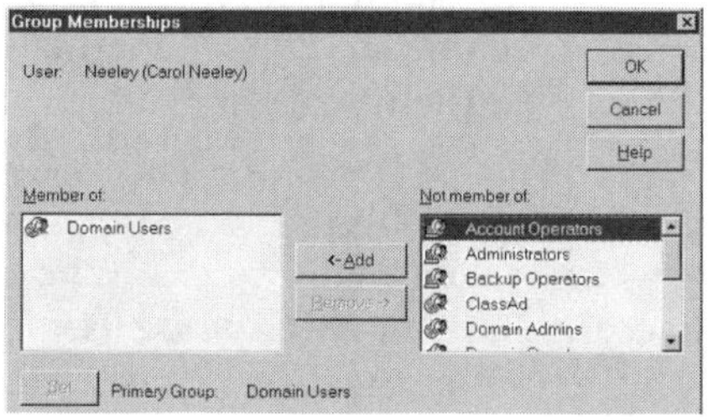

The Groups Membership window provides a very easy-to-use group management interface. You can instantly identify which groups the user belongs to, if any, and which group is their primary group.

To add the user to a new group, do the following:

1. Find the group in the Not Member Of list and highlight it.

2. Click the Add button.

To remove the user from the group, do the following:

1. Find the group in the Members Of and highlight it.

2. Click the Remove button.

Check This Out

There are four built-in Windows NT groups that you probably don't want to assign users to: Administrators, Backup Operators, Servers Operators, and Account Operators. Members from these four groups have substantial authority and can perform sensitive tasks. When you assign a user to any of these four groups, you're granting them a very high security clearance. Think twice before doing it.

The Profile Button: Setting the User's Profile Environment

After you assign a user's user name, password, identifying information, and groups, you must edit that user's profile environment. The profile environment describes the user's profile location, home directory, and so on.

Check This Out

A *profile* consists of customized settings such as the desktop's appearance or network connections. Profiles can be used to restrict users' access. For example, you can restrict users from changing the appearance of the desktop or their monitor type.

To edit a user's profile environment, click the Profile button in the New User screen. This launches the User Environment Profile window, shown in the following figure.

Use the User Environment Profile window to set the user's profile options.

The User Environment Profile window enables you to specify several options:

➤ *User Profile Path*   This tells NT where to find the profile information. You express this path in three parts—the server name, the profile folder, and the user's name: \\MyServer\profiles\bill.

➤ *Login Script Name*   Use this field to name the login script file. Note that not every user will have a login script, and that login scripts are not required. However, if you do assign users a login script, you must specify it here.

➤ *Home Directory*   It is here that you specify the user's home directory. If you've ever used UNIX you're probably familiar with this concept. On network operating systems, users must have their own directory where they can store files and run commands; this prevents users from accidentally mixing up their files. When the user saves files, the files are saved to this directory by default.

Typically, you name the directory after the user's user name or something similar. Moreover, it makes sense to place all user directories under a shared hierarchy. For example, you can create a directory tree called /myusers and assign all accounts beneath this root, such as /myusers/chris and /myusers/bill.

➤ *Connect To*   It is here that you specify the network drives to which the user will attach when they first log in.

Setting User Access Times: The Hours Button

Windows NT supports granular access control—not simply of files, directories, and resources, but also of times. Therefore, you can restrict the hours during which a user can access his or her account. To set user access times, click the Hours button in User Manager's New User screen. This launches the Logon Hours window, shown in the following figure.

Use your mouse to highlight access times, and then click Allow or Disallow. Your changes will be applied to the user's next session. Unless the Forcibly Disconnect Remote Users from Server When Logon Hours Expire button is checked in the account policy, the user will not be disconnected while they are still logged on. In other words, their current sessions continue until they log out. However, they will not be able to make any new connections.

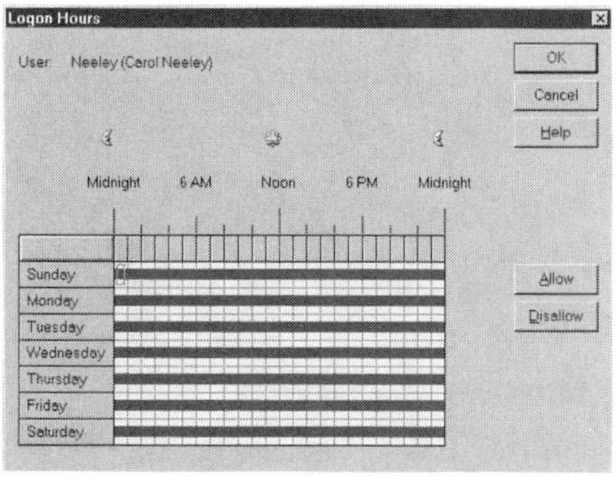

Use the Logon Hours window to set user access times.

The Logon To Button: Restricting User Access to Particular Machines

Windows NT enables you to control not only which account a user uses (and when they use it), but also which machines a user can access. To do so, click the Logon To button in User Manager's New User window. This launches the Logon Workstations window, shown in the following figure.

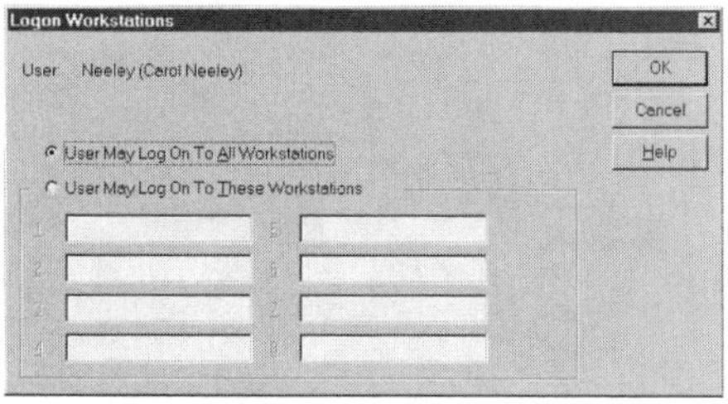

Use the Logon Workstations window to control which machines users can log on to.

Here you specify whether the user can log on to all workstations; alternatively, you can enter up to eight computers that the account can use.

The Account Button: Setting up Automatic Account Expiration

Sometimes you'll create temporary accounts, intended for use for two or three weeks only. When you do, it's nice to have them expire automatically. (When an account expires, it is completely disabled.) To set an account for automatic expiration, click the Account button in the New User window. This launches the Account Information window, shown in the following figure.

Enter the desired date, and then save your changes. The account will expire automatically. If you'd like to see what happens when an account expires, set up a test account today and set its expiration date for tomorrow. Then, go back and check the account tomorrow.

The Account Information
window.

The Dialin Button: Supporting Dial-In Access

In all likelihood, you'll support at least some dial-in access. Dial-in access can often be a lifesaver when you're trying to get that report in by Monday morning. However, dial-in access is also a twofold security risk. On the one hand, it invites roaming hackers to take a crack at your network. On the other, it enables nosy employees to snoop around at night. So you need to apply access control to your dial-up services, just as with files, directories, printers, resources, and accounts. To do so, click the Dialin button in the New User window. This launches the Dialin Information window, shown in the following figure.

The Dialin button is used
to grant dial-in permis-
sion.

If you allow dial-in access by checking the Grant Dialin Permission to User check box, you are presented with three options:

➤ *No Call Back* This specifies that when the user connects, the RAS server will not hang up and call the user back. This call is on the user's dime—but less secure because call-back both verifies the user's location and creates a record of his or her telephone number.

➤ *Set By Caller* After connecting, the user can specify a phone number for the RAS server to call. The RAS server then dials up the user, and this time the charge is on the RAS server's dime. This is a little less secure, because the caller can specify a cell phone or other temporary mobile number that might later be untraceable or a dead end.

➤ *Preset To* This is the preferred setting—and the most secure. This forces the user to access the RAS server only from a specific phone number. The RAS server will call back only to that number, so the user must be there.

Establishing Account Policy

Finally, establish stringent policies for the user's account, including passwords and such. To do so, choose Start | Programs | Administrative Tools | User Manager | Policies and the Account option. This invokes the Account Policy window, shown in the following figure.

The Account Policy dialog box.

You'll model your account policy around several security-related issues (to be discussed in a moment), so be sure to enforce the following settings:

➤ Always require passwords by deselecting the Disallow Blank Password option button in the Minimum Password Length area.

➤ Always require a minimum password length. The longer the password, the harder it is to break. Select the At Least option button in the Minimum Password Length area and enter the minimum password length in the corresponding field.

➤ Enforce password aging and expiration. You might want to consider setting passwords to expire in 60 days. To set an expiration, select the Expires In option button in the Password Restrictions area, and then enter the number of days a password can be used in the corresponding field.

➤ Force users to employ unique passwords. In other words, don't allow users to reuse a password after it expires. Click the Remember option button in the Password Uniqueness area and enter the number of expired passwords you want the user's system to disallow. In order to restrict reuse of passwords, you must leave the Do Not Keep Password History option unchecked.

➤ Enable account lockout by selecting the Account Lockout option button, and then entering a number in the Lockout After *x* Bad Logon Attempts field. This locks an account after *x* bad login attempts. To set the lockout duration, select the Forever (Until Admin Unlocks) option button. This ensures that you—and only you—control when an account is freed up.

167

➤ Choose to forcibly disconnect users if they're logged on and exceed their allowed access time by checking the Forcibly Disconnect Remote Users from Server When Logon Hours Expire check box.

The UNIX World: Getting to the Root of the Problem

Your first step to successful UNIX system administration is to understand how UNIX privileges are assigned.

UNIX is a multi-user system, meaning that many folks can use the same machine simultaneously. To keep track of multiple users, UNIX employs a very structured approach. Each user has an account consisting of a user name, a password, and a home directory (for example, /home/bwagner). When the user first logs in, she is positioned in her home directory. On a typical UNIX box in a corporate environment, there can be as many as 200 accounts and, therefore, some 200 home directories.

To manage these accounts, UNIX makes use of a special or *privileged* account; this account is called *root* or *superuser*.

It's a Bird, It's a Plane, It's SUPERUSER!

What makes root such a superuser? Here it is in a nutshell: Whereas regular users can generally make changes only to their own files, root can make changes to any file. In the larger picture, however, root is much, much more. To understand root and the power it wields you need a crash course in computer security.

In shared networked environments, users can check out files, directories, and other resources at will. To prevent that from getting out of hand, UNIX employs a technique called *Discretionary Access Control*, or *DAC*. DAC is present in any system that enables a centralized, human authority to incisively permit or deny users access based on file, directory, or machine. As root, you enforce these rules through *permissions*. There are different types of permissions:

➤ *Execute*   Execute permissions enable users to execute the specified file.
➤ *Read*   Read permissions enable users to read the specified file.
➤ *Write*   Write permissions enable users to alter the specified file.

These permissions are attached to files, directories, and devices. Each permission is represented by a token. Permission tokens are

➤ r   Read access
➤ w   Write access
➤ x   Execute access

To ascertain permissions on a file or directory, list the file in long format by typing the following at the command line:

```
ls -l
```

Here's some sample output:

```
drwxrwxrwx   2 bwagner   other        512 Jun 25 22:35 Consent
drwxrwxrwx   2 bwagner   other        512 Jun 25 22:35 Instructions
drwx------   2 bwagner   other        512 Aug  8 18:41 mail
-rw-rw-rw-   1 bwagner   other        324 Aug 11 16:34 ppp-off
-rw-rw-rw-   1 bwagner   other        121 Aug 11 16:34 ppp-on
-rw-rw-rw-   1 bwagner   other      46188 Aug 11 16:33 pppd-man.txt
-rw-rw-rw-   1 bwagner   other         58 Aug 11 20:43 pppkill
drwxrwxrwx   8 bwagner   other        512 Aug  1 01:32 public_html
```

For purposes of clarity, extract the fourth line:

```
-rw-rw-rw-   1 bwagner   other        324 Aug 11 16:34 ppp-off
```

Notice that the line is broken into fields. Here, the interest lies only with the first field, which consists of 10 characters:

```
-rw-rw-rw-
```

Let's break down what those ten characters mean. The first character tells you the type of file you're dealing with. There are two tokens for this:

➤ - Represents a file

➤ d Represents a directory

In the example, the first character is -; therefore, it is clear that this is a file.

The remaining nine characters are actually three sets of three. Let's break them down, three at a time. The first set (reading from left to right) represents the permissions of the current user:

```
rw-
```

In this case, the current user (that's me) has read and write but not execute permissions.

The second set (again, reading from left to right) represents the permissions of the current group:

```
rw-
```

Again, group users have read and write access.

Finally, the last set represents what permissions the rest of the world has:

```
rw-
```

169

As you can see, the rest of the world also has read and write access. So everybody has the same permissions on this file.

Suppose, however, that the first column of the permission table looked like this:

```
drwxr-xr-x
```

This is a different situation altogether. First, it is known that this resource is a directory because the first character is a d. Also, it is clear that root (the owner) has read, write, and execute privileges because the next three characters are rwx. However, the fact that the final six characters are r-xr-x indicates that both the current group and world can only read and execute; they cannot write.

So, to reiterate:

➤ The first character reports the file type (typically, a regular file or directory.)

➤ The next three characters reflect the owner's privileges.

➤ The second set of three reflects the group's privileges.

➤ The last set of three reflects the world's privileges.

Setting Permissions: the chmod Command

To set permissions on an individual file or directory, use the chmod command. chmod accepts three operators:

➤ -   This operator removes permissions.

➤ +   This operator adds permissions.

➤ =   This operator assigns permissions.

Table 11.1 summarizes what permissions these operators can remove, add, or assign.

Table 11.1 chmod Permissions

chmod Permission	Explanation
r	The r character adds or subtracts read permission. Example: chmod +r *filename* adds the read permission to *filename*.
w	The w character adds or subtracts write permission. Example: chmod +w *filename* takes away write permission from *filename*.
x	The x character adds or subtracts execute permission. Example: chmod +x *filename* adds the execute permission to *filename*.

chmod *and the Octal System*

Using letters (r, w, x) to assign permissions on individual files and directories is fine. Sometimes, however, you'll want to set permissions *en masse*. For example, you might want to set permissions for the file's owner, the owner's group, and finally, the rest of the world. For this, it's easier to use the octal system.

In the octal system, numbers represent permissions. Table 11.2 summarizes the octal number scheme and what each number represents.

Table 11.2 chmod **Octal Permissions**

chmod **Octal Permission**	**Explanation**
0	The octal value 0 is equivalent to - - - or no permissions at all.
1	The octal value 1 is equivalent to - -x, or only execute permissions.
2	The octal value 2 is equivalent to -w-, or only write permissions.
3	The octal value 3 is equivalent to -wx, or only write and execute permissions.
4	The octal value 4 is equivalent to r- -, or only read permissions.
5	The octal value 5 is equivalent to r-x, or only read and execute permissions.
6	The octal value 6 is equivalent to rw-, or only read and write permissions.
7	The octal value 7 is the whole shebang: It's equivalent to rwx, or read, write, and execute permissions.

You can use the octal scheme to perform widespread permission changes. For example, consider this command:

```
chmod 751 filename
```

In this case, filename has the following permissions:

➤ The owner can read, write, and execute it.

➤ The group can read and execute it.

➤ Outsiders can only execute it.

Be careful when applying permissions. You can accidentally place over-restrictive permissions, and then no one will be capable of accessing anything. Conversely, if your permissions are too liberal, folks can overwrite or access files they shouldn't.

171

Adding and Removing Users

Part of your job as system administrator is to add and remove users. For a first-time system administrator, these can be hazardous undertakings—but they needn't be. There are several ways to accomplish these tasks, depending on your configuration:

➤ *Using proprietary graphical tools* Many modern UNIX systems (including Solaris, AIX, HP-UX, and UNIXWare) have graphical tools for adding and removing users.

➤ *Using command-line tools or scripts* Some systems (such as Linux) have automated scripts or command-line programs to add and remove users.

➤ *Editing the* passwd *file manually* On many older systems, you have to edit the passwd file manually and create the /home directory for each user.

Consult your system manuals to determine which option is available to you. Because I cannot guess your specific configuration, I've offered an explanation of generic procedures here.

/etc/passwd: **The Password File**

User login and password information is stored in a central database called passwd. passwd is located in the directory /etc. On older systems, the /etc/passwd file looks like this:

```
root:uXonr7RoTwQWs8:0:0:root:/root:/bin/bash
bin:*:1:1:bin:/bin:
daemon:*:2:2:daemon:/sbin:
adm:*:3:4:adm:/var/adm:
lp:*:4:7:lp:/var/spool/lpd:
sync:*:5:0:sync:/sbin:/bin/sync
shutdown:*:6:0:shutdown:/sbin:/sbin/shutdown
halt:*:7:0:halt:/sbin:/sbin/halt
bwagner:yPf3M5qMgglUc:101:10:Bill Wagner:/home/bwagner:/bin/bash
```

That probably looks very confusing. In reality, however, the file's structure is really quite simple. Each line consists of seven fields, separated by colons:

➤ The user's login ID

➤ The user's password in encrypted form

➤ The user's user ID (uid), a numeric value to identify the user

➤ The user's group ID (gid), a numeric value to identify the group that user belongs to

➤ The user's real name

➤ The user's home directory

➤ The user's shell

Consider my entry:

```
bwagner:yPf3M5qMgglUc:101:10:Bill Wagner:/home/bwagner:/bin/bash
```

From this, you can ascertain the following:

➤ My user name is `bwagner`.

➤ My password, in encrypted form, is `yPf3M5qMgglUc`.

➤ My user ID is `101`.

➤ My group ID is `10`.

➤ My real name is Bill Wagner.

➤ My home directory is `/home/bwagner`.

➤ My preferred shell is `bash`.

To remove a user, you need only remove his entry from the `passwd` file and delete his home directory. Adding a user, however, is a bit more complicated. The following section discusses adding a user.

Adding a User

The only data in `/etc/passwd` that can't be entered manually is the password itself. Therefore, to add a new user, edit the `passwd` file and add the other six values by hand. For this, you can use any editor, although on BSD-based systems the preferred editor is `vipw`.

`vipw` is a simple tool for editing the `passwd` file. Its advantage is this: `vipw` does not save a `passwd` file that has a corrupted root entry. Because of this, `vipw` guards against root `passwd` lockouts. This is very important because it can prevent you from doing something really silly, such as accidentally bungling the root `passwd` entry.

Techno Talk

`vipw` behaves just like `vi`. If you don't know how to use `vi`, do not use `vipw` to edit the `passwd` file. There is a strong chance that if you have no experience with `vi`, you might potentially bungle the `passwd` entries. Furthermore, because `vipw` only checks for root entry integrity, you might accidentally lock out other users.

Step One: Add a New Line to the `passwd` File

Whatever editor you ultimately use, go to the end of the `passwd` file, where you'll be adding a new line. That new line is constructed as follows:

```
username:blank-password:userid:groupid:real-name:home-directory:shell
```

During this process, you have to carefully choose both the user ID (`uid`) and group ID (`gid`). The `uid` can be any number between 0 and 32767. In general, though, you need to make the `uid` greater than 100 but less than 19000. So long as the number is unique, however, it is sufficient.

173

Likewise, the gid can be any number between 0 and 32767. However, check /etc/group or /etc/groups to see what groups already exist. It's best to add new users to a group that already exists. This way, when you make global changes to that group the change affects all users in the group—making your life much easier. Following are the contents of a typical /etc/group file:

```
root::0:root
other::1:
bin::2:root,bin,daemon
sys::3:root,bin,sys,adm
adm::4:root,adm,daemon
uucp::5:root,uucp
mail::6:root
tty::7:root,tty,adm
lp::8:root,lp,adm
nuucp::9:root,nuucp
staff::10:
daemon::12:root,daemon
sysadmin::14:
nobody::60001:
noaccess::60002:
nogroup::65534:
```

Check This Out

You can make any directory home, but making it /home/username is a good idea. This way, when you need to automate a system administration task you can do so wholesale to all users in the /home directory hierarchy.

Step Two: Create the New User's Home Directory

After you add the user to the passwd file, the next step is to create his home directory. This is typically a subdirectory of /home. For example, for user bwagner, the home directory is /home/bwagner.

Step Three: Set the User's Initial Login Password

Finally, after you've added the user to /etc/passwd and created his home directory, set his initial login password. This is done with the passwd command, as follows:

```
passwd bwagner [some-password]
```

passwd prompts you for verification; commit the new password to the passwd database. That's it! You just created a new user.

Using Password Tokens

Newer UNIX distributions usually have special tools for adding new users. So in all likelihood, you'll never have to follow the procedure outlined previously. If you do, though, here's a tip: Many UNIX systems do not store the encrypted password in /etc/passwd. Instead, this password is replaced by a token. For instance, examine this sample passwd file:

```
root:x:0:1:Super-User:/:/sbin/sh
daemon:x:1:1::/:
bin:x:2:2::/usr/bin:
sys:x:3:3::/:
adm:x:4:4:Admin:/var/adm:
lp:x:71:8:Line Printer Admin:/usr/spool/lp:
smtp:x:0:0:Mail Daemon User:/:
uucp:x:5:5:uucp Admin:/usr/lib/uucp:
nuucp:x:9:9:uucp Admin:/var/spool/uucppublic:/usr/lib/uucp/uucico
listen:x:37:4:Network Admin:/usr/net/nls:
nobody:x:60001:60001:Nobody:/:
noaccess:x:60002:60002:No Access User:/:
nobody4:x:65534:65534:SunOS 4.x Nobody:/:
bwagner:x:101:10:Bill Wagner:/home/bwagner:/bin/bash
```

Notice that the character x occupies the password field. This is a placeholder for the real, encrypted password that resides elsewhere on the disk drive. When you edit the passwd file on such systems, add the token instead of a blank password field.

A Few Words about UNIX Security

This book is really too short to give you a decent primer on security (although this issue is covered in Chapter 13, "Security"). However, here are some basic rules to live by when maintaining a UNIX network:

➤ *Never give anyone the root password*   The root password gives you access to everything. If someone gets your root password, they can seize control of your machine. Protect that password with your life. Don't write it down, and make sure that it isn't easy to guess. For example, don't make the root password your birthday, your social security number, or even any word found in the average dictionary.

➤ *Back up the entire system on a regular basis* Backups often comprise the only evidence you'll ever have that a security breach has occurred. If you have more than a few users, back up weekly (at a minimum).

➤ *Buy a good book on security* UNIX security is a very complex field that's evolved over some 25 years. If you really intend to secure your server, you need expert advice. For this, check out *Practical UNIX and Internet Security* by Simson Garfinkel and Gene Spafford (published by O'Reilly & Associates). This takes you step-by-step through the paces of UNIX security. Alternatively, try *Maximum Security*, published by Sams Publishing.

Where To From Here

Network administration is a complex subject and this chapter only scratched the surface. Over time and through experience, you'll discover ways of improving centralization and simplifying management on your particular platform.

In the next chapter, "Disaster Prevention: Backing Up," you'll learn about backing up: why it's necessary and how it is done.

The Least You Need to Know

➤ Always enforce strong password policies. If you don't do it, nobody will. Users are lazy when it comes to these things.

➤ Exploit the convenience of group-based management whenever possible. This will save you many hours of work.

➤ Always apply the most stringent privileges.

➤ Never give anyone your administrative password.

## Chapter 12

Disaster Prevention: Backing Up

In This Chapter

➤ Understand why you need to back up your computer files.

➤ Learn how to perform simple backups.

➤ Find out what kinds of media are used to back up data.

➤ Learn what goes into creating a backup strategy.

Your computer might be struck by lightning. Your son might mistakenly erase the novel you've been working on for the past three years. Your laptop can fall into the lake.... If you've backed up your computer's data, these will be irritations rather than disasters.

As an individual, your data is important to you. To a business, data might be the company's lifeblood. Anyone can back up their personal computer files; to most businesses, however, backing up computer data is a necessity.

If your home or business computers are on a network, that network is probably the best way to make sure that everyone's files are backed up. Network backups can be more thorough, cost effective, and efficient than backups done individually.

This chapter describes the advantages of backups in general, and on networks in particular. It then describes how to go about planning and performing backups.

Why Back Up?

The reason for backing up your computer files is simple: Your files can be deleted or destroyed when you still need them. There are many ways in which your files can be lost:

➤ *Hard disk crash*   A computer's hard disk has elements that are electrical, magnetic, and mechanical. Any of those types of technology can fail, causing the disk to crash in such a way that data is not recoverable.

➤ *Deletions*   People delete files all the time, both intentionally and by mistake. If the deleted files existed at a time when the computer's files were backed up, the files can be retrieved later if it is found that they are needed.

➤ *Viruses*   A virus can infect the programs and files in a computer. This can result in files being destroyed or infected in such a way that they are no longer useful. A system backup from before the time the virus was introduced can return the computer system (and the data files) to a workable state.

➤ *Computers destroyed*   Fires, floods, or other natural—or unnatural—disasters can destroy computers as much as any other kind of property. The backup medium you created can be used to re-create the computing environment with the new or fixed equipment.

For some companies, the information contained on their computers is far more valuable than simply the cost of hardware. That information can include inventory records, accounts receivable, sales data, product specifications, and a variety of other things. Seeing that timely backups are done and managed is part of company policy.

Performing Simple Backups

Generally, a backup consists of copying one or more data files from their permanent location (typically a computer's hard disk) to another location (usually a removable medium, such as a cartridge tape or removable disk). The removable medium can then be stored in a safe place in case it is ever needed.

There are a few simple types of backups that you can do with existing software on your Windows 95/98 computer. Although these procedures do not enable you to perform complex or automated backups, they will help you realize that backups are not so scary.

A Simple Copy-to-Floppy

Perhaps the easiest backup—and the one done by most first-time PC users—is to copy a few important files to floppy disk. Let's say, for example, that you want to back up a folder containing your latest novel (`C:\mybook`) to floppy disk from Windows 95. The steps for doing so are as follows:

1. Insert a floppy disk into the floppy drive (usually A:).

2. Double-click the My Computer icon.

3. Double-click the C: icon; arrange the My Computer and C: windows on your desktop so you can see them both.

4. Drag and drop the mybook icon onto the 3.5 Floppy icon.

As long as the floppy disk can hold the amount of data contained in the folder, the files are copied to the floppy disk. At that point, you can pop out the floppy disk and store it in a safe place. That's it!

Using Windows 95 Backup

Although a simple copy-to-floppy technique is okay for a few files, more sophisticated tools need to be used in cases where there are a lot of files that must be backed up on a consistent basis. The Backup utility that comes with Windows 95 is a good tool for setting up a backup that you can run more than once. Here's an example of how to use the Backup utility:

1. Click on Start | Programs | Accessories | System Tools | Backup. After a few pop-up windows, the Backup window appears, as shown in the following figure.

Run simple backups with the Windows 95 Backup utility.

2. From the left frame, select the files and folders you want to back up.

3. Click Next Step. The window asks you to enter the location or device to which the files will be backed up.

4. From the left frame, select the backup device (tape drive, floppy drive, and so on) or location (folder).

5. Click Start Backup. A pop-up window asks you to put a label on the backup set. This name will help you identify the backup in case you need to restore the files later.

6. Type the name of the backup set you are creating. At this point, you also have a choice of adding a password to the backup set. If you add a password, the files can't be restored later by anyone who doesn't have the password.

Check This Out

Here's your opportunity to back up the files over the network. Any file servers on the network appear in the Network Neighborhood folder. Choose the file server to which you want to back up your files.

7. Click OK to begin the backup. When the backup is complete, you see a message telling you so.

8. Click OK.

Check This Out

During the backup process, you can click Save As, then save the backup settings to a file that can be used again. Saving backup settings is helpful because many people save all their data files to the same locations.

At this point, you can remove the backup medium and mark it with an appropriate name and date. If at a later time you need to restore the files from this backup, you can do so by using the Restore tab in the screen shown in the preceding figure.

Check This Out

One drawback to Windows Backup is that a single backup can't span more than one medium. In other words, if you fill up a 100MB Zip cartridge before the backup is done, you can't just pop in another cartridge and have it continue. To get around this problem, you can use the DOS utility Xcopy to do the backup. From a DOS window, first change the attributes to indicate that files are ready to be archived (the following line changes all files on your C: drive):

```
ATTRIB +A C:\*.* /S
```

Then, with the medium loaded into the drive (let's say the Zip drive in drive D:), type the following command:

```
XCOPY C:\*.* D:\ /S /M
```

Once the medium is full, a message tells you so. Put in another blank Zip cartridge and run the command again. Repeat the command until the command exits without showing you a disk full message.

Using Iomega 1-Step Backup

Simple backup tools are often delivered with the backup medium itself. For example, Iomega Zip and Jaz drives come with a 1-Step Backup utility. This utility provides a simple way to identify files to back up, run the backup, and save the backup settings for later use.

To start the Iomega 1-Step Backup, select Start | Programs | Iomega Tools | 1-Step Backup for Zip and Jaz. The utility assumes you are backing up to your Zip or Jaz drive, but enables you to select the files to back up. You can add password protection to the backup and compress the data (so more fits on the removable disk).

Why Network Backups?

The focus of this chapter is network backups, which entail a lot of issues you might want to consider. Network backups imply that you are dealing with multiple computers and users, so you need to think about

➤ How much data needs to be backed up? If you have a network of three PCs, you might get by with a 100MB Zip drive for all your backups. If the network has 100 PCs, you probably want at least one mass storage device.

➤ How critical is the information? If there is little new data being added to the computers, you might do a backup just once a week. If important data—such as financial or medical records—is being added constantly, you might need to do backups every day or even every few hours.

The more computers and users that are on your network, the more beneficial network backups can be. Many of the advantages you get from sharing other network resources also apply to centralizing your backup administration. Some of these advantages are

➤ *Shared hardware*   Instead of spending money on a removable drive for each PC, you can have one large backup device, such as a CD tower or tape device, that is shared on the network.

➤ *Central administration*   Because a company's information is so important, most companies have a policy about how and when computer files are backed up. Having one person responsible for running the backups and securely handling the backup medium helps ensure that backups get done properly for all computers and users. Using the network, the administrator can back up all the computers without actually visiting each one.

➤ *Convenient scheduling*   Using some of today's advanced backup tools, backups can be scheduled to run over the network at times when the computers aren't being used much. This can help prevent the performance hits that occur during backups.

Choosing a Backup Type

Different people who use computers change different amounts of data, add and delete different numbers of files, and place different levels of importance on their files. Each of these issues has an impact on the types of backup you need and how often those backups are run.

Most locations use a combination of backup types. The reason for doing different backups at different points in the backup schedule is to make your backups efficient. For example, if a computer has 1GB of data on it, but only 2MB of data changes between Monday and Tuesday, there is no reason to do a full backup of the computer each day. Therefore, on some days you do a full backup, whereas on other days you do either an incremental or differential backup.

Full Backup

With a full backup, you copy the entire contents of a computer (that is, its whole hard disk) to the backup medium. After a full backup is done, you have the capability to restore that entire hard disk to where it was when the backup was done.

Incremental or Differential Backups

A typical backup schedule backs up the entire contents of a hard disk once a week, then simply backs up the changes that occur on every other day of the week. The backups that are done on those other days are either incremental backups or differential backups.

For an *incremental backup*, the backup program determines which files have been added or changed since the previous (most recent) backup. Only the added or changed files are put on the incremental backup tape. The next backup will again store only those changes made since the previous incremental backup. This continues until the next full backup, at which time the next incremental backup uses the new full backup as the baseline.

For a *differential backup*, all backups that are done after the initial full backup track all changes since the full backup. So, for example, if a full backup is done on Sunday night, a differential backup on Monday contains all files that are new or changed since Sunday. The next differential backup done on Tuesday also contains all files that have changed since Sunday (including files changed on Monday and Tuesday).

The differences between incremental and differential backups include the number of backup media you use and the difficulty in restoring the files if necessary:

➤ *Backup amounts differ*   Incremental backups result in less information being stored each day than with differential backups. Therefore, with incremental you can use fewer media (fewer tapes or disks) and get each backup done faster. Think of Saturday's backup in the preceding example. With incremental, Saturday's backup includes changes between Friday and Saturday. With differential, Saturday's backup contains all changes since last Sunday.

➤ *Restore convenience differs*   With a differential backup you only need two sets of media to restore files from any day: the full backup and the day you want to restore to. Restoring with incremental media requires you to have the full backup (from the week being restored) and the backup media for each day up to the restore day.

Because most backups are done automatically overnight, the differential backup is usually the most convenient. By reducing the restore to two media, one full and one differential, the administrator's restore job is much easier.

Choosing Backup Media

Remember that a backup means creating a copy of a file or files in some place other than the original medium. Although this typically means a removable medium, a backup can also be done to a hard disk on another computer or to a second hard disk on the same computer. Various types of backup media are available:

➤ Hard disk

➤ Tape

➤ Recordable CD

➤ High-density floppies

➤ Removable disks

Check This Out

Although it is possible to back up files onto the same hard disk, that generally defeats the purpose; if the hard disk crashes, you lose both copies.

Hard Disk

It can be much faster to copy files to another hard disk—possibly even if that disk is on a network server—than it is to copy them to tape. This type of backup can be used for backing up data in real-time, where waiting until the night's backup isn't soon enough.

Although hard disks are more expensive than tape devices, prices have decreased significantly in recent years. If the data being protected is critical, ongoing backups can efficiently copy data to a file server's hard disk. That data can then be offloaded to tape when it is convenient.

This type of backup is sometimes referred to as *real-time replication*. Essentially, you are creating a replica of the data on another hard disk. That disk might be on a NetWare file server or a variety of other types of systems.

Tape

Before inexpensive removable disks and writable CD-ROMs were around, magnetic tape was the backup medium of choice. In fact, one of the first UNIX system backup utilities was called tar—short for tape archiver. Although there are still the old 60MB and 120MB cartridge tapes around, much higher capacity tape drives are available today for reasonable prices. These include

➤ *Digital Linear Tapes (DLT)*   DLT is considered to be the leading format for high-end tape backup. Although originally created by Digital Equipment Corp., DLT is an open standard for magnetic tapes. DLT is a half-inch tape. Its cartridge is 4.1 square inches and one inch high. A DLT 4000 can hold 20GB (or up to 40GB compressed), whereas a DLT 7000 can hold 35GB (or up to 70GB compressed).

➤ *QIC* QIC tapes use a 5.25-inch cartridge. The latest versions can hold up to 13GB of data.

➤ *DAT* DAT holds up to 8GB compressed data (DDS-2 format) or 24GB compressed data (DDS-3 format). These small cartridges are popular in part because they are compact and are produced by several different vendors.

➤ *8mm* This type of cartridge tape was created by Exabyte Corporation. Using 2:1 compression, 8mm tapes can hold up to 20GB of data.

DLT is becoming the most popular tape format for high-end operations. DAT is popular for inclusion on desktop units.

Recordable CD

There are two different types of recordable CDs available:

➤ CD-R (compact disc-recordable) enables you to write once to a CD, then read it as many times as you like. This type of media is referred to as *WORM* (write once-read many).

➤ CD-RW (compact disc-rewriteable) enables you to write and erase the CD multiple times.

Although both the media and the drives are more expensive with CD-RW, the ability to rewrite data can make CD-RW more cost-effective. However, one drawback to CD-RW is that discs cannot be read by all disc players, whereas CD-R can.

For more information about recordable CDs, refer to the CD-Recordable FAQ (`http://www.fadden.com/cdrfaq`). This FAQ contains a lot of information about the different formats and how you can use them.

High-Density Floppies

The SuperDisk 120MB floppy disk drives can be used to replace standard 1.44MB floppy drives. With the new drives, you can use either the new 120MB floppies or the standard 1.44MB floppies—so you can continue to use your old floppies. For low-volume backups, the 120MB floppy disks can be a good alternative to purchasing another backup medium.

Removable Disks

Like high-density floppies, removable disk cartridges came along to fill the huge hole between floppy disks (holding 1.44MB) and mass storage devices. These drives are fairly inexpensive, can plug into an existing parallel port, and use inexpensive media (under $12 for a cartridge).

185

Iomega is the leader in removable storage devices. An Iomega Zip drive uses 100MB cartridges. The more expensive Jaz drives can handle 1GB and 2GB cartridges. You can find Zip drives today for under $120 and Jaz drives for under $400. The major competitor to Iomega has been Syquest. (However, Syquest recently filed for Chapter 11 bankruptcy, putting its future as a leader in removable drives in question.) You can find Syquest SparQ 1GB removable drives for under $200. Their cartridges are also less expensive than those of Jaz drives.

Choosing a Backup Strategy

No single backup strategy fits all cases. Computers that contain constantly changing, critical data need a much more diligent backup schedule than low-use computers containing non-essential data. Large and small amounts of data benefit from different kinds of backup media. This section helps describe the issues that go into choosing a backup strategy.

What Needs to be Backed up?

Determining what data you need to back up is probably the best place to begin. The kind of information you want to back up from computers falls into two basic categories:

➤ *Data files*   These contain the information that users or applications generate, and can include word processing files, database records, and spreadsheets.

➤ *System files*   These contain data that is needed to reconstruct your computer system. System files can include information defining user preferences (such as screen layout and colors) and configuration information (such as network addresses).

If a computer is managed in an organized way, data files are fairly easy to back up. In a UNIX system, users tend to keep personal files in their own home directories. For example, a user named johnj might store his files in the /home/johnj directory. Windows 95 users tend to store files in folders that are specific to an application, although this still represents a limited number of locations.

System files, however, can be more spread out than data files. Although in a UNIX system there are separate configuration files for almost every feature, most of these files are in the /etc directory. For example, the following are UNIX configuration files that you need to back up to re-create your system:

➤ /etc/password   Contains user names and encrypted passwords for each user on the computer

➤ /etc/inittab   Contains the programs that are run (mostly system programs) when the computer starts up or enters a different run state

➤ /etc/printcap   Contains information about the printers that are configured to work on your computer

On a Windows 95 system, system information includes registry entries, user profiles, and INI files. An inexperienced user probably doesn't even know where most of this information resides. Luckily, there are backup utilities specifically designed to find and back up Windows 95 system information.

Techno Talk

There are a variety of backup utilities available to back up your Windows 95 system files so your computer can be re-created in the case of a disk crash. Safety Net Pro (http://members.aol.com/_ht_a/ron2222/snpro.htm) backs up your Registry, INI files, and startup files to disk. Emergency Recovery System (http://www.mslm.com) can also be used to back up Windows 95 system files.

How Often Is Backup Needed?

Both the kind and the amount of data being created on your computers have an impact on how often you need to back up. Following are a few examples of situations that require data to be backed up at different intervals:

➤ *Personal backups*   Say you have a few computers on a small LAN—perhaps in a home or a school—that are not used for anything critical. In this case, you might choose to back up the computers once a week on a regular basis, with an occasional special backup if someone has just created some important files.

➤ *Daily backups*   Some small businesses put their sales, inventory, scheduling, billing, and all other critical information on a few computers that are connected by a LAN. Although consistent backups are necessary in this case, once each workday is usually enough. Usually the backup is run after hours so as not to disrupt ongoing work.

➤ *Ongoing backups*   Sometimes the data on a company's computers is so critical that it must be constantly backed up. For example, a bank can't afford to go back to yesterday's backup medium to restore its data, as it would lose track of money that has come and gone from people's accounts. In this case, companies might use *mirroring*, where all the data on a hard disk is mirrored exactly on another disk. Both disks are updated simultaneously. (See the description of RAID later in this chapter.)

The amount of data you need to back up can help you determine the type of backup device you need. By backing up over a network, you multiply the backup volume you do for a single computer. For that reason, instead of using a single tape or CD device, you might want to purchase a unit that can handle multiple backup devices at the same time. This type of device is referred to as a *library*.

One advantage of using a library is that you don't need an operator to change tapes or disks during the backup operation. This is useful because backups are often run during the middle of the night, when it might not be convenient to keep an administrator near the machine. The tapes or disks can be removed, labeled, and stored the next morning.

When Should Backups Be Run?

Running a backup slows down the performance of the computer being backed up. For that reason, backups are often run late at night. However, for critical data (such as financial data), live backups might need to be run constantly—or at least several times a day.

To run backups late at night, UNIX systems use utilities called at or cron. With at or cron, an administrator registers the backup utility (such as cpio or tar) to be started at a particular time with a certain set of options. With Windows 95/98 and Windows NT systems, you can use the backup agent to run automatic backups. From the Network Properties window, you can add backup services such as Backup Exec (from Arcada Software) or ARCserv (from Cheyenne). Then, to enable the automatic backup, display the properties for the network service and select Enable Network Backup (in addition to any options you choose to set).

Backup Tips

The following are some tips to help you perform backups and manage backup media:

➤ *Cycle backup media*   You don't need to use a new tape or disk each time you run a backup. Besides being expensive and difficult to manage, it is also unnecessary. Rewritable media are designed to be rewritten. So, cycling media is the normal practice.

Have at least two sets of media that you cycle. By alternating them, you always have a good set of media in case the hard disk crashes in the middle of a backup.

Check the manufacturer's specifications for information on how often the medium can be rewritten. Some tapes can handle 100 backup and restore passes and might need to be replaced only once a year.

➤ *Label backup media*   If the day ever comes when you need to restore some or all of a computer's files, you will understand just how important a good label is. The label indicates: when the backup was done, where the data came from, the type of backup (full, incremental or differential), the backup tool used (cpio, tar, or other), and the number of the medium in the set (such as tape 4 of 7).

➤ *Store the media safely*   It doesn't help to have the backup medium on the desk next to the computer if the office burns down. Media need to be kept in waterproof and fireproof containers. For very important data, media need to be kept at another site.

➤ *Verify the backup media*   Try restoring a few files from your backup medium after the backup is complete. You don't want to find out that the medium was bad when you go to restore the files from a crashed hard disk.

➤ *Clean the drive*   Check the manual that comes with the tape drive for instructions on how and how often the drive needs to be cleaned.

Protecting Your Data

Although it's nice to be capable of recovering from disasters that can happen to your computer network, it's even better to prevent disasters in the first place. UPS and RAID technology can help you do just that.

RAID

When it is imperative that your data be protected and always available, *Redundant Array of Independent Drives (RAID)* might be your answer. A RAID unit is made up of two or more disks that appear as a single disk to the outside world. Data on the disks is redundant, so if one disk crashes, another can take over without missing a beat.

Having duplicate data available on several physical disks has other advantages. Performance can improve by allowing access to different records simultaneously, instead of one after another on a single disk. Also, if one disk needs to be repaired or replaced, it can be done without shutting down the system.

UPS

To prevent power problems from bringing down or damaging the computers on your network, you can use an *uninterruptible power supply (UPS)*. A UPS unit can protect your computers by

➤ Protecting against power surges and spikes

➤ Providing an uninterrupted flow of power during power outages

There are several different types of UPS systems available. A UPS system used with computers has a battery backup that immediately kicks in when the power goes out. This allows the computers to continue to work for a short period of time without interruption.

If the power outage lasts for a long time, the UPS can keep the computers up long enough that they can be shut down in an orderly way. If it's critical that the computers stay up, even in long power outages, the UPS can keep the systems up until a backup generator can be started to keep the power flowing beyond the battery capacity.

Where To From Here?

Keeping your data safe from disk crashes, fires, and floods can be done using the backup methods described in this chapter. Keeping your data safe from more insidious attacks, such as viruses and hackers, falls under the heading of security. Matters of security, and techniques for improving your security using passwords, firewalls, and other methods, are described in Chapter 13, "Security."

The Least You Need to Know

Right now, the least you need to know about backing up data is this:

➤ Computer backups, where data is copied from its permanent source to another medium, can prevent the loss of your vital computer information.

➤ For simple backups, no network is needed. You can simply copy to another medium using drag-and-drop or the Windows 95 Backup utility.

➤ Network backups can make backing up more efficient by allowing many computers to share backup devices and centralize administration.

➤ Backups are typically done with a combination of full backups (perhaps once a week) and incremental or differential backups (perhaps every day).

➤ Backups can be done from one hard disk to another. More often, however, the eventual destination of a backup is a removable medium (such as tape, recordable CD, high-density floppies, or removable disks).

➤ When you create your own backup schedule, you need to determine several things. You must decide what to back up, how often the data needs to be backed up, and when the backups are to be run.

## Chapter 13

Security

In This Chapter

➤ Learn about network security risks.

➤ Learn how to tighten your network security.

Chapter 12, "Disaster Prevention: Backing Up," discussed backups and disaster recovery. This chapter discusses network security and disasters that can result from poor security practices. Security is a complex subject and can take up several volumes instead of the single chapter you'll find here.

Do You Really Need Security?

Many folks argue that because their network is small, they really don't need much security. After all, the chance of attack in a closed network is slim—particularly if you maintain a home or office peer-to-peer network that's not wired to the Net.

However, if you rely on that network for your livelihood, you need to be more concerned. Network intrusions are more common than ever, and that trend will only continue. A 1998 Computer Security Institute survey reported that 64% of respondents experienced network security breaches in 1997. (That figure was up 16% from the previous year.)

Despite this fact, American businesses are not well prepared for attack. A 1998 survey by Ernst and Young found that

➤ More than 35% of respondents failed to employ basic intrusion detection.

➤ More than 50% of respondents failed to monitor network connections.

➤ More than 60% of respondents had no written policy for responding to a security incident.

Don't allow your network to become a statistic—institute at least basic security controls on your network. The remainder of this chapter focuses on those controls.

Generic Security Precautions

In the most sweeping sense, your security program starts with these three steps:

1. Choosing a network operating system
2. Identifying risks
3. Addressing those risks

Let's run through each now.

Choosing a Network Operating System

The operating system you choose has a weighty impact on your security. When making that decision, take the following into account:

➤ *Encryption*   Does your NOS encrypt passwords and other important data? If so, how strong is its encryption scheme?

➤ *Logging*   What if there's a security breach? Will your NOS record that event (and the intruder's subsequent activities)?

➤ *Access Control*   Does your NOS enable you to incisively deny access to files, directories, and network resources?

Table 13.1 compares several popular network operating systems and their out-of-the-box security tools.

Table 13.1   Comparison of Network Operating System Security Controls

Issue	Encryption	Logging	Access Control
Linux	Good	Very Good	Excellent
NetWare 2.x	Poor to none	Fair	Fair

Issue	Encryption	Logging	Access Control
NetWare 3.x	Good	Good	Good
NetWare 4.x	Excellent	Good	Excellent
Plan 9	Very Good	Very Good	Excellent
UNIX (General)	Very Good	Very Good	Excellent
VMS	Good	Very Good	Excellent
Windows 3	None	None	None
Windows 3.11	Perfunctory	None	None
Windows 95	Weak at best	None	Minimal/ineffective
Windows 98	Weak at best	None	Minimal/ineffective
Windows NT 3.x	Some but weak	Decent	Good but vulnerable
Windows NT 4.x	Good	Very Good	Excellent

Unless you have a reason not to, always choose the operating system with the most security (and naturally, one that you're familiar with). For example, if you're a Windows user, choose Windows NT.

Using Multiple Operating Systems

Another point to consider is whether your network is homogenous or heterogeneous. In the old days, this wasn't an issue. Most networks were homogenous, meaning that all machines ran the same operating system. In today's business world, however, networks are often composed of workstations running multiple operating systems. (Some offices house systems running NetWare, Microsoft Windows 95, Windows NT, MacOS, and UNIX—all under one roof). This naturally makes security more complex.

If you can stick with a homogenous network, do it. In such an environment, you'll enjoy centralization, a consistent application set, and a manageable series of well-known security vulnerabilities. But if you can't maintain a *completely* homogenous network, at least ensure that your servers run the same system.

Identifying Risks

Once you've chosen an operating system, your next step is to identify your risks. These risks naturally differ from platform to platform, but there are some constants. In general, your network can be attacked on four levels, each of which poses a special risk:

➤ The human level
➤ The hardware level
➤ The software level
➤ The network level

Risks at the Human Level

Security experts have consistently proven that human beings are the weakest devices in any security structure. Because of this, hackers can often "socially engineer" their way into your system.

Anti-Social Engineers

Social Engineering is a fancy term that describes the act of obtaining information through fraud. A typical example is a hacker calling your personnel department claiming to be a security administrator. During this initial conversation, the hacker obtains a list of valid users. From there, he calls each user, claiming that he needs to "verify" their password. Incredibly, most employees surrender their password without questioning the caller's authority. The victim of such a ruse has been *socially engineered*.

To understand how silly users are in this regard, consider this: Two months prior to this writing, a security expert tried this social engineering approach on a series of banks. In most cases, bank personnel unwittingly provided their passwords without a struggle.

Addressing Human-Level Risks

Your only defense against social engineering is to educate your users. At the very least, they need to adhere to the following simple rules:

➤ Never offer network information via telephone or email.

➤ Never transmit a password via email in clear text.

➤ Never discuss the network with non-company personnel.

➤ Never write down (or otherwise record) passwords.

Lecturing users on these points is one thing; getting them to adhere to them is another. One way to encourage compliance is to periodically run unannounced tests. In other words, have an outsider call up each department posing as a security administrator. See if your outsider can obtain any real passwords. After the test, post the names of those employees who failed.

Risks at the Hardware Level

Risks at the hardware level include

➤ Denial of service

➤ Data theft

➤ Data destruction

You Just Sank My Battleship!

In *denial of service* attacks, attackers render your system inoperable; they effectively blow a machine off the network by crippling its capability to respond to its peers.

Addressing Hardware-Level Risks

To prevent against these basic risks, take at least the following four steps:

➤ *Place your servers out of reach* To protect your servers against hardware attacks, house them in a secure location, such as a room that offers restricted access. (Ideally, only employees with a key have access.) When you finally develop a written on-site security policy, be sure to clearly specify which employees can physically access your servers and when such access is authorized. (Also, establish penalties for non-compliance. This protects you if you later decide to terminate an employee who violates policy.)

➤ *Secure your backup media* Many offices use backup devices to hedge against disaster. This is an excellent idea. However, remember that backups—especially total backups—pose a special security risk. (Often, such backups contain vital and sensitive information.) Unless your backups are completely encrypted, store them in a secure location.

➤ *Secure your installation media* If employees have access to your installation disks, they can bypass traditional access control. (Remember that installation routines place the user in a privileged mode. This enables them to alter file systems and access resources they can't otherwise reach.)

➤ *Use removable storage media whenever possible* Additionally, if your data is sensitive, I recommend using removable hard disk drives. These drives are typically encased in a carriage that slides along a track. This track leads to an extended data cable, inside the machine. Using these devices, you can remove your hard drives each night and place them in a safe.

Secure Your Wiring

Your network wire is yet another point of vulnerability. Certain network wiring schemes are susceptible to splice-in attacks. In this type of attack, someone splices a workstation or laptop into your network by attaching it to your network wire. This attack is more common in bus-based networks. However, it is possible to splice into other topologies.

To protect against splice-in attacks, carefully insulate your wire route from outsiders. For example, if your offices are located in a large building (and therefore co-exist with other offices adjacent, above, or below you), beware. Make certain that folks in other offices can't gain physical access to your wire.

Who Can That Be Knockin' at My Door?

On the off chance that you're extremely paranoid, I thought I'd mention *Transient Electromagnetic Pulse Emanation Standard* (*TEMPEST*). TEMPEST technology is the study of capturing electromagnetic emissions from computers. There are now TEMPEST tools that can capture signals from your monitor and reassemble them on a remote computer (up to two blocks away). If you're engaged in very sensitive work, you might want to outfit your network with TEMPEST-shielded computers. These are quite expensive but guarantee complete security from prying eyes (or antennae). To learn more about TEMPEST, visit

`http://www.yorku.ca/faculty/academic/neil/issue5/tempest.htm`.

About Console and BIOS Passwords

Console and BIOS passwords represent yet another risk. If you fail to set these passwords, anyone in your offices can gain access to the BIOS or command mode. From there, they can cause serious damage. Many BIOS systems now provide disk-formatting utilities or surface-analysis tools that can destroy drive data. Moreover, most modern BIOS systems provide access to serial and printer ports or other hardware that can be used to export or import information.

This problem is not confined to Intel-based architecture, either. Many UNIX workstations provide access to single-user or command mode through the PROM.

Depending on the workstation's design, users can perform a wide range of tasks from command mode including disk formatting, boot device assignment, serial communication, and so on. For this reason, you need to ensure that both PROM and BIOS passwords are set on all workstations.

Going to the PROM

PROM stands for *Programmable Read-Only Memory*. The PROM is to a UNIX machine what the BIOS is to a PC: It's a chip with firmware that manages the most basic tasks, including identifying disks, tabulating your machine's memory capacity, and so on.

Finally, if your system supports SCSI devices, you probably rely on a SCSI adapter card. Most SCSI adapter cards have their own BIOS or configuration environment. At bootup, you're given the option to enter this environment and set certain parameters including the boot device. (For example, you can either enable or disable bootable CD-ROM support.) Be sure to password-protect this environment if the card supports it.

Risks at the Software Level

Risks at the software level include

➤ Flawed applications

➤ Weak Passwords

➤ Viruses

Addressing Risks Associated with Flawed Applications

Many *commercial-off-the-shelf* (*COTS*) applications have poor security. There are two reasons for this:

➤ Security is an obscure concern, and one that's sometimes overlooked.

➤ Today's network applications often exceed 500,000 lines of code. Managing such a large project is difficult, and there's much room for error.

Another factor is the time-to-market schedule in software development. The software industry is highly competitive and has only become more so with the increased demand for networked applications. In the rush to market, many software manufacturers fail to adequately test their products for security controls. As a result, the industry is now flooded with insecure applications.

Worse still, because source code is rarely available, you have no way of finding out whether your COTS software is safe. Typically, insecure programs are exposed too late, only after hackers or crackers have already exploited the weakness.

Unfortunately, there's no easy solution to this problem. The best you can do is watch security mailing lists for vulnerability reports. The location of several such lists is provided at the end of this chapter.

Risks at the Network Level

Password security is an important issue. Weak passwords account for a high percentage of network security breaches. Make every effort to educate your users on good password choices. At a minimum, user passwords should never contain

➤ Proper names, birth dates, or social security numbers

➤ Any word that appears in a dictionary

➤ Strings of fewer than five characters

➤ All numbers

➤ All the same letter

➤ Any combination of the preceding

Additionally, institute a password aging system. This is where user passwords expire after so many weeks or months. The purpose of this is to periodically force your users to change their passwords, which reduces the chances of a password compromise.

Some network operating systems have password aging built into their security structure and others don't. If yours doesn't, consider obtaining third-party tools for this purpose.

There are several tools for testing password strength. These tools attempt to crack your network passwords, and their approach is quite effective: Whole dictionaries are encrypted using the same algorithm that your operating system uses. Each encrypted word is then compared to your network password. If the program finds a match, the password has been cracked.

Such tools are available for UNIX, Windows NT, and Novell NetWare. For these platforms, I recommend Crack, NTCrack, or NWPCrack. Let's briefly look at these utilities and what they do.

Crack

Crack is used to check UNIX networks for characteristically weak passwords. The author, Alec D. E. Muffet, explains the program's purpose:

> Crack is a freely available program designed to find standard UNIX eight-character DES encrypted passwords by standard guessing techniques...It is written to be flexible, configurable, and fast, and to be able to make use of several networked hosts via the Berkeley rsh program (or similar), where possible.

Crack runs on UNIX only. It comes as a tarred, g'zipped file, and is available at `http://www.users.dircon.co.uk/~crypto/`.

NTCrack

NTCrack performs high-speed brute force attacks. As reported by the folks at Somarsoft:

> The program...does about 1000 logins per minute, when run on a client 486DX-33 with 16MB of RAM, a server 486DX2-66 with 32MB of RAM, and a 10Mbps Ethernet. This is equivalent to testing 1,152,000 passwords per day. By comparison, there are perhaps 100,000 common words in the English language.

To prevent such attacks, Somarsoft suggests that you enable account lockout, rename the Administrator account, disable network logins for Administrator, and disable SMB over TCP/IP.

To try out NTCrack, get the source at `http://somarsoft.com/ntcrack.htm` or a compiled version at `http://somarsoft.com/ftp/NTCRACK.ZIP`.

NWPCRACK

NWPCRACK is a brute-force NetWare password cracker. It works in much the same manner as Crack, but is slower. You can find NWPCRACK at `http://www.digital-gangsters.com/hp/utilities/nwpcrack.zip`.

As a rule, test user passwords once every 90 days. Whenever you find a weak password, notify the user and request that they create a stronger one. This process effectively weeds out crackable passwords and thus increases your system's overall security.

Viruses

A computer virus is a program that attaches itself to files on the target machine. During attachment, the virus's original code is appended to victim files. This procedure is called *infection*. When a file is infected, it is converted from an ordinary file to a *carrier*. From that point on, the infected file can infect other files. This process is called *replication*. Through replication, viruses can spread themselves across a hard disk drive, achieving systemic infection. Often, there is little warning before such a systemic infection takes hold, and by then it's too late.

Different viruses perform different tasks. Some do nothing more than replicate and thus cause a little disruption of service. However, a limited number destroy data, format hard disk drives, or otherwise incapacitate their host system. A recent—and irritating—development is the emergence of data viruses. These are commonly called *macro viruses*. Macro viruses infect documents and document templates, particularly in Microsoft Word and Excel. Such infection invariably leads to the host application's poor (or sometimes bizarre) performance.

Got a Virus? Go to the Clinic!

One excellent place to learn about viruses is the Department of Energy's Computer Incident Advisory Capability Virus Database. The CIAC Virus Database lists thousands of viruses, their signatures, their file sizes, and what damage they can cause. To check out the Virus Database, go to `http://ciac.llnl.gov/ciac/CIACVirusDatabase.html`.

Viruses come from programmers who are either malicious or bored. Virus programmers usually release their code to the Internet (or another communal network), where the chances of proliferation and transport are high. From there, the virus might take any number of twists and turns before it gets to you. You might unwittingly download it directly from the Internet, or you might receive an infected disk. In most cases, you'll never know.

There are currently more than 10,000 viruses, the majority of which target consumer-oriented, PC-based operating systems. In particular, all Microsoft products and several Apple products are especially vulnerable. UNIX, on the other hand, is low-risk for virus infection—in fact, there are only two known viruses for UNIX. Does UNIX have some magical, inherent protection against viruses? No; rather, UNIX is a poor target for virus attacks because its access control is exceptionally stringent. Therefore, it's not possible for a virus to spread in a UNIX environment.

Addressing Risks Associated with Viruses

Protecting against viruses is relatively simple. To do so, install a quality virus-detection utility on each workstation. Most of these utilities can be programmed to scan a workstation's drive each time it boots.

Table 13.2 lists several well-known virus-detection utilities. We have experience using each of the entries in this list, and can recommend them all. Most employ similar techniques of detection.

Check This Out

An important, and often missed, point about virus scanners is that their effectiveness hinges greatly on time. New viruses are released every month; therefore, in order to protect your network, you must constantly keep up with virus-scanner updates.

Table 13.2 Popular Anti-Virus Utilities

Product	URL
FindVirus	http://www.drsolomon.com/
F-PROT Professional	http://www.DataFellows.com/
Integrity Master	http://www.stiller.com/stiller.htm
Iris Antivirus Plus	http://www.irisav.com/
Norman Virus Control	http://www.norman.com/
Norton Anti-Virus	http://www.symantec.com/avcenter/index.html
PC-Cillin II	http://www.checkit.com/
Sweep	http://www.sophos.com/
Thunderbyte Anti-Virus	http://www.thunderbyte.com
ViruSafe by Eliashim	http://www.eliashim.com/
VirusScan by NAI	http://www.nai.com/default_mcafee.asp

External Security: The Internet

Internal security is very important and, traditionally, this is the focus of most LAN security schemes. However, the rules drastically change after you establish Internet connectivity. Internet servers often run the full gamut of TCP/IP services, which means that if you don't use a firewall (a subject to be discussed momentarily), anyone can connect to your system.

This is very different from a traditional private LAN, where known users can connect, but only at certain times of day. Hence, you can easily identify the source of an intrusion. Moreover, you can quickly identify unauthorized after-hours activity. Conversely, with an Internet server, both known and unknown users can connect 24 hours a day, seven days a week.

Sacrificial Hosts

If you establish a Web server purely for distributing generic information (promotional materials about your company, for example), securing your site is simple enough. This arrangement is sometimes called a *sacrificial* or *bastion host*. Sacrificial hosts don't house sensitive or even dynamic data, which means that disaster recovery is quick and painless: Simply restore the hard disk drive and you're good to go.

Additionally, folks rarely spend much money to secure sacrificial hosts. Security on such servers is typically limited to absolute requisites. Sacrificial hosts—at worst—can be brought down by denial of service attacks. If this happens, you simply implement a disaster-recovery plan.

If, however, you intend to establish Internet connectivity for your entire network, you'll need a firewall.

Firewalls

A *firewall* is any device designed to prevent outsiders from accessing your network. This device is typically a standalone computer, a router, or a firewall-in-a-box (proprietary hardware device). This unit serves as a single entry point to your site. As connection requests are received, the firewall evaluates each one. Only connection requests from authorized hosts are processed; the remaining connection requests are discarded.

Firewalls can also analyze incoming packets of various protocols. Based on that analysis, a firewall can undertake various actions. Firewalls are therefore capable of performing conditional evaluations ("If this type of packet is encountered, I will do this.") These conditional constructs are called *rules*. Generally, when you erect a firewall, you furnish it with rules that mirror access policies in your own organization.

201

For example, suppose you have both accounting and sales departments. Company policy demands that only the sales department can have access to your Web site. To enforce this policy, you provide your firewall with a rule; in this case, the rule is that connection requests from accounting are denied.

In this respect, firewalls are to networks what user-privilege schemes are to operating systems. For example, Windows NT enables you to specify which users can access a given file or directory. This is discretionary access control at the operating system level. Similarly, firewalls enable you to apply such access control to your networked workstations and your Web site.

However, that is only a part of what modern firewalls can do. For instance, most commercial firewalls enable you to screen content. You can exploit this capability to block Java, JavaScript, VBScript, ActiveX, and cookies at the firewall. In fact, you can even create rules to block particular attack signatures.

Techno Talk

Attack signatures are command patterns common to a particular attack. For example, when a user Telnets to port 80 and begins issuing command-line requests, this "looks" a particular way to your machine. By training your firewall to recognize that series of commands, you can teach it to block such an attack. This can also be done at a packet level. For example, some remote exploits generate specialized packets that are easily distinguished from other, non-malicious packets. These can be captured, recognized, and acted on.

Types of Firewalls

There are two types of firewalls:

➤ Network-level firewalls

➤ Application gateway firewalls

Network-Level Firewalls

Network-level firewalls are typically routers with powerful packet-filtering capabilities. Using a network-level firewall, you can grant or deny access to your site based on several variables, including

➤ Source address

➤ Protocol

➤ Port number

➤ Content

Router-based firewalls are popular because they're easily implemented. (You simply plug one in, provide some rules, and you're done.) Moreover, most new routers do a superb job of handling dual interfaces, where IP from the outside must be translated to some other protocol on the inside.

Additionally, a router-based firewall is a perimeter solution. That is, routers are external devices, so they obviate the need to disrupt normal network operation. If you use a router-based firewall, you don't have to configure a dozen machines (or a dozen services) to interface with it.

Application Gateway Firewalls

Another type of firewall is the *application-proxy firewall* (sometimes called an *application gateway*). When a remote user contacts a network running an application gateway, the gateway proxies the connection. In this instance, IP packets are not forwarded to the internal network. Instead, a type of translation occurs, with the gateway acting as the conduit and interpreter.

The advantage of application gateways is that they prevent IP packets from tunneling into your network. The disadvantage is that they demand high overhead and substantial involvement on your part. Here's why: A proxy application must be configured for each networked service including FTP, Telnet, HTTP, mail, news, and so forth. Additionally, inside users must use proxy-aware clients. (If they don't, they'll have to adopt new policies and procedures.)

Do You Really Need a Firewall?

Firewalls are expensive (typically costing $2,000 to $100,000). Before you consider buying a firewall, therefore, ascertain whether you really need one. In fact, there are many instances in which firewalls are impractical.

For example, if your network is an otherwise open environment that must accept connections from varied sources, a firewall is probably not the best solution. Universities and Internet service providers are good examples. Often, these networks house mail servers that perform relay services. This enables remote users to check their mail from anywhere in the world (an Internet café, another school, or a friend's home). Because these connections can come from virtually anywhere, there is no feasible way to establish an approved IP address list. Therefore, instituting firewall policies simply isn't possible.

Also, perhaps your company is using the Internet merely as a conduit, a sort of private leased line. In such an environment, you probably won't accept any traffic from the outside world. If so, you might not need all the functionality offered by a full-fledged firewall. Instead, you might choose a *virtual private network* (*VPN*) solution. VPNs are systems that allow encrypted traffic between two or more points (regional offices, for instance) and are typically less expensive than firewalls. The best VPN solution we're aware of is NetFortress. You can learn more about NetFortress at `http://www.fortresstech.com`.

Resources Roadmap

The security procedures you undertake depend on many factors, including your operating system, hardware, and application set. To provide you with a small roadmap of where to start, here is a list of resources, including

- ➤ Security checklists
- ➤ Security mailing lists
- ➤ Security newsgroups

These resources will get you pointed in the right direction. Furthermore, as you use the Internet more, you'll find a treasure chest of security information. In fact, the Internet houses most of the computer security information now available.

Security Checklists

Here you'll find a wide variety of security checklists:

- ➤ Microsoft MS-DOS Security Checklist by Bryan Thatcher, USAF
  `http://kumi.kelly.af.mil/doscheck.html`
- ➤ Microsoft Windows Security Checklist by Bryan Thatcher, USAF
  `http://kumi.kelly.af.mil/wincheck.html`
- ➤ UNIX Computer Security Checklist by AUCERT
  `http://www.bive.unit.liu.se/security/AUSCERT_checklist1.1.html`
- ➤ LAN Security Self-Assessment by Computer Security Administration—University of Toronto   `http://www.utoronto.ca/security/lansass.htm#lansass`
- ➤ Generic Password Security Checklist by Lindsay Winsor
  `http://delphi.colorado.edu/~security/users/access/goodprac.htm`
- ➤ CERT Coordination Center Generic Security Information Checklist by Computer Emergency Response Team   `http://ird.security.mci.net/check/cert-sec.html`
- ➤ TCP/IP Security Checklist by Dale Drew
  `http://ird.security.mci.net/check.html`
- ➤ Informix Security Checklist (author unknown)
  `http://spider.osfl.disa.mil/cm/security/check_list/appendf.pdf`

➤ Cisco IP Security Checklist by Cisco Systems, Inc.
  http://www.cisco.com/univercd/cc/td/doc/cisintwk/ics/cs003.htm

➤ Security Policy Checklist by Barbara
  Guttman and Robert Bagwill
  http://csrc.nist.gov/isptg/html/
  ISPTG-Contents.html

Security Mailing Lists

Table 13.3 identifies key security mailing lists.
The majority of these issue up-to-the-minute
advisories.

Check This Out

I recommend merging all lists that
apply to your network configuration.

Table 13.3   Mailing Lists for Holes and Vulnerabilities

List	List Name and Subjects Discussed
8lgm-list-request@8lgm.org	**The Eight Little Green Men Security List.** Detailed discussion of UNIX security holes, exploits, and fixes. To subscribe, send a message that has the command subscribe 8lgm-list in the body.
alert@iss.net	**The Alert List at Internet Security Systems.** Alerts, product announcements, and company information from Internet Security Systems. To subscribe to this and other ISS lists, go to http://iss.net/vd/ maillist.html#alert.
bugtraq@netspace.org	**The BUGTRAQ Mailing List.** Members here discuss vulnerabilities in the UNIX operating system. To subscribe, send a message with the command SUBSCRIBE BUGTRAQ in the body.
firewall-wizards@nfr.net	**The Firewall Wizards Mailing List.** Maintained by Marcus Ranum, this list is a moderated forum for advanced firewall administrators. To subscribe, go to http://www.nfr.net/ forum/firewall-wizards.html.

continues

Table 13.3   Continued

List	List Name and Subjects Discussed
`linux-alert-request@RedHat.com`	**The Linux Alert List.** This list carries announcements and warnings from Linux vendors and developers. To join, send a message with the command `subscribe` in the subject line.
`linux-security-request@redhat.com`	**The Linux Security List.** Now maintained by RedHat, this list focuses on Linux security issues. To subscribe, send a message with the command `subscribe` in the subject line.
`majordomo@lists.gnac.net`	**The Firewalls Mailing List.** This list focuses on firewall security. (This was previously `firewalls@ greatcircle.com`.) To subscribe, send an email message with the command `subscribe firewalls` in the body.
`majordomo@toad.com`	**The Cyberpunks Mailing List.** Members discuss issues of personal privacy and cryptography. (If a major cryptographic system is broken, you'll probably hear it here first.) To subscribe, send a message with the command `SUBSCRIBE` in the body.
`majordomo@uow.edu.au`	**The Intrusion Detection Systems List.** Members of this list discuss real-time intrusion-detection techniques. To subscribe, send a message with the command `subscribe ids` in the body.
`listserv@listserv.ntbugtraq.co`	**The NTBUGTRAQ List.** Maintained by Russ Cooper, the NTBUGTRAQ list tracks vulnerabilities in Microsoft Windows NT. To subscribe, send a message with the command `subscribe ntbugtraq` *firstname lastname* in the body.
`risks-request@csl.sri.com`	**The Risks Forum.** Members of this list discuss a wide variety of risks which are inherent to an information-based society. (Examples include invasion of personal privacy, credit-card theft, cracking attacks, and so on.) To subscribe, send a message with the command `SUBSCRIBE` in the body.

Security Newsgroups

You can also collect important security information from USENET security groups. Table 13.4 lists a few good haunts in that regard.

Table 13.4   USENET Newsgroups Related to Security

Newsgroup	Topics Discussed
alt.2600	Hacking and cracking
alt.computer.security	General computer security
alt.security	General security issues
alt.security.espionage	For the truly paranoid
comp.lang.java.security	Java programming language security
comp.os.netware.security	NetWare security
comp.security	General computer security
comp.security.firewalls	Firewall technology
comp.security.unix	UNIX security
microsoft.public.cryptoapi	Microsoft cryptography

Where To From Here

In this chapter, you learned about securing your network from outsiders. In the next chapter, "Troubleshooting Your Network," you'll learn what steps to take when your network acts hooey.

The Least You Need to Know

Securing a network is no easy task; as mentioned, much depends on your specific configuration. However, there are some basic steps you can take to improve your network security:

➤ Place your servers in a secure location.

➤ Educate users on good password practice.

➤ Regularly check the strength of user passwords.

➤ Secure your backups and installation media.

➤ Protect your wire and hardware.

➤ Run virus scans frequently.

➤ If you establish an Internet server, consider a firewall.

➤ If you use the Internet as a leased line, consider a VPN.

## Chapter 14

Troubleshooting Your Network

In This Chapter

➤ Common networking problems

➤ Approaches to troubleshooting

➤ Common troubleshooting tools

Well, I've got good news and bad news—I'll give you the bad news first. The bad news is that no matter how many networking books you buy, and no matter how careful you are, your network is never going to work perfectly the first time out. Furthermore, over time you're going to encounter dozens of network errors. The good news is that this chapter covers many of the common problems you'll encounter.

Approaches to Troubleshooting

When you're first confronted with a network error, the experience can be pretty daunting. After digesting various error messages, you look around the office and see a dozen machines wired up. In that instant, you suddenly realize the worst: The problem could be *anywhere*.

Well, you'll be happy to know that there's a rigid methodology for isolating and fixing errors. It rests on two rules:

➤ Problems can only arise in cabling, hardware, or software.

➤ Most problems are not inherently complex or widespread.

In other words, most problems arise for a single reason, at a single workstation. Therefore, when approaching a networking problem assume the simplest and most likely cause first. Only if your suspicions don't check out should you expand your probe to more complex systems.

The first thing you need to check is whether the problem affects only the current workstation or if others are also involved. After you've established that, perform the following steps on one or more workstations:

➤ Verify that the NIC is properly installed.

➤ Verify that the network cable is properly attached to the NIC.

➤ Verify that the workstation recognizes the NIC.

➤ Verify that the NIC's driver software is properly loaded.

➤ Verify that the software has been properly configured.

➤ Verify that the NIC can send and receive packets.

➤ Verify the route.

➤ Check hubs, routers, bridges, and switches along the route.

By taking this approach (working from the inside out), you not only increase your chances of success; you also guard against undertaking unnecessary procedures. Half the time, you'll find simple problems with even simpler solutions; for example: The network cable was accidentally knocked loose.

Because you might be using different network operating systems and disparate hardware, the solutions here are generic (there's a section at this chapter's end that deals with specific network errors). However, you'll find that you can diagnose most network problems with the tools and techniques discussed here.

Troubleshooting Your Cable Paths

Let's start with cabling. Network cable is susceptible to various hardships, including age, abuse, normal wear-and-tear, and so on. Over time, these can damage cable and reduce its capability to transmit a clear, robust signal. Therefore, whenever you perform system upgrades, always take stock of your existing cable—and that includes newer cables.

Believe it or not, even brand-spanking-new cables can sometimes be damaged or faulty. What looks like perfectly a healthy cable might in fact be harboring a short or break. To find out, you need a time domain reflector.

Time Domain Reflectors

Time domain reflectors (*TDRs*) are devices that diagnose various cable types (including power and network cables). TDRs rely on a technology called *pulse echo reflection* (*PER*). When you test a cable, your TDR sends an electronic pulse down the cable wire. This pulse is then measured and results are displayed graphically on a screen.

As you watch the screen, you can easily see the status of the electronic pulses, much like watching an EKG of a heart patient. When you see a dramatic change in the pulse strength—which means a change in the pulse's velocity—you know that a fault or defect exists in the wire. The TDR can pinpoint the defect's actual physical location within two feet or so. This distance is gauged by the time it takes for signals to echo back to the TDR.

You'll probably never need a TDR because they're employed chiefly in large networks. To learn more about these tools, though, contact a TDR vendor. I recommend Riser-Bond Instruments of Lincoln, Nebraska. You can contact Riser-Bond's staff at:

Riser-Bond Instruments, Inc.
5101 N. 57th Street
Lincoln, NE 68507 (USA)
(800) 688-8377
http://www.riserbond.com/

Beyond Cables: Diagnosing Hardware, Software, and Protocols

After determining that your cables are trouble-free, your next step is to isolate other possible causes, which might include faulty hardware, misconfigured software, user error, and so on. This section covers the tools and techniques used to diagnose network problems.

Ping: Checking for Signs of Life

Ping is a tool for testing whether a host is alive and well. Ping's name was derived from submarine lingo. During WWII, submarines found one another by sending sonar waves across the ocean. Whenever those waves struck a submarine, a sonar wave was echoed back to the sender (this noise was the *ping*). This notified the sender that another sub was nearby.

Similarly, Ping sends out a special packet to the specified address and waits for a response. Following is an example:

```
C:\WINDOWS>ping 207.171.0.111

Pinging 207.171.0.111 with 32 bytes of data:
Reply from 207.171.0.111: bytes=32 time=183ms TTL=247
Reply from 207.171.0.111: bytes=32 time=164ms TTL=247
Reply from 207.171.0.111: bytes=32 time=168ms TTL=247
Reply from 207.171.0.111: bytes=32 time=156ms TTL=247
```

In this case, you know that 207.171.0.111 is alive and well. It took 156 milliseconds to respond with 32 bytes of data. But what happens if you ping a downed, disabled, or non-existent host? Take a look:

```
C:\WINDOWS>ping 172.16.0.1

Pinging 172.16.0.1 with 32 bytes of data:
Reply from 144.228.79.49: Destination host unreachable.
Reply from 144.228.79.49: Destination host unreachable.
Reply from 144.228.79.49: Destination host unreachable.
Reply from 144.228.79.49: Destination host unreachable.
```

From this, you know that something is wrong. 144.228.79.49 is not responding and, therefore, either the route is bad or the host is down. If you ping one of your hosts and get a negative response, check the host's physical connections. Perhaps a wire came loose or the NIC was inserted incorrectly. If these investigations turn up nothing, check to see whether all requisite protocols have been loaded and bound to the NIC. If everything seems fine at the workstation, there might be a problem with the network route. For this, try using Traceroute.

Ping

To use Ping, you must issue the ping command plus your desired address at a command prompt. This is true of both UNIX and Windows.

Traceroute: Checking for Trouble on the Line

Traceroute is a tool for checking the route between two machines. It is used to locate where the problem is. Traceroute performs this task by dropping special packets at each stop that echo back to the sender. In this way, Traceroute builds a network map of the precise route taken between two machines. Following is an example:

```
C:\WINDOWS>traceroute 207.171.0.1

Tracing route to cisco-t3.pacificnet.net [207.171.0.1]
➥over a maximum of 30 hops:
1 149 ms   137 ms   137 ms   tnt1.isdn.jetlink.net [206.72.64.13]
2 141 ms   136 ms   125 ms   jl-bb1-ven-fe0.jetlink.net [206.72.64.1]
3 147 ms   143 ms   139 ms   166.48.176.17
4 138 ms   135 ms   137 ms   core1.Bloomington.cw.net [204.70.4.161]
5 141 ms   139 ms   145 ms   lang1sr2-4-0.ca.us.ibm.net [165.87.156.174]
6 140 ms   138 ms   137 ms   165.87.157.129
7 149 ms   143 ms   135 ms   ded1-fe0-0-0.lsan03.pbi.net [206.13.29.196]
8 161 ms   157 ms   152 ms   cisco-t3.pacificnet.net [207.171.0.1]

Trace complete.
```

Pretty interesting stuff. In the preceding trace, the two machines (206.72.64.13 and 207.171.0.1) are only several miles apart—but it still took eight hops to complete the trace. But even that's considered a healthy trace. What about a trace where problems are revealed? Let's try it. I'll trace the route between the Central Intelligence Agency and me. Here's the output:

```
C:\WINDOWS>traceroute www.cia.gov

Tracing route to www.odci.gov [198.81.129.99]
➥over a maximum of 30 hops:1 140 ms 124 ms 127 ms
➥tnt1.isdn.jetlink.net [206.72.64.13]
2 214 ms 239 ms 169 ms jl-bb1-ven-fe0.jetlink.net [206.72.64.1]
3 145 ms 134 ms 134 ms ana-3-0-2xT1.sprintlink.net [144.228.79.9]
4 136 ms 141 ms 154 ms 144.232.1.37
5 138 ms 135 ms 136 ms  sl-bb4-ana-4-0-0.sprintlink.net
➥[144.232.1.30]
6 151 ms 140 ms 39 ms t16-0.Los-Angeles.t3.ans.net [207.25.133.1]
7 199 ms 211 ms 205 ms f2-1.t60-81.Reston.t3.ans.net [140.223.60.142]
8 213 ms 207 ms 205 ms  f0-0.c60-13.Reston.t3.ans.net
➥ [140.223.60.215]
9 222 ms 215 ms 205 ms  enss3624.t3.ans.net [207.25.139.38]
10 225 ms 219 ms 220 ms  207.27.2.46
11 *          *          *       Request timed out.
12 *          *          *       Request timed out.
13     *      *          *       Request timed out.
14     *      *          *       Request timed out.
15     *      *          *       Request timed out.
16     *      *          *       Request timed out.
17     *      *          *       Request timed out.
18     *      *          *       Request timed out.
19     *      *          *       Request timed out.
20     *      *          *       Request timed out.
21     *      *          *       Request timed out.
22     *      *          *       Request timed out.
23     *      *          *       Request timed out.
24     *      *          *       Request timed out.
25     *      *          *       Request timed out.
26     *      *          *       Request timed out.
27     *      *          *       Request timed out.
28     *      *          *       Request timed out.
29     *      *          *       Request timed out.
30     *      *          *       Request timed out.
```

Hmmm...Something's amiss. I wonder what it could be. To find out, you'd have to begin with the last viable address; in this case, that is 207.27.2.46:

```
1 140 ms 124 ms 127 ms tnt1.isdn.jetlink.net [206.72.64.13]
2 214 ms 239 ms 169 ms jl-bb1-ven-fe0.jetlink.net [206.72.64.1]
3 145 ms 134 ms 134 ms ana-3-0-2xT1.sprintlink.net [144.228.79.9]
4 136 ms 141 ms 154 ms 144.232.1.37
5 138 ms 135 ms 136 ms  sl-bb4-ana-4-0-0.sprintlink.net
➥[144.232.1.30]
6 151 ms 140 ms 39 ms t16-0.Los-Angeles.t3.ans.net [207.25.133.1]
```

213

```
7 199 ms 211 ms 205 ms f2-1.t60-81.Reston.t3.ans.net [140.223.60.142]
8 213 ms 207 ms 205 ms  f0-0.c60-13.Reston.t3.ans.net
➥[140.223.60.215]
9 222 ms 215 ms 205 ms  enss3624.t3.ans.net [207.25.139.38]
10 225 ms 219 ms 220 ms  207.27.2.46
```

Similarly, on your network, if you run a `traceroute` query and receive timeouts, start with the last viable address. Somehow, between that host and your intended target, there's a problem. Trace the physical and logical connections for a possible breach. (For example, a wire might have come undone.) If you can't find any immediate cause, you might need to search even deeper, to the packet level. If so, you'll need a protocol analyzer. (Please see the section in this chapter titled "Protocol Analyzers: Getting Down to the Nitty-Gritty.")

In particular, Traceroute is useful for diagnosing network bottlenecks and gateway errors in just a few seconds. For example, take a look at these four lines:

```
1 40 ms 44 ms 47 ms tnt1.isdn.jetlink.net [206.72.64.13]
2 34 ms 64 ms 69 ms jl-bb1-ven-fe0.jetlink.net [206.72.64.1]
3 45 ms 89 ms 77 ms ana-3-0-2xT1.sprintlink.net [144.228.79.9]
4 36 ms 41 ms 54 ms 144.232.1.37
```

Notice that the turn-around times are pretty short. The packets went smoothly through the entire route—the longest response time was 89 milliseconds. But what if the Traceroute table looked like this:

```
1 40 ms 44 ms 47 ms tnt1.isdn.jetlink.net [206.72.64.13]
2 34 ms 64 ms 69 ms jl-bb1-ven-fe0.jetlink.net [206.72.64.1]
3 245 ms 289 ms 277 ms ana-3-0-2xT1.sprintlink.net [144.228.79.9]
4 236 ms 241 ms 254 ms 144.232.1.37
```

Notice that the turn-around times increase dramatically after the packets reach `144.228.79.9`. That is precisely where the problem starts: `144.228.79.9`. So, by examining response times, you can often identify where to begin your serious investigation.

Traceroute

Traceroute is a command native to UNIX. To use it, you can simply issue the `traceroute` command followed by the desired address, like this: `traceroute 207.171.0.111`. On Windows, however, the command is `tracert` instead (therefore, the command would be `tracert 207.171.0.111`). Finally, note that to use `tracert` on Windows, you need to run it through a DOS or Command Prompt window.

If You Don't Have Traceroute or Ping

If you're not using UNIX or a Windows variant, you might not have Traceroute or Ping. Table 14.1 provides locations of these tools for other operating systems.

Table 14.1   Traceroute and Ping tools for Other Operating Systems

Application	Description/Location
AtcpTraceroute (Amiga)	Traceroute tool for Amiga enthusiasts, located at `ftp://wuarchive.wustl.edu/pub/aminet/comm/tcp/AtcpTraceroute.lha`.
MacTCPWatcher (Macintosh)	Ping/Traceroute utility (with extended TCP/IP debugging) located at `ftp://ftp.tidbits.com/pub/tidbits/tisk/_MacTCP/mactcp-watcher-20.hqx`.
Trumpet TCP (DOS)	A Traceroute tool for DOS, located at `ftp://ftp.trumpet.com.au/tcp-abi/tcp201.zip`.
WhatRoute (Macintosh)	TCP/IP utility that provides Traceroute, available at `http://homepages.ihug.co.nz/~bryanc/beta/whatroute-150b15-fat.hqx`.

The `netstat` Command: Checking the Routing Table and Connections

The `netstat` command is useful for troubleshooting protocol problems. For example, `netstat` allows you to examine protocol statistics. Following is a sample report:

```
C:\WINDOWS>netstat -s

IP Statistics
  Packets Received            = 55
  Received Header Errors      = 0
  Received Address Errors     = 0
  Datagrams Forwarded         = 0
  Unknown Protocols Received  = 0
  Received Packets Discarded  = 0
  Received Packets Delivered  = 55
  Output Requests             = 58
  Routing Discards            = 0
  Discarded Output Packets    = 0
  Output Packet No Route      = 0
  Reassembly Required         = 0
```

```
Reassembly Successful              = 0
Reassembly Failures                = 0
Datagrams Successfully Fragmented  = 0
Datagrams Failing Fragmentation    = 0
Fragments Created                  = 0

ICMP Statistics
Received     Sent
Messages                     0            0
Errors                       0            0
Destination Unreachable      0            0
Time Exceeded                0            0
Parameter Problems           0            0
Source Quenchs               0            0
Redirects                    0            0
Echos                        0            0
Echo Replies                 0            0
Timestamps                   0            0
Timestamp Replies            0            0
Address Masks                0            0
Address Mask Replies         0            0


TCP Statistics
   Active Opens                    = 5
   Passive Opens                   = 0
   Failed Connection Attempts      = 0
   Reset Connections               = 0
   Current Connections             = 0
   Segments Received               = 51
   Segments Sent                   = 54
   Segments Retransmitted          = 0

UDP Statistics
   Datagrams Received    = 4
   No Ports              = 0
   Receive Errors        = 0
   Datagrams Sent        = 4
```

If you pull such a report and find many receive or transmit errors, the local workstation's NIC might be malfunctioning. Another possibility is a faulty network driver.

netstat also allows you to view the routing table. To do so, issue the netstat command plus the -r (route) switch, like this:

```
netstat -r
```

Here's some sample output:

```
Route Table

Active Routes:

Network Address  Netmask          Gateway Address
➥Interface       Metric
0.0.0.0          0.0.0.0          208.19.49.121    208.19.49.121   1
127.0.0.0        255.0.0.0        127.0.0.1        127.0.0.1       1
208.19.49.0      255.255.255.0    208.19.49.121    208.19.49.121   1
208.19.49.121    255.255.255.255  127.0.0.1        127.0.0.1       1
208.19.49.255    255.255.255.255  208.19.49.121    208.19.49.121   1
224.0.0.0        224.0.0.0        208.19.49.121    208.19.49.121   1
```

If the reported gateway address is incorrect—different from your gateway's actual address—you'll need to change it.

Protocol Analyzers: Getting Down to the Nitty-Gritty

Protocol analyzers are devices that capture network packets. Their legitimate purpose is to analyze network traffic and identify potential areas of concern. For example, suppose that one segment of your network is performing poorly—packet transport seems incredibly slow or machines inexplicably lock up on a network boot. To determine the precise cause, use a protocol analyzer.

Protocol analyzers vary in functionality and design. Some analyze only one protocol, whereas others can analyze hundreds. As a general rule, though, most modern protocol analyzers can analyze at least the following protocols:

➤ Standard Ethernet

➤ TCP/IP

➤ IPX

➤ DECNet

Protocol analyzers are always a combination of hardware and software. Proprietary protocol analyzers are typically expensive but offer superb technical support. Freeware protocol analyzers, in contrast, are cheap but offer little or no support.

How Do Protocol Analyzers Work?

Protocol analyzers work by capturing the date, time, request, and result of each packet sent across the network. More importantly, however, protocol analyzers actually debug the protocol exchanges between machines. For example, let's look at a Telnet session from my machine to a host named `traderights.pacificnet.net`. Following is a capture from the first two seconds of that session:

```
00:53:01:038 gethostbyname ("traderights.pacificnet.net")
➡returns (NO ERROR)
hostent.h_name = "traderights.pacificnet.net"
        .h_aliases = NULL
        .h_addrtype = AF_INET
        .h_length = 4
        .addr[0]= 207.171.0.111 returns (NO ERROR)
00:53:01:038 WSALookupSeviceBegin(... )
00:53:01:045 WSALookupServiceNext(... )
00:53:01:045 WSALookupServiceEnd(... )
00:53:01:045 getservbyname ("telnet", "tcp") returns (NO ERROR)
servent.s_name = "telnet"
        .s_aliases = NULL
        .s_port = 5888
        .s_proto = "tcp" returns (NO ERROR)
00:53:01:045 socket (af=PF_INET, type=SOCK_STREAM,
➡protocol=0) returns (SOCKET=118)
00:53:01:045 bind (SOCKET=118, SOCKADDR.length=16,
                            .family=AF_INET
                            .port=0
                            .address=0.0.0.0)
➡returns (NO ERROR)
00:53:01:045 ntohs (0x1700) returns (0x0017)
00:53:01:045 getsockopt (SOCKET=118, SOL_SOCKET, SO_TYPE=1)
➡returns (NO ERROR)
00:53:01:045 inet_ntoa (0x6F00ABCF) returns (207.171.0.111)
00:53:01:201 connect (SOCKET=118, SOCKADDR.length=16,
                            .family=AF_INET
                            .port=23
                            .address=207.171.0.111)
➡returns(NO ERROR)
00:53:01:297 WSAAsyncSelect (SOCKET=118, hWnd=0x00000B08,
➡wMsg=0x05F4, lEvent=0x00000027) returns (NO ERROR)
00:53:01:310 notification AsyncSelect (hWnd=0x00000B08,
➡wMsg=0x05F4, SOCKET=118,FD_WRITE)
00:53:01:457 notification AsyncSelect (hWnd=0x00000B08,
➡wMsg=0x05F4, SOCKET=118,FD_READ)
00:53:01:458 recv (SOCKET=118, buf=0x00407D4C,
➡len=4096, flags=0x0000) returns (15 bytes)
```

```
0000:    FF FD 18 FF FD 1F FF FD    23 FF FD 27 FF FD 24
➥          ........#..'..$
00:53:01:458 send (SOCKET=118, buf=0x0062FAB4, len=3, flags=0x0000)
➥returns (3 bytes)
0000:    FF FB 18       ...
00:53:01:458 send (SOCKET=118, buf=0x0062FAB4, len=3,
➥flags=0x0000) returns(3 bytes)
0000:    FF FC 1F       ...
00:53:01:458 send (SOCKET=118, buf=0x0062FAB4, len=3,
➥flags=0x0000) returns(3 bytes)
0000:    FF FC 23       ..#
00:53:01:458 send (SOCKET=118, buf=0x0062FAB4, len=3,
➥flags=0x0000) returns(3 bytes)
0000:    FF FC 27       ..'
00:53:02:061 recv (SOCKET=118, buf=0x00407D4C, len=4096,
➥flags=0x0000) returns(54 bytes)
0000:    0D 0A 0D 0A 55 4E 49 58    28 72 29 20 53 79 73 74
➥          ....UNIX(r).Syst
0010:    65 6D 20 56       em.V
00:53:02:339 notification AsyncSelect (hWnd=0x00000B08,
➥wMsg=0x05F4, SOCKET=118,FD_READ)
00:53:02:340 recv (SOCKET=118, buf=0x00407D4C, len=4096,
➥flags=0x0000) returns(16 bytes)
0000:    FF FB 01 FF FB 03 FF FD    01 6C 6F 67 69 6E 3A 20
.........login:.
```

At first glance, the output looks like simple gibberish. However, if you break it into smaller parts it's more digestible. For example, you know that during the logged session, the local machine was trying to reach `traderights.pacificnet.net`. Take a look:

```
00:53:01:038 gethostbyname ("traderights.pacificnet.net") returns
➥(NO ERROR)
hostent.h_name = "traderights.pacificnet.net"
```

Before actually contacting `traderights.pacificnet.net`, the machine first performs a reverse IP lookup to obtain the numeric IP address:

```
.h_aliases = NULL
      .h_addrtype = AF_INET
      .h_length = 4
      .addr[0]= 207.171.0.111 returns (NO ERROR)
00:53:01:038 WSALookupSeviceBegin(... )
00:53:01:045 WSALookupServiceNext(... )
00:53:01:045 WSALookupServiceEnd(... )
```

219

Having obtained a valid IP address, the system next tries to connect using telnet:

```
00:53:01:045 getservbyname ("telnet", "tcp") returns (NO ERROR)
servent.s_name = "telnet"
        .s_aliases = NULL
        .s_port = 5888
        .s_proto = "tcp" returns (NO ERROR)
00:53:01:045 socket (af=PF_INET, type=SOCK_STREAM,
➥protocol=0) returns(SOCKET=118)
00:53:01:045 bind (SOCKET=118, SOCKADDR.length=16,
                                .family=AF_INET
                                .port=0
                                .address=0.0.0.0) returns
➥(NO ERROR)
00:53:01:045 ntohs (0x1700) returns (0x0017)
00:53:01:045 getsockopt (SOCKET=118, SOL_SOCKET, SO_TYPE=1) returns
➥(NO ERROR)
00:53:01:045 inet_ntoa (0x6F00ABCF) returns (207.171.0.111)
00:53:01:201 connect (SOCKET=118, SOCKADDR.length=16,
                                .family=AF_INET
                        .port=23
                        .address=207.171.0.111) returns
➥(NO ERROR)
```

Finally, `traderights.pacificnet.net` responds by issuing an operating system flag and a login prompt:

```
0000:   0D 0A 0D 0A 55 4E 49 58   28 72 29 20 53 79 73 74
➥        ....UNIX(r).Syst
0010:   65 6D 20 56         em.V
00:53:02:339 notification AsyncSelect (hWnd=0x00000B08,
➥wMsg=0x05F4, SOCKET=118,FD_READ)
00:53:02:340 recv (SOCKET=118, buf=0x00407D4C, len=4096,
➥flags=0x0000) returns(16 bytes)
0000:   FF FB 01 FF FB 03 FF FD   01 6C 6F 67 69 6E 3A 20
.........login:.
```

This is what the user actually sees in his or her Telnet session:

```
UNIX(r) System V
login:
```

As you can see, even minor traces of TCP calls can produce volumes of information. But that's not all; good commercial protocol analyzers capture and report on every byte passed across the network—even passwords.

220

Protocol analyzers are most useful in diagnosing large networks at the hardware or network level. (For example, they can be used to analyze whether NICs, routers, switches, hubs, and gateways are working correctly.) It's unlikely that you'll need a protocol analyzer for a small network. However, I've assembled a small list of commercial and non-commercial protocol analyzers just in case that need arises.

Warning!

Protocol analyzers capture passwords in plain text. For this reason, you should never share your trace logs with outsiders.

Commercial Protocol Analyzers

The following protocol analyzers are commercial, but many companies offer demo versions. Prices range from $200 to $3,000.

ATM Network Analyzer from Network Associates

Internetwork Analyzer decodes more than 250 LAN/WAN protocols, including but not limited to AppleTalk, Banyan VINES, DECnet, IBM LAN Server, IBM SNA, NetBIOS, Novell NetWare, OSI, Sun NFS, TCP/IP, 3Com 3+Open, X Window, and XNS/MS-net. Network Associates can be reached at

> Network Associates, Inc.
> 3965 Freedom Circle
> Santa Clara, CA 95054
> Phone: (408) 988-3832
> URL: http://www.networkassociates.com/

PacketView by Klos Technologies

PacketView is a DOS-based protocol analyzer that is ideal for Ethernet, Token Ring, ARCNET and FDDI environments. The demo version is located at
ftp://ftp.klos.com/demo/pvdemo.zip.

> Klos Technologies, Inc.
> 604 Daniel Webster Highway
> Merrimack, New Hampshire 03054
> Phone: (603) 424-8300
> Fax: (603) 424-9300
> Email: sales@klos.com
> URL: http://www.klos.com/

EtherPeek

EtherPeek is widely recognized as the premier Macintosh protocol analyzer (although a Windows version is also available).

The AG Group, Inc.
2540 Camino Diablo, Suite 200
Walnut Creek, CA 94596
Phone: (510) 937-7900
Email: ricki@aggroup.com
URL: http://www.aggroup.com/

NetMinder Ethernet

NetMinder Ethernet is a Macintosh-based protocol analyzer that offers automated, real-time HTML output reports. A demo version is available at
http://www.neon.com/demos_goodies.html.

Neon Software
3685 Mt. Diablo Blvd. Suite 253
Lafayette, CA 94549
Phone: (800) 334-NEON
Email: info@neon.com
URL: http://www.neon.com

NetXRay Analyzer

NetXRay Analyzer is one of the most comprehensive protocol analyzers and network monitoring tools available for Windows NT.

Cinco Networks Inc.
6601 Koll Center Parkway Suite 140
Pleasanton CA 94566 USA
Phone: (510) 426-1770
Email: marketing@ngc.com
URL: http://www.cinco.com/

NetAnt Protocol Analyzer

NetAnt Protocol Analyzer decodes all popular protocols including TCP/IP, IPX/SPX, NetBIOS, AppleTalk, SNMP, SNA, ISO, BPDU, XNS, IBMNM, RPL, HTTP, FTP, TELNET, DEC, SunRPC, and Vines IP. NetAnt Protocol Analyzer also runs on Windows 95 and exports to popular spreadsheet formats, making human analysis very convenient.

People Network, Inc.
1534 Carob Lane, Suite 1000
Los Altos, CA 94024
Email: sweston@people-network.com
URL: http://www.people-network.com/

Freely Available Protocol Analyzers

There are also many freeware/shareware protocol analyzers available. These are perfect if you want to learn about network traffic without spending any money.

Gobbler

Gobbler runs on MS-DOS and Windows 95 (through a shell window). You can run Gobbler on a single workstation, analyzing only local packets, or you can use it to monitor an entire network. The program offers complex packet filtering functions, and you can specify alerts based on the type of packet encountered. You can even start and stop Gobbler by configuring it to wait for a specified packet type before it begins logging.

Gobbler provides real-time monitoring of network traffic and is an excellent tool for diagnosing network traffic jams. Altogether, Gobbler is a great tool to learn about protocol analysis; you can get Gobbler at `http://www.computercraft.com/noprogs/gobbler.zip`.

Esniff

Esniff is a standard, generic UNIX-based protocol analyzer that can be obtained at `http://www.asmodeus.com/archive/IP_toolz/ESNIFF.C`.

Using Esniff

To use Esniff you need a C language compiler and IP header files. These tools come standard with most UNIX distributions. However, unless you specify these items to be installed, they generally aren't. If you have doubts, check your documentation.

Also, on UNIX you can check whether you have C by issuing the command cc. If you receive a `File not found` error message, you probably don't have C installed. To be absolutely certain, go to your root directory [/] and issue the following command: `find . -name "cc"`. This searches your entire drive for C. If you still discover that C hasn't been installed, install it.

ETHLOAD

ETHLOAD is a freeware packet sniffer written in C for Ethernet and Token Ring networks. It runs well with any of the following interfaces:

➤ Novell ODI

➤ 3Com/Microsoft Protocol Manager

➤ PC/TCP/Clarkson/Crynwr

Furthermore, it analyzes the following protocols:

➤ TCP/IP

➤ DECnet

➤ OSI

➤ XNS

➤ NetWare

➤ NetBEUI

ETHLOAD is an excellent protocol analyzer for DOS and Novell platforms. Get it at `http://www.computercraft.com/noprogs/ethld104.zip`.

Troubleshooting in the Trenches: Some Extra Tips

When maintaining your network, you might encounter any of a thousand network problems and errors. Unfortunately, there isn't room to address them all here; however, Table 14.2 lists some common network problems and errors and possible solutions. (Network error messages are italicized).

Table 14.2 Common Network Problems and Possible Causes

Problem	Likely Cause and Possible Solution
An intranet host is unreachable	Check to see that you properly assigned both IP addresses and subnet masks. For quick and easy intranet setups, assign your root server an address of 172.16.0.1. All subsequent workstations can be 172.16.0.2, 172.16.0.3 and so on. For a subnet mask, try 224.0.0.0. If this does not immediately remedy the problem, verify that your gateway address (for your subnet) is correct.
Cannot Find Specified Name	You misspelled the server name. Try again.
Connection reset by peer	This could be several things. If this occurs while you're connected to the Internet via Dial-Up Networking, it might be your

Problem	Likely Cause and Possible Solution
	modem. To cure this, try a different initialization string. For AT&T modems, try `AT&F/Q3/N3`. For Hayes compatibles, try `AT&F&C1&D2&Q5&K3S46=136`. If that doesn't work, it might be a problem on the server side. (Sometimes, servers that set cookies have this problem if the cookie data comes back corrupted.) In this case, simply reload the Web page and continue surfing.
Cross-device link	This indicates that you're trying to access or create a link across two hosts, one of which either doesn't support linking or doesn't have the specified file or directory. If you've previously accessed linked files or directories on the remote host, check your spelling and try again. Otherwise, contact the remote host's administrator. Perhaps they disabled shared links, or maybe the directory or file has been moved.
Dialup host keeps dropping you	This happens when you attempt to connect using Dial-Up Networking in Windows. The actual error message is `You have been disconnected from the computer you dialed. Double-click the connection to try again.` This invariably means that you failed to install TCP/IP. Solution: Choose My Computer | Control Panel | Network | Add | Protocol | Microsoft | TCP/IP. This installs Microsoft TCP/IP. Next, reboot and try again. Everything should work beautifully. (If not, it's possible that the remote host is expecting an encrypted login. Check with the system administrator at the remote host.)
Excessive packet collisions	If you run a protocol analyzer and discover an inordinate number of packet collisions, your cable might be damaged, or one or more segments might be incorrectly terminated (using bus topology somewhere, perhaps). Check your cable and your terminators. If neither of these pan out, check for duplicate hardware addresses. Some Ethernet cards/software allow the user to manipulate MAC addresses. Although it is unlikely, two NICs could have the same hardware address. This can cause serious trouble, collisions, and packet delivery failure. Solution: Replace the current MAC address with one that is unique.

Table 14.2 CONTINUED

Problem	Likely Cause and Possible Solution
File Creation Error	This is a security violation message; it means that you attempted to create a file on a network drive to which you had no privileges. Solution: Get higher privileges.
FTP Error 57	This indicates that the FTP server is currently overloaded. Try again later.
Host name lookup failure	This error indicates that you're either not connected to the network (or Internet) or that you failed to specify a domain name server. (Without a name server, your system cannot resolve hostnames.) Solution: Verify that you're connected. If so, check your DNS setup or, if you use UNIX, check /etc/resolv.conf for a valid name server address. (In Windows, you might check your lmhosts or hosts files. It's possible that one or more hostnames or addresses are misspelled. Therefore, when your system tries to reach those hosts, it fails.)
Host or Gateway not Responding	Check your spelling of the hostname. Otherwise, check your assigned gateway's address. It might be incomplete or incorrect.
Illegal buffer length	This is a NetBIOS error. It means that the system tried to send a unit larger than 512 bytes. This rarely happens, and is usually a benign error (you simply resend). However, if you continue to get this error from a particular application, it could be the programmer's fault. If so, discontinue use of the product and notify the vendor.
IPX not installed	This is a NetWare (or NetWare client) error. As it suggests, IPX is not installed. Choose My Computer I Control Panel I Network I Add I Protocol and install either Novell's or Microsoft's IPX.
Memory Errors	Memory errors are rare and usually occur only in DOS or DOS/Windows 3.11 environments. Try commenting out EMM386.
Network unreachable	This TCP/IP error typically signifies that your gateway is down, or that there's a routing problem. Check to see that the route to the gateway is correctly assigned. To do so (on both UNIX and Windows), issue the command netstat -r, which displays the routing table. Check the real gateway

Problem	Likely Cause and Possible Solution
	address against the one in your `netstat` query. If they differ, change the Gateway settings. (In Windows, this is done by choosing Control Panel | Network | TCP/IP | Properties | Gateway.)
No route to host	This TCP/IP error indicates that your network connection is down. Check your network connection and whether your interface (Ethernet, PPP, and so on) is working correctly. On UNIX, you can do this with the `ifconfig` command. In Windows, issue the command `winipcfg` and check that your interface is up. (If you discover your interface is down, activate it or investigate further.)
Session terminated	This indicates that the remote host died, reset, or killed the connection. Check the remote host. (There's nothing wrong at your end.)
Transmission of garbage	If a single workstation starts spontaneously transmitting high volumes of garbage or malformed packets, the workstation's cable or NIC has most likely malfunctioned. Solution: Troubleshoot both and replace the offending hardware.
Unable to create directory	This is a security violation message; it means that you attempted to create a directory on a network drive to which you had no privileges. Solution: Get higher privileges.
Workstation(s) often freeze up	First, determine whether the problem is isolated, local, or global. If the problem is isolated, it's almost certainly due to a faulty cable, connection, NIC, or driver on the troubled workstation. Check these first. If the problem is local or global, however, check your hubs, switches, routers, or other networking hardware.
You can't access a network drive	The network drive might not be shared out. See Chapter 10, "Case Study: Building a Windows SOHO System," for the section "Setting up Your Shared Resources" and double-check that all shares are properly assigned. If this doesn't work, verify that the target workstation is currently connected and accessible.

HTTP and Web Errors

While building an intranet, you might encounter many strange HTTP errors. Unfortunately, default HTTP client and server installations seldom have extensive error explanations. Table 14.3 lists a few common errors and the reasons for them.

Table 14.3 Common HTTP and Web Errors and What They Mean

HTTP Error	Reason
Connection Refused by Host	See 403 Forbidden.
Failed DNS Lookup	Either the nameserver couldn't be reached (unlikely) or the site no longer exists.
File Contains no Data	The URL probably calls a script that doesn't currently generate output. Therefore, the server cannot return anything. You'll get these errors in the wee hours when folks are fine-tuning their scripts. Try again later.
Invalid Host or Unable to Resolve	The FTP site is down or no longer exists.
NTTP Server Error	The news server is probably down. Try again later.
TCP Error Encountered	Your hardware is malfunctioning. Check your connections. (This can sometimes happen when your connection has been dropped.)
400 Bad Request (Client error)	The server couldn't understand the specified request. This usually arises from a malformed directive (as opposed to a bad URL).
401 Unauthorized (Client error)	This error indicates that you failed to authenticate yourself. This is commonly seen on password-protected Web sites that rely on challenge-response authentication. Solution: Reconnect and enter the proper username/password pair.
403 Forbidden (Client error)	This error indicates that your request is forbidden and there's no further information. You'll get this error if you try to access an off-limits directory. There is no solution.

HTTP Error	Reason
404 Not Found (Client error)	The document no longer exists. There is no solution. However, if the document was a presentation of some kind, and its name was unique, you might try searching for it elsewhere on the Internet.
500 Internal Server Error	This indicates an unspecified server error. Many times, this is the result of a malformed server-side script. If you're responsible for debugging the script, check your syntax and ensure that all statements have been closed. Otherwise, notify the party maintaining the site.
501 Not Implemented	This indicates that the request method is faulty. If you receive this error while testing your own Web pages, check your `method` property in your `form` tag. Following is an example of a fudged request: `<form action="myscript.cgi" method="poist">`. In this case, `poist` should be `post`. If the site isn't yours, notify the maintainer.
502 Bad Gateway	This is generally a proxy error. Notify the site administrator.
503 Service Unavailable	The server is either busy or down. Try again later.

Where To From Here

In this chapter, you've learned that network troubleshooting is all about the process of elimination. Often the problem is exactly what you expect it to be: simple and easily fixed. In the next chapter, "Upgrading and Expanding the Network," you'll learn how to upgrade and expand your network, as well as glean some tips on saving money and time.

The Least You Need to Know

Right now, the least you need to know about troubleshooting your network is

➤ First, strive to isolate the affected machines. Often, this will lead you directly to the problem.

➤ Confine your investigation to the affected machines until you find some evidence to expand your inquiry.

➤ Subject each affected machine to identical diagnostic and repair procedures, and always exhaust testing of each machine before moving on to the next.

➤ If many machines become suddenly affected, check your hardware first. A hub, switch, bridge, or router might have failed.

## Chapter 15

Upgrading and Expanding the Network

In This Chapter

➤ Assessing your network

➤ Tips and tricks on saving money and time

➤ Expanding and upgrading your system

The French have a saying: "Plus ca change, plus c'est la meme chose." It means, "The more things change, the more they stay the same." Is it true? You be the judge.

When I was a teenager, cars were the rage. My friends and I sat around gawking at hot rod magazines. "Man, when I get some more money, it's all about twin overhead cams and mag wheels!" It didn't even matter if you knew what mag wheels were. You knew they were cool, and that's what counted. I'm happy to report that we've since grown up...Or have we? Today, we sit around looking at computer magazines. "Man, when we decide to upgrade, it's all about twin Pentiums and SCSI-III hard drives!" Yes, indeed. Plus ca change, plus c'est la meme chose.

In the computing world, things move fast—so fast that by the time you get your new computer home, it's obsolete. This—coupled with an endless barrage of advertising—probably has you wondering: Do you need to upgrade? That's what this chapter is all about.

Taming the Upgrade Monster: Do You Really Need to Upgrade or Expand?

Your local hardware dealer has probably told you a dozen times that what you need to increase work production is an upgrade. At first blush, that sounds reasonable; after all, bigger disks, faster processors, and more RAM are bound to improve computing performance.

Before you spend a lot of money, though, there are some things you ought to know. First, unless your existing hardware is hopelessly outdated, it's probably more than sufficient. You can't word process much faster with a 333MHz processor than you can with a 266MHz processor. In fact, unless you're doing high-performance computing— such as compiling, extensive number crunching, or high-end graphics—the difference is negligible.

Moreover, there are many hidden costs to upgrades. For example, upgrades can often be time consuming. When performed during business hours, a full network upgrade can bring production to a complete halt. That's not all: If compatibility or reliability issues surface later, a bad upgrade can set you back big time.

I favor upgrading in a gradual fashion, concentrating most of my efforts on servers. This is a particularly efficient and economical approach when outfitting client/server networks where servers shoulder the greater workload.

With respect to individual workstations, focus on efficiency and maximizing processor power. For example, stations used for word processing need far fewer resources than those used for computer-aided design. By wisely and judiciously distributing your processor and memory power where they're most needed, you can save thousands of dollars.

Nonetheless, you'll still inevitably need to upgrade one or more of the following devices or tools:

➤ Hard disk drives

➤ Motherboards and processors

➤ Communication devices

➤ System software

Upgrading to New and Bigger Hard Disks

When upgrading to a new hard disk, you have two choices:

➤ Install the new hard disk as a secondary drive

➤ Install the new hard disk as your primary drive

Most folks decide to upgrade only after their existing hard drive is hopelessly jam-packed with software. Therefore, they usually take the first approach—mainly because it's convenient. They designate their new disk as a secondary drive and, in doing so, they quickly and painlessly obtain greater storage capacity. This, of course, leaves their primary disk unchanged. More adventurous users, however, take the high road and designate the new drive as their *primary* disk. This frees up the old drive, which can be used elsewhere. However, this approach demands that you reinstall critical software.

Which approach will you take? That depends on what you're trying to accomplish. If you simply need more storage space, then designate the new drive as a secondary storage device and leave it at that. On the other hand, if you're aiming for high performance (or want to retire or reuse your smaller hard drives) you'll need to undertake the more complicated approach. The next sections cover both techniques.

Adding an IDE Secondary Hard Disk Drive

To add a secondary internal IDE drive, you must perform four steps:

1. Alter the jumper settings to designate the drive as a slave.
2. Add the drive to the disk drive cable.
3. Set the disk's parameters.
4. Partition and format the disk.

Altering the Jumper Settings

Whenever you use more than one IDE drive, you must specify your *master* or *primary* drive. This tells your machine which disk to use when searching for boot instructions. If you fail to specify your master drive, your system won't boot properly. With few exceptions, IDE drives rely on hardware-based master/slave designations. You set these options using jumpers. *Jumpers* are tiny on/off switches on your hard disk drive's main circuit board (see the following figure).

Metal jumper pins jut out from the hard disk drive's main circuit board.

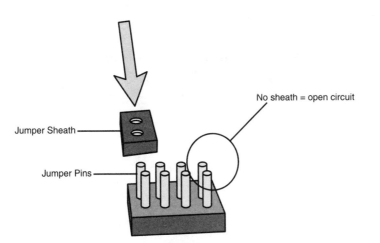

No sheath = open circuit

Jumper Sheath

Jumper Pins

233

Jumper pins are arranged in pairs; each pair governs a single circuit. While the jumper pin pair is unsheathed, the circuit is open. You can close this circuit by applying a sheath to the specified jumper pin pair (see the following figure).

To close the circuit, cover the jumper pin pair with a sheath.

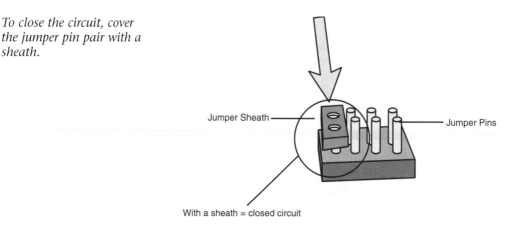

To find the master-slave jumpers on your IDE hard disk drive, turn the drive to reflect a rear view (see the following figure). As illustrated in the following figure, most IDE hard disk drives have the cable connector, power connector, and jumpers at the rear. Typically, there are three clearly-marked jumper pairs:

➤ Master (M or C)

➤ Slave (S or D)

➤ Cable Select (CS)

The cable connectors, power connectors, and jumpers are generally located at the rear of the hard disk drive.

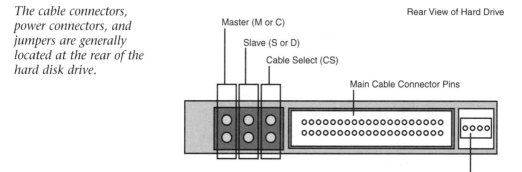

Once you've identified which jumper pin pair you need, set the drive to slave status. You do this by either applying or removing a sheath to the proper jumper pin pair.

Adding the Drive to the Disk Drive Cable

Next, you'll need to connect the drive to your system. For this, you must open your box to expose the disk drive connector cable. Once you remove the system casing, you will see the hard disk drive cable. In older computers, this cable extends from an insertable hard disk controller card (such as the one depicted in the following figure) to the hard drive. In newer systems, however, the hard disk con-

Check This Out

Not every hard disk manufacturer adheres to these conventions. If you can't immediately make out what each jumper pair does, check the drive's documentation. Also, this information is sometimes printed on the drive's surface (usually on the top, on a peel-off sticker).

troller is on-board and, therefore, the hard disk cable extends from the motherboard to your existing hard disk.

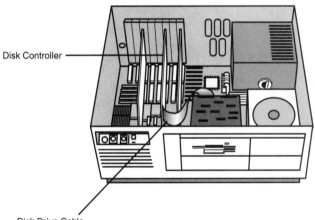

Disk Controller

Disk Drive Cable

Finding the disk drive connector cable.

The hard disk drive cable will look much like the one depicted in the following figure. The cable will have at least three connectors—two for hard drives and one for the controller. Attach your slave hard disk drive to an empty connector on the ribbon cable, plug in the drive, and secure it. You probably don't want to permanently mount the drive yet because you might need to remove it again before installation is complete.

Walking the Thin Red Line

When connecting a ribbon cable, be sure that it goes in right-side-up. You can quickly determine this by locating the thin red strip on the cable. This strip signifies the location for pin 1 on the drive and motherboard (or card controller). Ensure that you match up the red strip with pin 1; otherwise, the connection will be incorrect—up-side-down—and the system won't recognize your drive.

A typical connector ribbon cable with three connection points.

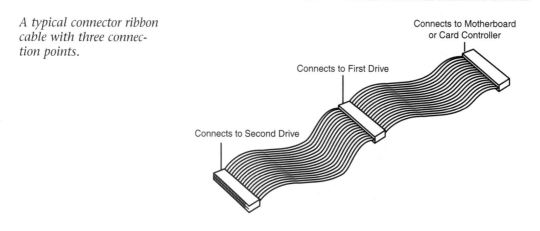

Connects to Motherboard or Card Controller

Connects to First Drive

Connects to Second Drive

Setting the Disk's Parameters

Next, you'll need to set the disk's parameters and geometry, including some—or perhaps all—of the following values:

➤ *The landing zone* Landing zones are blank spaces on the hard disk drive's surface, reserved for temporarily parking the head or heads. This prevents the head from accidentally writing to recordable portions of the disk.

➤ *The number of cylinders* Cylinders are collections of associated tracks on a hard disk drive's surface.

➤ *The number of heads* Heads are tools that read and write data from the disk.

➤ *The number of sectors* Sectors are small areas of the disk contained within tracks. These sectors house the smallest possible space used to record data. There are usually at least eight sectors per track.

➤ *The number of tracks* Tracks are similar to grooves in an LP record. They extend completely around the disk's surface. Within each track are several sectors.

Years ago, users had to specify this information manually, a complex and often difficult task. Have no fear, though. Most modern systems collect this information without human intervention.

Once you have the drive connected, restart your machine and enter your system BIOS (or PROM). Depending on your machine's manufacturer, you might have to take different steps to do this. On most PCs, you can strike the Delete key any time before the system actually boots. This brings you to a CMOS screen.

In your CMOS, find the Hard Disk Drive Auto Detection option. On some systems, this is one menu deep, usually in the Advanced Settings section. On other systems, it's immediately available from the main menu. Once you find this option, click it and the machine automatically detects your new disk's parameters (including heads, cylinders, sectors, landing zones, and size). Your machine then asks whether you accept these parameters. Click Yes, save your changes, exit, and reboot.

Techno Talk

On older systems, the BIOS might not offer hard disk auto-detection. If you own such a system, you'll have to manually set the drive's parameters. To do so, copy down the parameters from the drive's peel-off sticker (or accompanying documentation). Be sure to have these values ready before entering the BIOS. Once there, enter the values manually, save the configuration, and reboot.

Partitioning and Formatting the Disk

Most new hard disk drives already come with a viable partition. In many cases, therefore, you can format the drive immediately upon reboot. To do so in Microsoft Windows, double-click the My Computer icon, right-click your new disk's icon, and choose Format. If your new disk does *not* contain a valid partition, you'll need to create one. To do so, go to the Start menu and choose Programs | MSDOS Prompt. This opens an MS-DOS window (see the following figure).

Once you've opened the MS-DOS Prompt window, issue the following command:

```
fdisk
```

The MS-DOS Prompt window.

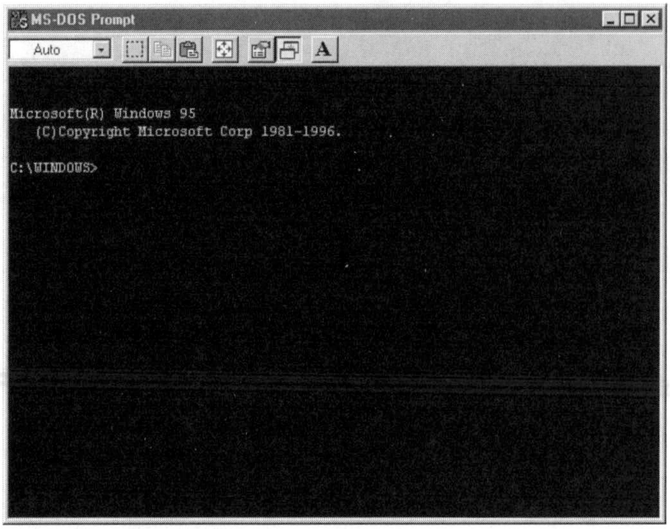

This starts FDISK, the disk-partitioning tool that comes with Windows. At this point, if you're using Windows 95, you'll see the following advisory:

```
Your computer has a disk larger than 512MB. This version
of Windows includes improved support for large disks, resulting
in more efficient use of disk space on large drives, and allowing
disks over 2GB to be formatted as a single drive.

IMPORTANT: If you enable large disk support and create any new
drives on this disk, you will not be able to access the new
drive(s) using other operating systems, including some versions
of Windows 95 and Windows NT, as well as earlier versions of
Windows and MS-DOS. In addition, disk utilities that were not
designed explicitly for the FAT32 file system will not be able
to work with this disk. If you need to access this disk with
other operating systems or older disk utilities, do not enable
large drive support.

Do you wish to enable large disk support (Y/N)...........? [N]
```

If you see this advisory, choose Y (N is the default). This takes you into FDISK's main menu. You then see a screen similar to the one in the following figure.

The FDISK main menu.

From here, there are six remaining steps:

1. Choose Create DOS Partition or DOS Logical Drive.
2. Choose Create Primary DOS Partition.
3. Specify that you want the maximum available space.
4. Choose Yes.
5. Exit FDISK.
6. Reboot.

If you survived all that, you have installed a new secondary IDE hard disk drive.

Adding a New Primary IDE Drive

The procedure for adding a new primary IDE disk drive is almost identical to the process for adding a secondary one. The only real procedural difference is that you leave the jumpers alone when installing a new primary drive. However, the *preparation* for upgrading your existing primary drive is different.

239

A Gentle Warning

First, before you do anything, *back up the existing drive*. This is to ensure against potential disaster during the upgrade process. Although the likelihood of disaster is slim, stranger things have happened. You might accidentally drop the drive while removing it, or you might unwittingly expose it to excess static electricity. This can damage or incapacitate components. Once, I was hot-swapping two disks (like a complete idiot) and inadvertently dropped the primary disk into the box. The drive lodged itself between the motherboard and the Ethernet card. I reached in to get the drive but quickly recoiled. Before I was able to pull the plug, the drive fused itself to the motherboard and the network card (arc-welding, anyone?). Needless to say, the data on that drive was unrecoverable. To learn about backing up your system, refer to Chapter 12, "Disaster Prevention: Backing Up."

Next, before upgrading, take stock of your software. Are there irreplaceable software programs on your existing primary drive? If so, are those applications critical to your business? If your answer to both questions is yes, you need to carefully consider upgrading. Here's why: If you designate your existing primary drive as a slave, many of its software programs will not work anymore. Applications have system calls hard-coded into their design that expect certain files to be on certain drives. For example, when you first install a software program, it unpacks its resource files to the primary drive. A record is then made of their location (in this case, `C:>`). If you later change your drive's logical designation (from drive C to drive D, for instance), important resource files are no longer where they're supposed to be. Therefore, when applications look for those files, their search fails. (Typically, the program throws up a dialog box explaining that files are "Not Found".) This results in a fatal error. So before you replace your existing primary drive, ensure that you have original installable versions of all critical software.

The CD-ROM Problem

It's now time to answer the number one technical support question of all time! Today, most commercial software is distributed on CD-ROM. Therefore, when you install a new drive which has absolutely no software on it, you need to install the CD-ROM drivers. If you don't, you end up with an empty drive and no way to install your applications.

If you have the original CD-ROM software installation disks, you have no worries. After you format the drive, you simply install the CD-ROM software and that's that. From there, you can install Windows, Office, and so on. But what if you only have the CD-ROM drivers, and no installation disks? How do you make a boot disk that catches the CD-ROM? I can't tell you how many times I've been asked that question. The following steps provide an answer:

1. Take a clean, formatted floppy disk and convert it into a system disk. You can do this in one of two ways:

   ➤ *In Windows*   Double-click My Computer, right-click your desired floppy disk's icon, and choose Format I Full I Copy System Files.

   ➤ *From a prompt*   Issue the following commands:

   ```
   sys a:
   cd c:\windows\command
   copy *.exe a:
   copy *.com a:
   ```

2. Locate your CD-ROM drivers. If you're uncertain where these reside, check the contents of your CONFIG.DOS file. Typically, it contains a line similar to this:

   ```
   DEVICE=C:\DEV\HIT-IDE.SYS /D:MSCD001
   ```

   In this case, my CD-ROM driver is located in the directory C:\DEV. After you locate your CD-ROM driver, copy it to your floppy disk; for example:

   ```
   copy c:\dev\hit-ide.sys a:
   ```

3. Create two files on your floppy disk: CONFIG.SYS and AUTOEXEC.BAT. In the CONFIG.SYS file, specify your CD-ROM driver as a device. Using the previous example, your CONFIG.SYS file looks similar to this:

   ```
   DEVICE=HIT-IDE.SYS /D:MSCD001
   ```

   In your AUTOEXEC.BAT file, you'll initiate the MSCDEX.EXE command, which drives CD-ROMs. Hence, your AUTOEXEC.BAT file looks similar to this:

   ```
   MSCDEX.EXE /D:MSCD001 /m:8
   ```

4. Test the disk. Make certain that the floppy disk is inserted into the floppy drive and reboot. Your system will boot from the floppy and load the CD-ROM driver. From there, you can format and partition the drive and then proceed with a complete software installation.

Notes On SCSI Hard Disk Drives

The process of upgrading to a new SCSI hard disk drive is very similar to the procedure in the preceding section, but with one exception: If you're installing a secondary SCSI drive, you might need to alter the new drive's SCSI ID.

The SCSI interface enables you to daisy chain SCSI devices with ease. A *daisy chain* connects six or seven SCSI drives to the same computer. In order to keep track of these multiple devices, the SCSI controller relies on *SCSI IDs*—addresses where each device can be found. Typically, most SCSI drives are capable of occupying IDs 0 through 7.

Most PC SCSI controllers attempt to boot from SCSI ID 0, or the first available SCSI device. Many new SCSI drives are set to ID 0 at the factory. Hence, if you're adding a new SCSI drive and want to designate it as a secondary disk, you'll need to change the drive's ID from 0 to any higher number. If you don't, there will be a SCSI conflict because the controller finds two devices registered at ID 0.

To change your new hard disk drive's SCSI ID, you'll need to either apply, relocate, or remove one or more jumpers. To find out which jumper (or jumpers) to remove, check your new drive's documentation.

Manually Determining the New Drive's SCSI ID

If you purchased a SCSI drive without documentation, you can still manually determine the jumper settings. Simply attach the drive, reboot, and watch the error messages from your SCSI adapter. In particular, note the SCSI ID that the adapter automatically detected for the secondary drive. Then turn off the machine, alter the drive's jumpers, and try again.

If this technique fails, try visiting the Web site of the drive's manufacturer. Most SCSI manufacturers post jumper settings and other schematics for all their current products, and occasionally for their ancient ones. For example, someone recently gave me a RAID array of SCSI disks that were manufactured in 1991. I had no trouble finding their jumper settings at Seagate's Web site.

Upgrading Motherboards and CPUs

Another common upgrade path is to replace your motherboard, your CPU, or both. This is an economical way to obtain better performance without replacing the entire workstation. (These days, you can buy a motherboard/CPU upgrade for as little as $150).

Upgrading the Motherboard

Your motherboard is your computer's largest and most important circuit card. This board houses the *Central Processing Unit* (*CPU*), the computer's memory, and the important firmware (BIOS) used to perform basic hardware configuration.

In desktop systems, this board is located at the very bottom of the machine, as depicted in the following figure. In tower and mini-tower systems, the motherboard is located on either side.

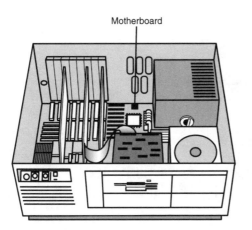

Motherboard

The motherboard is gener-ally fastened to the bot-tom of the machine.

Often, other devices (including the power supply, disk drives, and so on) obstruct open access to the motherboard. Therefore, you might have to remove these devices to perform the upgrade. Before you do, though, check to see whether access is pro-vided through the bottom or side of the computer's casing.

When you do gain clear access to the motherboard, you'll see that it houses many important slots, bays, and ports. Some of these are identified in the following figure.

243

The motherboard houses serial ports, parallel ports, on-board disk controllers, memory bays, and so on.

Chances are, your motherboard also houses several expansion cards. These fit into expansion slots (see the following figure).

Expansion cards (typically green or dark green) fit into slots on the motherboard.

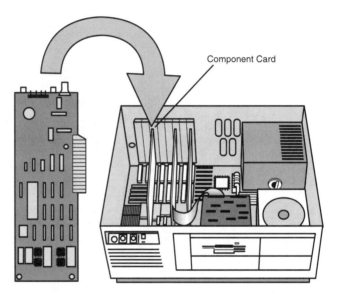

Component Card

Before removing the old motherboard, you must first disconnect all expansion cards and power cables. (To disconnect expansion cards, you'll need a Phillips-head screwdriver.) When removing expansion cards, handle them gently and make every effort to protect them from excess static electricity.

Once you've disconnected all expansion cards and cables, you're ready to remove the motherboard. Most motherboards are secured to the computer case with screws or plastic fasteners. These are generally located at the corners (see the following figure).

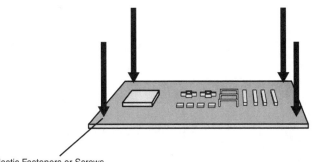

Screws and fasteners are usually located at the corners.

Plastic Fasteners or Screws

Once you've removed all screws and fasteners, you can safely lift out the old motherboard and install the new one.

CPU Upgrades

There are two basic CPU upgrade types:

➤ *Upgrading to an overdrive processor*   Overdrive processors are an inexpensive solution to upgrading very old systems. (A good example is converting a 486DX66 to a 486DX100). While overdrive processors offer only marginal speed gains, they can provide the extra oomph needed to upgrade a system from Windows 3.11 to Windows 95 (barely).

➤ *Upgrading to a new processor*   In contrast, upgrading to a new processor presents a world of possibilities (including any range of speeds, from 133MHz to 450MHz). However, new processors can be expensive.

About Those Overdrive Chips...

Many folks opt for overdrive chips as an inexpensive way to upgrade older boxes, such as 486 systems. Personally, I'd advise against it. I've never seen an overdrive chip that can offer the same performance as a new chip with the same clock speed. For example, installing an 80MHz overdrive chip into a 40MHz Sparc IPX achieves only a moderate speed increase—certainly less than a regular non-overdrive 80MHz chip. This is equally true of X86 chips. In essence, it's worth the extra $150 or so to really upgrade to 133 or 166.

Several factors influence your choice of CPU upgrade, but none so much as the make and model of your motherboard. For example, older motherboards might offer you little or no upgrade path. This is especially so with certain proprietary 386 and early 486 models. Let me demonstrate why...

As depicted in the following figure, the typical legacy processor has pins that fit into holes on a processor carriage. There are two types of carriage: slotted and non-slotted. *Slotted* carriages are designed for convenience and enable you to swap processor chips (you simply pull out the old chip and insert a new one). Conversely, *non-slotted* carriages are not flexible—the chip is usually welded in—and, therefore, prohibit processor upgrades.

The typical legacy processor.

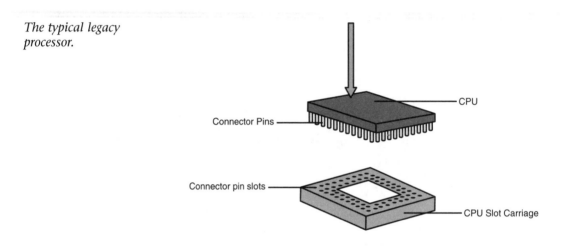

Before you decide to upgrade those old 386 and 486 boxes, open them up and take a close look. If your system has a non-slotted carriage, forget it. The only way you'll upgrade that processor is to replace not only the processor but the entire motherboard, too. (Of course, if you only want a modest upgrade—to 166MHz, for example—this is still a pretty economical move). If your system *is* slotted, there are still other considerations. For example, many system boards support only Pentium—and not Pentium II—processors; worse still, they'll only handle up to 200MHz.

Since there are so many different motherboards and so many different processors, it is difficult to describe a generic procedure for processor upgrades (other than to suggest replacing the old chip with a new one). So, instead, here are some general tips that apply to all CPU upgrades:

➤ *Watch your voltage*   Different chips take different voltages; most modern motherboards support either 3.5 or 5 volts. If your chip requires 3.5 volts and your motherboard is set to 5, you might damage your processor. (You'll know if that happens: You'll see very strange results on the screen, such as characters broken in half and logos fragmented into fuzzy shapes.) To avoid accidentally frying your processor, consult your motherboard's manual. Invariably, you'll find that jumpers on the motherboard govern voltage. Really good motherboards provide visual notification of this. Typically, the voltage count is burned into the board, adjacent to the jumper. Also, in most cases, the chip's required voltage is visible on the chip's surface. Be certain to set your motherboard to the correct voltage prior to starting the machine.

➤ *Handle the chip with care*   Processor chips (like most computer components) are especially sensitive to static electricity. Older chips in particular (486, and early Pentium 100, 133, and 166MHz units) come with their pins embedded in an anti-static pad for this very reason. It's worth supporting your board with a rubber pad—or other non-static surface—while you perform the upgrade.

➤ *Provide the chip with adequate cooling facilities*   Most processors get pretty hot under extensive use. When you upgrade from an older chip to a new one, take this into account. Older chips (486 models and some early Pentiums) require only a small fan to keep them cool. However, newer chips often require more extensive measures (including heat synchs or, in the extreme, miniature internal refrigeration systems). Make certain that you employ the proper cooling procedure for your chip. If you don't, it overheats and burns out. (You'll know if your cooling system is inadequate; your system will chronically fail, reboot, or freeze at intervals ranging from 30 seconds to three minutes.)

➤ *If you don't have the original documentation on your current motherboard and processor, get it*   And certainly don't attempt an upgrade until you do. Here's why: Many proprietary systems—particularly from companies such as Acer, Compaq, and Packard Bell—tie key functionality of the processor to the system BIOS. Some systems are simply not compatible with certain chips (such as AMD's K6, for example). To prevent spending money that you might not recover, be absolutely certain that the upgrade processor you choose is compatible with your current motherboard.

Upgrading Communication and Networking Hardware

It's unlikely that you'll upgrade communication or networking hardware during your network's first year of operation. As your network grows in size and scope, however, this might change. In particular, as you add more workstations you'll need additional hubs, switches, or routers. Since your network's growth cannot be anticipated, only generalized tips and tricks can be offered in this regard:

➤ *Apply prudent topology choices whenever possible*   For example, by chaining star segments together (or by daisy chaining), you can often avoid purchasing more expensive hardware.

➤ *Inquire vigorously*   For example, suppose you're concerned with security and a vendor pitches you on an "intelligent hub." Press that vendor on the hub's features, especially regarding segmentation. Does the hub *really* perform segmentation, or does the sales pitch take liberties?

➤ *Pay that extra dollar*   In networking, you often get precisely what you pay for. In other words, it's better paying a few extra dollars for quality equipment and guaranteed reliability. As your network grows, reliability becomes a very serious issue. When many people rely on a network, you can't afford to have it go down.

➤ *Stick to a standard*   When purchasing hubs, routers, switches, or bridges, buy them from the same vendor—or at least make certain that they offer very similar management features and functionality. By doing so, you'll avoid a new learning curve and you'll be less likely to encounter problems.

Software Upgrades

Upgrading software is rarely a necessity—avoid it if possible. Here's why: Software manufacturers (particularly in the Windows world) often radically change their software, which can introduce an entirely new learning curve. As a result, installing such software can sometimes hinder productivity.

A good example is Microsoft's migration from Windows 3.11 to 95. Windows 95 drastically differed from 3.11 not only in a superficial sense (the visual interface worked differently), but also in more profound ways (the new system used a Registry instead of simple configuration files). Many of my clients didn't adjust well to that change and waited as long as possible before upgrading on a grand scale.

A good formula for determining whether you really need an upgrade is to weigh the following issues:

➤ Does the upgrade offer important functionality that was previously lacking?

➤ Does the upgrade fix problems that have plagued your system?

➤ Does the upgrade enhance your security?

➤ Is the upgrade a requirement to use mission critical applications you intend to introduce?

Unless one of these four statements is true, you probably don't need the upgrade. Moreover, you need to assess the upgrade for negative points. For example, what if the upgrade *takes away* important functionality? Either way, whenever performing a software upgrade (or, for that matter, a hardware upgrade), test that upgrade first. The following section covers testing issues.

Testing Upgrades

As part of your upgrade strategy, you need to test proposed upgrades before implementing them. This prevents you from inadvertently propagating a faulty upgrade throughout the entire network. Remember that in a network, you must preserve a stable computing environment. In this respect, maintaining a network is more structured than maintaining your own machine; you can't afford as many mistakes.

For testing purposes, always have one or two knock-around machines. These needn't necessarily have the exact same hardware as your other workstations, but they should be configured as closely to other workstations as possible.

Oddly, your main concern (and the greatest chance for error) is with software upgrades. Although a rare occurrence, some software upgrades can cripple your existing configuration by damaging or replacing key system files with either newer or older versions.

Windows Ninety-Ate My Drivers!

A good example is Microsoft's release of Windows 98. Because many older systems were incompatible with 98 (a fact not widely publicized), thousands of users upgraded only to have their computers malfunction. This led some large vendors (including Dell) to post advisories on their Web sites, warning users of possible dangers.

By first testing such upgrades on a throwaway machine, you greatly increase your chances of identifying and eliminating potential hazards. To effectively perform this task, outfit your test machines with

➤ The same network operating system as other workstations

➤ The same applications currently installed on other workstations

➤ The same protocol support

➤ The same security settings

This guarantees that your test machines have a very similar (or identical) Registry and shared library configuration.

Each time you perform a test run, check that every application, all protocol support, and all security settings are still valid and operational. Only then should you institute that upgrade network-wide.

Where To From Here

In this chapter, you learned how to upgrade your system. In the next chapter, you'll learn the pros and cons of telecommuting, the types of available telecommuting sites, the kinds of hardware and software needed for telecommuting, and the policies you'll need to put in place in order to support telecommuters.

The Least You Need to Know

Upgrades can lead to greater efficiency and productivity, but they're also expensive and time consuming. Here are a few tips to help you maximize your potential and minimize cost:

➤ Always perform a test run on a throwaway test machine to identify possible upgrade incompatibilities or problems.

➤ Always perform full backups before attempting any upgrade.

➤ Try to standardize as much as possible. Maintaining a consistent hardware set is as important as maintaining a consistent application set. For example, using switches made by a single manufacturer will reduce the time you spend configuring or upgrading them later.

➤ When performing a partial upgrade (where some existing hardware remains), make certain that the new and old components are compatible.

➤ When upgrading software, be certain that the new software reads old data flawlessly and that the learning curve is moderate.

➤ When upgrading workstations, do so judiciously by distributing your processor power and storage capacity where they're most needed.

➤ Whenever possible, try to limit your costs by upgrading servers first.

## Chapter 16

Enabling Telecommuting

In This Chapter

➤ Understand the pros and cons of telecommuting.

➤ Learn the different types of telecommuting sites.

➤ Understand the kinds of networking hardware and software needed for telecommuting.

➤ Determine what policies must be in place to support telecommuters.

If you're just going to sit in front of a computer screen all day, why not do it in the comfort of your own home? With tremendous improvements in computing and networking technology, working away from the company's main site can be a cost-effective—and pleasant—alternative for both employers and employees.

Telecommuting is the practice of working away from the primary workplace by using telephone lines—or faster network media—to communicate with co-workers and access company computing resources. Telecommuting can take place from home, from satellite offices, or from independent *telework centers* (temporary rented workspaces).

This chapter focuses on the computing and networking equipment and software you need to help make telecommuting a reality.

Understanding Telecommuting Issues

Telecommuting is a practice that is growing in the United States. Because telecommuting is not only beneficial to the individual, a variety of government agencies and commercial organizations are encouraging the practice.

Advantages of Telecommuting

Following are some of the advantages of telecommuting for individuals:

➤ *Avoids long commutes*   If you have an hour commute to work and an hour back, you immediately save two hours a day by working from home.

➤ *Saves commuting costs*   Money spent on fuel or wear and tear on the car can be saved or put toward equipment costs.

➤ *Allows greater flexibility*   With a fully-equipped office set up at or near your home, you can more easily put in those extra hours or work around personal matters that come up during the day.

Having some employees telecommute can also have benefits for companies:

➤ *Saves office space*   Companies can save money by having telecommuters either share or do without office space at the home office. Likewise, less parking space is needed.

➤ *Fewer absentee days*   Studies have shown that employees who telecommute miss fewer work days and put in more hours overall than employees who work only at the company site.

➤ *Attracts skilled labor*   Telecommuting can offer skilled people who cannot come to an office every day (due to disabilities or other special needs) the option to work from home.

There are government agencies that also have an interest in telecommuting. There are several reasons why local and federal agencies are interested in telecommuting:

➤ *Crowded highways*   The more people that are taken off the streets at rush hour, the more smoothly traffic can flow. Large-scale telecommuting can reduce pressure in and around crowded metropolitan areas.

➤ *Pollution*   By reducing commuter traffic, telecommuting can also reduce the resulting air pollution.

Locations can benefit most from telecommuting if they are difficult to get to but have access to a high-speed communications infrastructure. Metropolitan areas that are technologically advanced but highway-impaired are well suited for telecommuting.

Disadvantages of Telecommuting

Telecommuting isn't for everyone. Some jobs are just not suited for telecommuting. There are issues that have to be worked out before an effective telecommuting program can be put into place.

Telecommuting can be particularly beneficial to those whose jobs don't require much personal contact. People who do much of their work independently, such as graphic artists, technical writers, and editors, can benefit from telecommuting. However, telecommuting is less appropriate for people who require personal contact (such as retail sales) or special equipment (such as manufacturing workers).

Following are a few drawbacks of telecommuting:

➤ *Loss of contact*   A lot of what happens in a company happens informally. Information that comes from running into people in the hall or sitting down at lunch can be lost for people offsite.

➤ *Loss of exposure*   It can be more difficult for an employer to evaluate the effectiveness of an employee who has limited contact with management and co-workers.

➤ *Distractions*   With your home—and chores—around you all the time, you can become distracted from your business.

➤ *Support*   Getting help for computer and networking problems can be difficult when there is no expert onsite to help. Not having company services such as personnel staff and stock rooms nearby can also be inconvenient.

With a little diligence with regards to keeping up contacts and staying focused on your work, these negatives can be less of a problem. Also, because many telecommuters only do so part time, the most appropriate times and types of work can be chosen for telecommuting.

Is Telecommuting Right for You?

To evaluate whether telecommuting might benefit you or someone in your organization, check out the Symantec Telecommuting Resource Center. There is an "Are You Ready to Work Anywhere?" site (http://www.symantec.com/telecommute/ howto.html) that asks questions to help you through the evaluation process.

Telecommuting Organizations

The following are some organizations that have an interest in supporting telecommuting:

➤ *AT&T*   AT&T claims to have 36,000 U.S.-based managers that are telecommuting at least part time. The company supports a telework site that discusses telecommuting issues: `http://www.att.com/ehs/telecom.html`.

➤ *International Telework Association*   A non-profit organization that promotes the benefits of teleworking. Its Web site is located at `http://www.telecommute.org/index.html`.

➤ *European Community Telework/Telematics Forum*   Resource for telecommuting projects and studies. You can visit their Web page at `http://www.telework-forum.org`.

Besides these organizations, there are many networking equipment vendors that offer products and information relating to telecommuting. These companies include 3Com, Cisco Systems, MCI/WorldCom, and Lucent Technologies.

Locations for Telecommuting

By far, the most common location for telecommuting is the employee's home. A variety of economic and environmental issues, however, have made telecommuting from different types of locations a viable solution. The following sections describe the different types of telecommuting locations that have arisen in recent years.

Home Telecommuting

Some estimate that nearly 80% of all telecommuting is done from the home. Home telecommuting can offer cost and efficiency benefits to employers and time and lifestyle benefits to employees. Telecommuting can be done full-time, part-time, or on an after-hours basis.

Telecommuting equipment for the home can be as simple as a computer with a modem. In such cases, the home office might just be used for situations that require simple communications (such as email and Web browsing) and basic applications (such as word processing and spreadsheets).

For full-time telecommuting from the home, more equipment and sophisticated integration with the company computing resources might be necessary. So, from a PC, modem, and telephone line, either the employee or the company might want to choose some of the following enhancements:

➤ *Higher-speed connections* An old 28.8Kpbs modem might perform poorly when using more demanding applications, such as videoconferencing. Upgrading to a 56Kbps modem or an ISDN connection can make a big difference.

➤ *Special communications software* Software packages are available to simplify communication with the company computing resources. By setting up a virtual private network, the home telecommuter can be assured of a secure connection to the company's computers. Software, such as pcTelecommute from Symantec, makes it easier to communicate directly with the employee's LAN.

➤ *More equipment* Everything an employee takes for granted at the office—FAX machines, copiers, printers, scanners—can be sorely missed by the telecommuter. With a network connection to the main office, some equipment can be shared (and possibly picked up the next day at work).

➤ *Special support software* When something goes wrong with your computer, you probably won't have a friendly neighborhood technician down the hall to help you. Luckily, you can add software to your computer to allow others to dial in and debug your problems. The computer can also be used to access an online company help desk, if one is available.

➤ *Critical company applications* If you need to run programs that only reside on company computers or that access company database records, some special setup might be required. You many need to install company software on your home computer. However, there are ways an administrator can allow you to launch an application that runs at the main office but displays on a remote computer.

As a part-time telecommuter, you can often rely on equipment from the home office or, on special occasions, commercial copy centers to get things done. If you plan to use your home office for those tasks that require limited resources but concentrated work (such as writing a report or sending emails), it can be implemented with minimal extra effort.

Satellite Office

When downtown offices become crowded and adding space is prohibitively expensive, some companies choose to set up satellite offices. A satellite office typically has the following attributes:

➤ Located away from the company's more expensive main site, typically in a suburban location near where employees live.

➤ Fully-equipped office that is owned and operated by the company.

➤ Used by employees as a place to work one or more days a week, as an alternative to driving into the main office.

A reduction in wear and tear on the employees is one of the major advantages of the satellite office. From a quality-of-life standpoint, satellite offices also serve to take some commuters off the roads, reducing highway congestion and pollution.

Satellite offices can also save on more expensive office space at the company's main site. Shared office space is more of an option when employees are scheduled to be off-site for several days a week.

From a networking standpoint, a part- or full-time administrator can be placed onsite to set up equipment and keep it running. This arrangement offers the company the greatest level of control over resources in a telecommuting environment.

Hoteling

For companies with many employees who are mobile, *hoteling* is a means of drastically reducing the office space needed. With hoteling, employees have no full-time office location. Instead, when they know they are going to be at their company's office, they call ahead and reserve a work space (just like reserving a room at a hotel).

Companies (such as accounting and sales firms) who frequently send their employees to customer locations are good candidates for hoteling. Typically, an office coordinator makes sure that when employees are going to be in the office they have the office space, telephones, computers, and supplies they need.

To support hoteling, employees are typically set up with a *virtual mobile office*, or *VMO* (described later). From a computing standpoint, the VMO enables users to have access to any software and data that they have at the company office.

Telework Center

A telework center is similar to a satellite office except that the telework center is not maintained by the employee's company. Telework centers tend to be private companies that rent out office space to anyone who needs it.

In addition to space, the telework center allows you to rent whatever office equipment you need. Space and equipment are typically rented per day. Employees who use these centers typically choose one that is close to their homes. Like other telecommuting options, telework centers save commuting time and effort.

Suburban areas outside of Washington, D.C. and parts of California—where commuting is difficult—are popular areas for telework centers. Besides offering such facilities as reception areas, conference rooms, private offices, board rooms, and presentation rooms, telework centers often offer the following computing facilities:

➤ Personal Computers

➤ High-speed modem connections

➤ Popular publishing and presentation application software

➤ Personal email and voicemail

➤ Postal mailroom services

➤ Printing, FAX, and copying equipment

Although telework centers don't enable a company to tailor employees' computing needs exactly to the job, they do offer a low-maintenance way for employees to occasionally save on commuting.

Anywhere (The Virtual Mobile Office)

Very often telecommuting is done not to save on commuting time, but rather to enable an employee to connect to company computer resources from wherever that employee might be. The virtual mobile office is a way of setting up an employee's computer so that by dialing into the company, the employee can have access to all the resources available at the office.

Following are some of the things that a virtual mobile office might enable an employee to do:

➤ Download email or voice mail messages.

➤ Dial into the company LAN, enabling the employee to access all networking resources that he or she has access to at the office.

➤ Dial into his or her PC, enabling the user to have total control over the PC.

➤ Run important company applications to do such things as access sales reports, billing data, or employee records.

Some features needed by the virtual mobile office, such as MS Windows NT, are already built into PC operating systems and require only some configuration to work. See the section "Communications Software for Telecommuting" for information about Windows features that provide mobile computing services.

Network Approaches to Telecommuting

Companies need employees to concentrate on their work and not be bogged down in the technicalities of getting connected to the networks and computing resources they need. Telecommuting adds challenges to setting up these networks.

For the computing resources the employee sees while on the road to look as much as possible like what they see at the main office, some special setup is required. Following are a few approaches to setting up a network that result in workable network connections for telecommuters:

➤ *Virtual private network* (*VPN*)   A VPN is a way for a network administrator to create a private network that passes over public network media. With a VPN, a telecommuting employee can rely on a secure connection that results in the same level of connectivity he or she gets in the main office.

➤ *Remote node* By adding remote node software, a telecommuter can connect to the company's network in a way that makes the telecommuter's computer appear to be on the company's local network.

➤ *Remote control* With remote control software, a telecommuter can connect to his or her own PC back at the office (usually via a modem that's attached to the office PC). With the remote connection established, the user has access to everything that is accessible when the user is sitting in front of the computer at work.

Virtual Private Networks

Although virtual private networks can help address the needs of telecommuters, VPNs can go far beyond that by creating a cost-effective, flexible way to expand access to a company's network. Every day company networks are providing access to more mobile users, satellite offices, and client locations. VPNs are a way of managing that growth.

VPNs rely on public computer networks, particularly the Internet, to connect remote users to the company's network. While using the public network (which provides an inexpensive and accessible method of communication), the connection between the user and the company network looks like a dedicated link.

A method called *tunneling* is used to achieve connectivity between VPN nodes (such as the user's PC and the entry to the company network). With tunneling, the *tunnel initiator* uses the public network to set up a connection with a *tunnel terminator*. Following is an example of how this might work:

1. An end user with a laptop (tunnel initiator) dials up a local *Internet service provider (ISP)* and establishes a connection to the Internet using a dial-up protocol that is VPN-enabled.

2. Across the Internet, the dial-up software establishes a connection to a tunnel terminator device on the company's enterprise network.

3. Requests for all services are encapsulated and directed to the tunnel terminator, which is often located at the company's firewall. Even requests for Internet resources are directed to the tunnel terminator, then directed back to the Internet. In other words, nothing that a user of a VPN-enabled computer requests from the Internet or the company's network is interpreted until it reaches the tunnel terminator.

Tunneling enables users located anywhere to act as members of a company's LAN (hence the term *virtual LAN*). To protect the security of the connection between the user and the virtual LAN, a variety of encryption schemes can be used so that someone snooping on the public network can't read the transmissions.

The features for connecting to a VPN from a Windows 95/98 or Windows NT computer are available for each of those operating systems. To see if VPN support is installed on your PC, open the Network window (Start | Settings | Control Panel, then open the Network icon). You can see a Dial-Up Adapter labeled with VPN Support in the following figure.

Windows 95 supports dial-up connections to VPNs.

Check This Out

Dial-up VPN was not fully supported in the original release of Windows 95. If you do not see VPN support in your Network window, you probably need to install the Dial-Up Networking 1.3 upgrade. Download the file `Msdun13.exe` from the Microsoft Web site and install it.

Remote Node (Connect to Remote LAN)

Like VPNs, *remote node* connections enable a remote user to connect to the company's network as though the user's computer were physically connected to that network. Typically, with remote node connections the user dials a modem that is directly connected to the company LAN.

LANLynk from Lynk (`http://www.soholynk.com`) is an example of third-party software that makes a remote PC into a workstation on the network. By allowing the PC to transmit standard LAN data, several remote computers can connect to a single LAN-connected host.

Remote Control (Connect Directly to PC)

Instead of remotely connecting to a company network, remote control features enable you to directly dial a modem connected to a PC. Once you are connected, you can operate that PC remotely as though you were there locally.

Remote control software can enable you to

➤ Transfer files between the remote and local PCs.

➤ Synchronize files between the remote and local PCs.

➤ Manage remote peripherals (printers, servers, and so on).

➤ Troubleshoot problems on the remote computer.

The Microsoft Remote Access Service (RAS) software is included in Windows 95/98/NT operating systems. Configuring RAS, however, is somewhat difficult—and there are no special features available for remote control (such as file synchronization).

Check This Out

The Digital Planet Web site has information for configuring different RAS clients. Try this Web address: `http://www.digital-planet.net/citrix/html/tips/wfrm/ctx00020.htm`.

There are several third-party software products available for providing remote control of a PC, including

➤ LapLink Professional from Traveling Software (`http://www.travsoft.com`)

➤ pcAnywhere from Symantec Corporation (`http://www.symantec.com/telecommute`)

➤ ReachOut from Stac Inc. (`http://www.stac.com`)

➤ Carbon Copy from Compaq (`http://www.compaq.com/carboncopy`)

Network Hardware for Telecommuting

The networking and computing hardware you set up to allow for telecommuting depends on many factors. To start with, you need a computer, a modem, and a network connection. After you are connected to the main office, the peripheral hardware you add depends on how much you need with you and how much you can use over the network.

Setting up the Telecommute Site

If you just use your home computer to browse the Web, you might get by with your old 28.8Kbps modem. When you need the computer for serious telecommuting, however, you might need higher speed connections to support resource-hungry applications such as videoconferencing.

Choosing Analog Modems

Line speed is the first choice you will make. Today, analog modems (that communicate over standard telephone lines) are available at speeds of up to 56Kbps. As of February 1998, there is an industry standard defining 56Kbps transmissions—V.90. Before that time, there were two different 56Kbps methods:

➤ K56flex from Rockwell Semiconductor Systems and Lucent Technologies

➤ x2 Technology from 3Com

You might want to check with your ISP to make sure that it supports V.90, although they might also support the other two technologies. Manufacturers that used K56flex and x2 technology are offering ways to upgrade to V.90 compliance to smooth the transition.

Check This Out

Rockwell Semiconductor Systems offers several white papers describing how to upgrade a K56flex modem to the current V.90 standard. You can find those white papers at `http://www.nb.rockwell.com/K56flex`.

Choosing Digital Connections

For higher-speed connections from your telecommute site, you need digital lines from your site. Although digital lines cost more than analog lines, you can get much faster connections. Following are a few choices:

➤ *Digital Subscriber Lines (DSL)*   Provide voice and high-speed data services on a copper wire pair between two locations. ADSL (asynchronous) allows for fast data download speeds (up to 15.44Mbps) and slower upload speeds (up to 128Kbps). SDSL (symmetrical) allows transmission speeds of 384Kbps in both directions.

➤ *Integrated Services Digital Network (ISDN)*   Unlike analog phone lines, ISDN allows multiple communications to travel on a single line. Speeds of up to 128Kbps are supported for a range of data, voice, and packet services.

➤ *Frame relay*   Supports data transfer rates of 1.544Mbps and 45Mbps. It employs a packet-switching protocol that can take advantage of high-speed T1 and T3 lines.

Choosing Computers

People who telecommute from home often use their home computer to do so. Typically, the setup is a PC running some version of MS Windows. If the applications you use for work require a more powerful operating system, such as UNIX, you might need to install some version of UNIX to run the applications you need. There are several UNIX versions that run on personal computers. It is possible to install several different operating systems on your hard disk, and then boot the one you need.

In terms of the components of the computer you are using, if you need to use business applications that are very graphics intensive (such as drawing programs or video conferencing) you might want to have a video card with a lot of RAM. The more video RAM, the faster images can be displayed on your screen.

Choosing Peripherals

If your home or other off-site office location becomes your primary place of business, you might find yourself wanting easy access to the same kinds of equipment available at the main office. A nearby mail service or copy center might offer some of the services you need.

Another thing to consider, however, is that when you are networked into your company office you can access many of the devices that are connected to that network. Following are some of the equipment devices you might either want to get for your home office or find a way to access at work:

➤ Printer
➤ Fax machine
➤ Scanner

➤ Tape or removable disk backup device

➤ Voice mail service

➤ Photocopier

Setting Up Company Network for Telecommuters

Configuring the corporate network to enable telecommuters to access company computing resources requires a lot of planning. Threats of outsiders hacking into their systems have encouraged many companies to institute restrictive firewalls to keep out all but the most necessary outside traffic.

For those companies that allow their employees to dial in to the company network, modem pools are often used to allow that access. A modem pool can enable those dialing in or out of a location to share the same set of modems. Typically, between 10 and 20 modems can handle up to 100 users. Modems must be of the type (analog or ISDN) and speed (28.8Kbps, 56Kbps, or higher) that matches the needs of the remote users.

For security of the dial-in connections, many companies use a *Remote Authentication Dial-in User Service* (*RADIUS*) server. The RADIUS server authenticates the user names and passwords entered by the remote user. If that information is correct, the RADIUS server authorizes access to the network.

Communications Software for Telecommuting

A speedy connection to your company network won't do you much good if you don't have the applications you need to take advantage of it. Many of the features needed to use your home computer or portable PC for telecommuting are already built in. Still others are quite easy to add.

Telecommuting Features in Windows

Using features that are already in Windows 95/98/NT, you can perform many of the most basic telecommuting functions. Following are some of the features built into your PC's operating system that are useful for telecommuters:

➤ *Dial-up networking* Enables you to specify everything you need to connect to a remote modem using SLIP or PPP protocols over telephone lines. Other protocols, such as Novell's IPX/SPX, are also supported.

➤ *Remote access service (RAS)* Enables you to set up your computer to allow remote computers to dial in. This is a good feature for allowing remote diagnostics of your computer if you are having a problem while away from your company technicians.

➤ *Direct cable connection*   With this feature, you can directly plug your computer into another computer, using a cable between the two computers' parallel or serial ports. No network is needed to exchange files between two computers.

➤ *Deferred printing*   This allows your portable computer to print, even when you are not connected to a printer or network. With this feature, print jobs are saved on the hard disk until a printer connection is available.

➤ *Briefcase*   Using this feature, you can copy files from your computer at work to a laptop, update the files, and later resynchronize the files with those on your computer at work.

➤ *Docking detection*   Windows can tell whether your portable computer is currently connected to a docking station. With this feature you can use different configurations for when the computer is docked.

Applications for Telecommuting

To communicate with people back at the main office, clients, or anyone else reachable by the network, you probably need a combination of common Internet tools and applications that are specific to your job. You can get many of the Internet tools you need by simply installing Netscape Communicator or Internet Explorer.

Regardless of which tools you choose, following are the common features you need to communicate with others over the Internet or other TCP/IP-based network:

➤ *Email*   Used to send messages and attached documents or graphics to another person on the network.

➤ *Web browser*   Used to display Web pages and a variety of other types of information on the Internet.

➤ *File transfer*   Used to copy files from one computer (typically an FTP server) to another (typically your computer).

➤ *News reader*   Enables you to participate in online newsgroups by displaying, sending, and managing sets of messages that pertain to a particular topic of discussion.

➤ *Video conferencing*   Enables you to participate in video conferences over the Internet.

➤ *Data conferencing*   Enables the users participating in a conference call to view the same running application from their own computer. If allowed by the person running the program, remote users might be capable of manipulating the program as well as viewing it.

➤ *Whiteboard*   Enables all the users in a conference to draw in a shared window that all participants can see.

Although these are some of the applications that might be useful to telecommuters, each telecommuter needs to speak to the company's system administrator to determine what other applications employees will need to get their jobs done.

Supporting Telecommuting

All the safety and support issues that a network administrator can normally resolve at the company office become more difficult with employees who are telecommuting. A network administrator will probably help put together a guide to help employees protect their computing resources when they work off site.

Some kind of protection checklist can help keep data from being lost and destroyed. For example, the checklist needs to recommend using surge protectors for computing equipment. Also, guidelines ought to be set down for virus protection. Incoming dial-up setup (such as RAS) can be set to enable the administrator to do remote diagnostics.

For employees that need to punch a time clock, some sort of time tracking software can be added to the telecommuter's computer. A scheme for handling data backup also needs to be put in place.

Finally, because system administrators are busy enough without being bothered by every little problem that occurs, access to online help will probably be established. This might include access to the company help desk or connections to vendors that support the tools the employee is using.

Where To From Here?

This chapter has helped you understand telecommuting issues, particularly as they relate to keeping connected to company networking and computer assets. You now understand the types of challenges faced and tools that can be employed in telecommuting.

The next chapter, "The Internet, Intranets, and Extranets," describes the kinds of public and private networks that exist today, based on TCP/IP protocols. In particular, the next chapter describes the Internet, intranets, and extranets.

The Least You Need to Know

Right now, the least you need to know about telecommuting is this:

➤ How telecommuting can benefit employees and employers by creating a more flexible and efficient total work environment.

➤ How telecommuting can be done from home, satellite offices, hoteling arrangements, telework centers, or anywhere you can travel with a portable PC.

➤ Different network approaches that can be taken to telecommuting, including Virtual Private Networks (VPN), remote node connections, or remote control connections.

➤ The types of networking hardware (such as modems and other peripherals) you need to set up telecommuting both at the main office and offsite.

➤ What applications software you need for telecommuting.

➤ Support issues related to having a telecommuting site.

Part 5
The Internet and Beyond

You wouldn't believe what you can do with a network these days! When you chat, email, and surf, you only scratch the surface of what can be accomplished. This section discusses the ways in which using intranets, extranets, the Internet, and email can boost your business.

The Internet, Intranets, and Extranets

There are so many kinds of "nets" these days that it is hard to keep them all straight. Everyone has heard of the Internet—even those who don't yet know what it is. But as if the Internet isn't enough, new words such as intranets and extranets have begun popping up.

This chapter will help demystify what the Internet, intranets, and extranets are and when they are used. It will also explain the common standards that the three types of networks are based upon.

Understanding the Internet, Intranets, and Extranets

Intranets and extranets were created as a natural evolution from the public Internet. They reflect the desires of organizations to leverage the value of the widely-accessible Internet with the need to communicate with employees and partners in a secure way.

It helps to describe the features that are common to the Internet, intranets, and extranets. The most basic similarities between these networks are

➤ They are all built using TCP/IP protocols. These protocols define rules for such things as how messages are routed on the network and what types of services are supported.

➤ They use the same methods of identifying computers and users on the network. Names are organized in a hierarchy referred to as the *domain name system* (*DNS*) and numerical representations of those names are referred to as *IP addresses*.

➤ Because they use the same protocols and naming methods, the different types of networks can use the same network-ready applications (such as Web browsers and email), security methods, and system administration tools.

Differences Between the Internet, Intranets, and Extranets

If the Internet, intranets, and extranets sound similar, you might wonder what it is that makes them different. The truth is that from a technology standpoint, these types of networks are pretty much the same. The primary differences come from the way that the networks are used. Following is an explanation of how the Internet, intranets, and extranets differ:

➤ *The Internet*   The Internet is a wide-open network, made up of many public and private networks joined together. The vast majority of resources on the Internet are intended for public access. Users can view Web pages, send email, and access FTP sites associated with thousands of organizations all over the world.

➤ *Intranets*   An intranet is a private network that is controlled by a business or organization. It is intended for company business and is generally inaccessible to the outside world. Usually, people within the company communicate with each other using many of the same tools used on the Internet: Web browsers, network administration tools, and various collaborative programs.

➤ *Extranets*   An extranet is actually an intranet (privately maintained) that extends its network to remote users, suppliers, or other businesses or organizations with which it wants to collaborate. To extend outside of the company intranet, extranets often enable collaborators to connect to the intranet using secure connections over the public Internet.

The Domain Name System

The domain name system ensures that the computers on the Internet have unique names and IP addresses. Domain names are organized in a hierarchy that is probably familiar to you by now; these days, it seems that every business has a .com (dot-com) Internet address.

Well, that .com is just one of many top-level domain names. Each top-level domain name represents a category of domains under which many individual domain names exist. For example, following are some top-level domain names you might be familiar with:

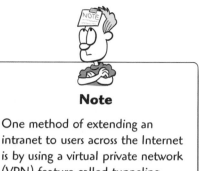

Note

One method of extending an intranet to users across the Internet is by using a virtual private network (VPN) feature called tunneling. Chapter 16, "Enabling Telecommuting," describes tunneling and VPNs.

➤ .com   Includes commercial domains, such as large corporations, wholesalers, and small businesses.

➤ .gov   Includes many United States government domains.

➤ .org   Includes various kinds of organizations.

➤ .edu   Includes educational institutions, particularly colleges and universities.

➤ .net   Includes organizations associated with computer networks, such as Internet service providers.

Because the first top-level domains were created for companies, government agencies, and universities in the United States, as organizations from other countries joined the Internet, top-level domains were added for each country. Following are some examples of top-level country domains:

➤ jp   Japan
➤ uk   United Kingdom
➤ ca   Canada
➤ de   Germany

Assigning Domain Names

After an organization is assigned a domain name under a top-level domain, it is within the organization's control to organize and name all their computers under that domain name. For example, for a commercial domain named handsonhistory, the domain name is

```
handsonhistory.com
```

Any computers within that domain can either be added directly to the domain name or to additional subdomains. For example, computers named decoys and baskets might be called decoys.handsonhistory.com and baskets.handsonhistory.com. Or, you might add a subdomain of crafts and have the computers named decoys.crafts.handsonhistory.com and baskets.crafts.handsonhistory.com.

Assigning IP Addresses

The IP address is used to actually communicate with a computer on the Internet. Domain names are translated into IP addresses before requests to communicate with a computer are made (a DNS server does the actual translation).

The IP address is made up of four numbers (from 0 to 255), separated by dots. Each number is referred to as an *octet* because it consists of eight bits. The following is an example of an IP address:

    123.45.67.89

Because any given organization usually has many computers, every organization is usually given a set of IP addresses to assign to its computers. The numbers assigned are divided into Class A, Class B, and Class C network addresses, each containing a different number of host addresses.

Part of each IP address represents a *subnetwork*, and the other part represents a particular computer on that subnetwork. The trick is that, depending on the network class, the parts of each address that represent the network and computer change.

A Class C network address contains up to 256 host addresses (the last of the four octets); a Class B network contains 65,536 host addresses (the last two of the four octets); and a Class A network contains more than 16 million host addresses (the last three of the four octets).

Needless to say, this was a fairly inefficient way of assigning addresses. In fact, whole Class A and Class B addresses are no longer assigned. Now you need to make a case for the number of IP addresses your organization gets.

IP addresses are running out, requiring that some tricks be used (such as assigning IP addresses dynamically as needed) until the next generation of the Internet is put in place. The next generation has a virtually limitless number of IP addresses.

Domain Names and Addresses in Intranets

That was a quick description of how Internet names and addresses work, but you might wonder how that relates to intranets and extranets. In terms of host names, most intranets and extranets organize their computers under the company's domain name. However, requests from the Internet for most computers on the intranet will be refused by the company's firewall (depending on how security is set up).

As for IP addresses, a special set of IP addresses is available to be used by any intranet. Because most or all of the computers on the private part of the company's network might not be reachable from the Internet, this same set of IP addresses can be used by all intranets. Internet routers know that these addresses are never accessible from the Internet.

IP Addresses for Private Networks

IP addresses that are allocated for private networks are defined in RFC 1918. These include

➤   `10.0.0.0` through `10.255.255.255`

➤   `172.16.0.0` through `172.31.255.255`

➤   `192.168.0.0` through `192.168.255.255`

The first set of numbers represents a single Class A network. The second set represents 16 Class B networks. The third set represents 256 Class C networks. Requests for these numbers are never routed off of the local subnetwork.

The Internet

The Internet is a massive computer network consisting of thousands of subnetworks and millions of computers worldwide. Although it began as a United States military project in the 1960s (used primarily by government agencies, universities, and government contractors), today it encompasses a vast range of commercial, educational, and recreational uses.

The World Wide Web

Although the number of computers and users on the Internet has grown since its inception, its greatest growth period began in the late 1980s with the creation of the World Wide Web. The Web placed a simplified framework over the Internet that enabled non-technical people to use the Internet for the first time.

The Web did several things to make the Internet more accessible to the masses:

➤   *Created Hypertext Markup Language (HTML)*   This enabled users to build graphical documents that contained images, formatted text, and links to other documents on the Web. Now HTML documents can include sound, video, and other content as well.

➤ *Created a simplified way of identifying Web resources*   Using uniform resource locators (URLs), a user can ask for a resource (such as a Web page or an FTP directory) directly from a server. Before, users had to log in to a computer, search for what they wanted, download a file, and then open it using an appropriate program.

The Web began naming computers with the same conventions used by the domain name system. However, prefixes were often added to identify different types of service requests. For example, Web servers were often preceded with www (such as www.whatever.com) and FTP servers were often preceded with ftp (such as ftp.whatever.com).

Tacked on in front of a Web address was the type of protocol associated with the content. For Web pages, Hypertext Transfer Protocol (http://) appeared in front of the address. For File Transfer Protocol the prefix ftp:// was added. The location of the resource on the server was placed at the end of the address. For example, a file called readme.txt in the /pub directory of an ftp server is added on as /pub/readme.txt. The whole address appears as follows:

```
ftp://ftp.whatever.com/pub/readme.txt
```

The program of choice for accessing these resources on the Web is called a *Web browser*. Although browsers were first intended primarily to display Web pages (in HTML format), browsers have turned toward a one-program-fits-all approach. By adding additional code, such as plug-ins and ActiveX controls, browsers can display and manipulate a wide range of data types.

How the Internet Works

Many of the design considerations that went into the early versions of ARPAnet, the predecessor to the Internet, are still apparent in the Internet of today. Because it began as a military project intending to ensure that computing resources had the capability to continue to respond during a nuclear attack (so that the government could shoot back), the network had to have the following attributes:

➤ *Keep running no matter what*   There could be no single point of failure that caused the network to stop running. Even if whole areas of the network were destroyed, the remaining parts had to continue to communicate.

➤ *Join together incompatible equipment*   Communication needed to occur between computing systems of different agencies that were often incompatible. Usually they weren't even capable of sharing files, let alone of communicating over networks in any meaningful way.

To meet the first criterion, the government decided to make the network a packet-switching network. Rather than have two communicating computers set up a connection and send data across that connection (like a telephone call), data is broken up into packets, with each packet labeled with the source and destination address of the data (like sending a letter at the post office).

The advantage of packet switching is as follows: Because each item of data knows where it is going, information can take any available route to reach the destination, and then be reassembled when the packets get there. If part of the network goes down, packets can take another route because communication doesn't rely on a particular connection staying up during the course of a communication.

As for the criterion of connecting incompatible computing systems, instead of replacing existing networks and computers, the new network acted as an umbrella by placing new protocols over existing ones. As a result, the many networks of today—including Ethernet and Token Ring LANs, Novell IPX/SPX networks, and wide-area networks such as X.25—can all be part of, and carry data for, the Internet.

The impact of this design on today's Internet is that the Internet can continue to grow by adding faster, higher-bandwidth backbones—like adding superhighways to a road system. Older, less efficient networks can be retired. Internet traffic can be routed to networks that are less congested. Furthermore, even though it might be slower, the Internet itself can continue to work when parts of the network go down.

Resources on the Internet

The transformation of the Internet that was brought about by the Web marked a major change not only in who was using the Internet, but also in the way the Internet was used. Originally, users tended to be technical workers or students, as opposed to today's potential user—anyone with a PC and a modem. Furthermore, Internet programs were command-oriented instead of graphical.

With the transition to the Web, traditional technical and educational uses have given way to entertainment, shopping, and a wide range of business applications. The following sections describe both the traditional and current uses of the Internet.

Traditional Internet Uses

If you were using the Internet BW—Before Web—here are some of the things you were probably doing:

➤ *Email* Mail messages were plain text, with an occasional attachment containing a binary file, such as a small program. You probably needed to know how to use a command such as uudecode to decode the attachment.

➤ *Newsgroups* This was, and remains today, a popular resource for exchanging ideas and information on topics of interest. Although some improvements have been made over the years, such as threads (to group together responses to a particular question) and HTML messages (which people with old newsreaders find annoying), newsgroups continue to operate today much as they did before the Web was created.

➤ *FTP*   To download software and documents from other computers, you can use the ftp command to access computers that are set up as FTP servers. After you log in, usually using an anonymous login, you can go up and down the directory structures to find and download the files you want.

FTP servers are still supported today, although Web pages are often used to navigate documents and download sites to simplify the task of finding the right resources.

➤ *Gopher, WAIS, Archie*   Even before the Web, people realized that it was difficult to find documents by accessing one computer at a time and looking at file names using ftp. To solve that problem, facilities for storing and indexing documents were created with programs such as Gopher, WAIS, Archie, and others.

Users did keyword searches to find documents of interest, then followed a sort of link to the site and got the document. Since the inception of the Web, however, with its tools that organize and search for documents much more effectively, facilities such as Gopher, WAIS, and Archie are becoming obsolete.

Besides the services mentioned in the preceding list, there were also a variety of commands that were used with the Internet. For example, commands that can be run between two computers include telnet and rlogin (for remote login), rcp (for remote file copy), and rsh (to run commands remotely). These commands are used primarily between trusted computers on UNIX and Linux systems.

Today's Internet Uses

In the United States, it's practically impossible to find a major corporation, educational institution, or government agency that doesn't have a presence on the Web. From these organizations' Web sites, there is a dizzying array of information, products, and services being offered.

As noted earlier, the Web browser is the primary tool for using the Internet. Products such as Microsoft Internet Explorer and Netscape Communicator have become full Internet access suites. Besides browsing, these products also contain tools for using email, participating in news groups, conferencing, creating Web pages, publishing Web content, and playing a variety of special content (such as video and audio).

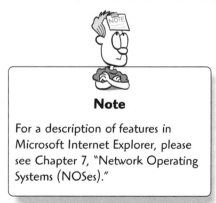

Note

For a description of features in Microsoft Internet Explorer, please see Chapter 7, "Network Operating Systems (NOSes)."

Although the space allotted here can't begin to cover all the resources available on the Internet, the paragraphs that follow describe several of the major uses of the Internet today. If you are about to make your first journey onto the Internet, know that you need a connection to the Internet, a PC, and a Web browser to start. Following are some of the things available to you on the Internet:

➤ *Shopping sites*   Many expect online shopping and other types of commerce to become one of the major uses of the Internet. Online shopping offers convenience (it's open 24 hours a day), easy price comparisons, detailed product descriptions, and sometimes links to reviews and other supporting information. Also, most anything you can think of can be purchased online—equipment, clothes, videos, food, automobiles, and so on.

Methods for carrying out secure transactions have become quite good. Enter a credit card number, mailing address, and a few other pieces of information, and your order can appear at your door within a few days.

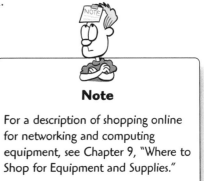

Note

For a description of shopping online for networking and computing equipment, see Chapter 9, "Where to Shop for Equipment and Supplies."

➤ *News and information*   All the major news services, newspapers, and other information media have Web sites where you can get the latest news, entertainment, and sports information. You can even tailor many of those sites to show you news on particular topics or regions of the country. Examples of these sites include `cnn.com`, `abc.com`, and `usatoday.com`.

➤ *Search engines*   Find information by searching the Web for sites containing certain keywords or sites that fall into specific categories. Search engine sites include `yahoo.com`, `lycos.com`, `excite.com`, `hotbot.com`, `altavista.com`, and several others.

➤ *Financial sites*   You can bank online, trade stocks, or apply for loans to name just a few of the financial services available on the Web. There are also tremendous (yet dangerous) resources for researching investment opportunities.

➤ *Education*   Most colleges, universities, and even K–12 schools have sites available on the Web. These sites can be resources for information about those institutions as well as a source for research information.

➤ *Entertainment*   Everything you might ever hope to know about movies, music, television, books, and other entertainment media can be found on the Web.

➤ *Gaming*   You can download games and play them against online competitors right from your PC. There are traditional board games (such as chess), card games (such as bridge), and monster-killing games (such as Quake II and Doom).

➤ *Sports*   Major sports organizations (NBA, NFL, and Major League Baseball) have Web sites with tons of articles, pictures, and statistics. There are also many sports news organizations and plain old sports fanatics with Web sites.

➤ *Travel*   There are hundreds of Web sites that can help you find the perfect vacation spot, scope out its accommodations and tourist spots, and sometimes even book the travel arrangements.

➤ *Chat rooms*   These sites enable you to type messages or talk online to strangers all over the world. Chats associated with certain topics of interest can actually be quite useful. Sometimes you can join chat rooms where you can ask questions of entertainers, athletes, or politicians. One warning: Chat rooms are also magnets to Internet weirdos, so be careful what you divulge about yourself, and to whom.

These are just some of the general resources available on the Internet. To look into more resources on your own, go to one of the search engines that enables you to step through categories of topics (such as the Yahoo.com site). Then just start clicking on topics that look interesting to you.

The following figure shows the Yahoo! home page (http://www.yahoo.com).

Find Internet resources from Yahoo! and other search sites.

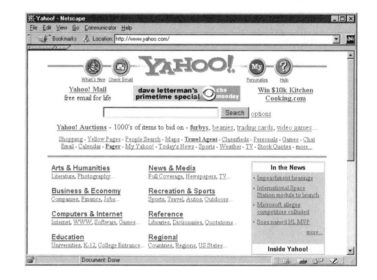

You might notice that the topics discussed here regarding the Internet are mostly those relating to organizations that want to make their resources available to the general public. By contrast, intranets and extranets are networks that want to limit network access to people within an organization, or to those who work closely with an organization.

Intranets

Most companies can't expect to hook employees up to the Internet and have the companies' networking needs met; at the same time, however, Web browsers and Internet protocols can be great tools for a company's network. Someone creating a network for a private company needs to consider the following:

➤ Security measures are needed to protect company information, such as financial data and strategic planning information.

➤ For employees to get their jobs done, companies need to have the capability to manage and protect the performance and reliability of their networks.

An intranet is one way of allowing network connectivity with a company, at the same time protecting those resources from the outside world. In general, an intranet is a private network that uses the same components that are used to create and run the Internet.

With an intranet, a company can build its network using well-known, well-tested Internet protocols and tools. Employees don't need special knowledge to set up or use the network. Information can be shared using common applications, with a Web browser typically acting as the centerpiece of the user interface.

Besides being relatively easy to implement, intranets can also be more cost-effective than proprietary networks. An intranet's use of standard protocols enables you to choose from a variety of network hardware and software vendors. Almost all off-the-shelf network applications for collaborating and accessing databases work using TCP/IP (Internet) protocols. If a company is just creating a company intranet, chances are it already has in-house expertise and resources from Web content already created for the company.

Security for Intranets

With an intranet, a company can manage network resources and determine the level of security with which it is comfortable. In many cases, this means secure local area networks and wide area networks connected to the outside world in a limited fashion through mechanisms known as firewalls.

Likewise, firewalls can also be used within the company intranet. For example, you might want to allow the engineering and human resources departments to have access to some company databases, but not allow the departments to access each other's LAN.

If more stringent security measures are required within the intranet, a variety of encryption techniques are available to keep particularly sensitive information from any but the intended parties. Basic levels of security can be enforced using standard password protection— maintaining users' rights to protect their own files and server policies—to restrict access to services to particular users.

Intranet Uses

Using an intranet, relevant and timely company data can be distributed to employees quickly and efficiently. The network can also serve as a means for collaboration on projects. The following are some ways of effectively using an intranet within a company:

➤ *Employee services*   Intranets can be used for online company phone directories, bulletin boards, company policy documents, and information on corporate locations and internal services.

➤ *Conferencing*   Intranets can offer software that supports video conferencing, audio conferencing, online chats, whiteboards, and application sharing. These features can be used together so that employees at different locations can hear and see the same information.

➤ *Project management tools*   Scheduling tools, workflow software, project timelines and a variety of other tools that chart the productivity of a project can be shared on an intranet.

➤ *Libraries*   Online libraries can be maintained so that documents that are relevant to engineers, marketers, sales, and management are easily accessible within the intranet.

➤ *Databases*   Databases of sales data, financial information, inventory, and various kinds of analysis can be selectively made available to employees on the intranet.

➤ *Web pages*   Instead of just sending memos, employees can publish appropriate information on Web pages (HTML format). This might include technical discussions of a project, company activities, or just something personal about the employee.

Anything that can be done on the Internet can also be done on a company intranet. It is up to each company to implement the policies to decide how the intranet is to be used and to allocate the computing and network resources to support those policies.

Check This Out

For information on choosing services and otherwise planning a corporate intranet, visit the Netscape Intranet Deployment Guide at `http://cgi.netscape.com/missioncontrol/idgindex.html`.

Extranets

An extranet extends the concept of intranets outside of a single company. With an extranet, the company network is extended to other companies, agencies, or individuals that need to collaborate with the company on an on-going basis.

One factor that typically characterizes an extranet is the way in which the extranet extends the company intranet. This means that those who are connecting from outside the intranet are usually doing so over a public network (in particular, the Internet). Although this can result in some performance hits, it can be a cost-effective solution because inexpensive Internet connections are widely available.

What the extranet does require, however, are some special security considerations. To ensure that corporate computing assets are safe, off-site users typically use such techniques as encryption or tunneling to keep their communications secure.

In general, extranets are thought of as more permanent than virtual private networks (see Chapter 16 for a description of VPNs). They are also less expensive than creating and maintaining leased lines.

A major drawback of extranets is that the performance of the network is out of the hands of the local company. For that reason, applications that require real-time response, such as banking and airline reservation applications, might not get the performance they need by communicating over the Internet.

Extranet Uses

For many applications, an Internet connection from a high-speed modem is quite acceptable. These are applications that, in a pinch, can wait a few extra seconds for a response. The following are some items a company might want to offer its partners on an extranet but not make available to the general public:

➤ Wholesale pricing lists

➤ Project plans and milestones

➤ Inventory availability information

➤ Special partner/dealer programs, including discounts, sales incentives, and promotions

➤ Company internal contact information

➤ Product specifications

➤ Marketing reports and studies

➤ Product support literature, including technical support databases

Building Security into an Extranet

Because important company assets are being exposed outside the boundaries of the corporate intranet, special attention needs to be paid to security issues. That attention will be focused on making sure that

➤ Remote users are who they say they are.

➤ Connections between the remote users and the intranet are secure.

➤ The scope of the information and resources available to the remote user are limited.

To verify the identity of a remote user, the first line of defense is still a user name and password. When a more rigorous identification is necessary, digital certificates can be required. A digital certificate more stringently establishes the identity of the user. A digital certificate can also satisfy the second item by enabling the two parties in the communication to establish an encrypted communication session.

Establishing certificates was once an expensive and complicated job. Now there are ways for a company to be its own *certificate authority* (*CA*) and issue digital certificates.

When it comes to the third item, a company can use the same measures to secure its resources against unauthorized access from its extranet partners as it does against unauthorized access from employees within the company. Access to secure LANs can be blocked using firewalls and password protection can be used to protect sensitive data.

As with access to resources by employees within an intranet, a company needs to set up security standards and performance requirements for its extranet. By doing this properly, a company can provide the information its partners need in a timely manner and still protect other computing resources.

Where To From Here?

After reading this chapter, you understand how the Internet, intranets, and extranets are used. In particular, you understand the types of resources best suited to each type of network and different security considerations associated with each network type.

To refresh your memory on topics related to the Internet, intranets, and extranets, you can refer to the discussion of virtual private networks in Chapter 16. Or, to review more basic issues relating to computer networks, refer to Chapter 2, "Why do You Need a Network?"

The Least You Need to Know

Right now, the least you need to know about the Internet, intranets, and extranets is this:

➤ All three types of networks are based on TCP/IP protocols and naming conventions.

➤ The domain name system (DNS) and IP addresses are used to identify host computers and other network resources in each of the network types.

➤ The World Wide Web made the Internet accessible to the general population.

➤ Some legacy Internet applications, such as email and newsgroups, are still popular today. Older document search and storage methods, such as Gopher, Archie, and WAIS, are becoming obsolete.

➤ The uses of the Internet are too numerous to describe; some popular uses include online shopping, online gaming, Internet searching, news access, and online chats.

➤ Intranets are closed networks that use the same protocols and addressing style used by the Internet.

➤ Extranets are networks that are maintained by a company, but extend beyond the physical boundaries of the private network so partners and suppliers can access some level of information from that network.

## Chapter 18

Email

In This Chapter

➤ Learn what to expect from an email program.

➤ Find out what features are included with popular email programs such as Netscape Messenger, Microsoft Outlook Express, and Qualcomm Eudora Light.

➤ Work with email addressing and attachments.

➤ Understand email protocols, such as POP3, IMAP4, and SMTP.

Electronic mail (*email*) is a quick and easy way to send a message to just one person, or to hundreds of people simultaneously. In most cases, the message arrives at the person's mail server within minutes, ready to be read. Since the first computer networks were created, email has been—and continues to be—one of the most important uses for computer networks.

In this chapter, you will learn how to use popular email programs to send, receive, and manage your email messages. The chapter will also tell you something about how electronic mail works. In particular, it describes the transfer protocols needed to carry a message across computer networks.

Email Basics

In its most basic form, an email message consists of some plain text and an address. The address identifies the recipient in a form that is recognizable by the network that forwards the mail to the recipient.

The first email messages were created with simple text editors (such as the UNIX `ed` or `vi` commands) and could be read on dumb character terminals (in other words, no fancy graphics or colors). Although mail messages can still be just as simple, today's programs for composing and reading mail offer a lot more features. Following are some examples:

➤ *HTML format*   The latest email programs enable you to create email messages in either plain text or HTML formats. By allowing HTML, you can add images, color, font changes, and text formatting. You can even include an entire Web page in a mail message.

➤ *Attachments*   Any type of computer file can be attached to an email message. When an attachment arrives with the message, the recipient can choose to save the attachment or open it in a program that is designed to play or display the file.

➤ *Address book*   Most email programs come with a way of storing the names and email addresses of the people you send mail to. You can also gather names together into an email group so you can send a message to a group of people at once. Some address books also enable you to store other information about each person, such as their address, job title, phone/fax numbers, and Web page location.

➤ *Mail download*   When the computing world was mostly mainframes, mail was usually stored on the same computer where you did your work. However, with more people working on PCs, to receive email the user often sends outgoing messages and downloads incoming messages by connecting to a mail server. Many mail readers use the *Post Office Protocol* (*POP3*) or *Internet Message Access Protocol* (*IMAP4*) to get messages from the mail server.

➤ *Multiple email accounts*   Some people have several email accounts (possibly one work and one personal account). Some mail programs enable you to query several mail servers for your email.

➤ *Managing messages*   Some people get so much email that managing the messages they receive is a big issue. Most mail programs offer a way to save messages to your hard disk or sort them to special mail folders you create. Within folders, there are also ways to sort messages by subject, time/date received, and sender.

➤ *Managing newsgroups*   Because newsgroups really just consist of a bunch of email messages grouped together, many mail message programs offer a way of reading and working with newsgroups as well as email. Some special features (such as allowing threads that follow the responses to a particular message) are included to be used for working with newsgroups.

When you go to choose your own mail message program, consider some of these special features to distinguish between the different programs offered. Because most mail readers today are either free or available on a trial basis, you might as well try out a few.

Choosing an Email Program

If you have an Internet browser on your computer, chances are an email program came with it. Netscape Communicator and Microsoft Internet Explorer each have email programs that work quite well (Netscape Messenger and Outlook Express, respectively). A popular email program that you can add on is the Eudora Light email reader, a free version of Qualcomm's Eudora Pro email program.

Netscape Messenger

With Netscape Messenger, you can read, send, and manage your email using the Messenger Mailbox window. If you have Netscape Communicator installed, you can open the Messenger Mailbox by clicking Mailbox on the Netscape component bar or by selecting Communicator | Messenger Mailbox from the Navigator window.

The following figure shows an example of the Netscape Messenger Mailbox window.

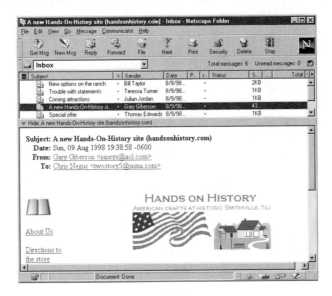

Read, send, and manage mail messages with Netscape Messenger.

Mail messages that have been received appear in the upper part of the Messenger Mailbox window. Select one of the messages and the contents of the message appear in the lower window. You can sort the messages by Subject, Sender, Date, Priority, Status, or Size by clicking on the heading above the column.

Check This Out

Notice that the message shown in the preceding figure contains an HTML page. Instead of just black on white text, the message contains colors, different fonts, and several images.

Following are some of the things you can do with Netscape Messenger:

➤ To download your messages from the mail server, click the Get Msg button.

➤ To create a new mail message, click the New Msg button. From the Composition window that appears, add the recipient's address, the subject of the message, and text. You can also add attachments and change the fonts. When the message is complete, click Send.

➤ To reply to a message, click the message and then click the Reply button. Then select either Reply to Sender or Reply to Sender and All Recipients. A Composition window appears with the recipient and subject filled in, and the message you're replying to included in the text pane.

➤ To forward a message, click the message and then click the Forward button. A Composition window appears with the message you are forwarding added as an attachment.

While you are composing a message, there are a lot of features you can use. Click Address to choose recipients from the address book. Click Attach to attach a file to the message. Click Spelling to spell check your message. Click Security to find out how to add security features, such as passwords and certificates, to the message.

Microsoft Outlook Express

Outlook Express is a reduced-feature version of Microsoft's Outlook 98. Although Outlook 98 has some advanced features for collaborating with others and integrating with Microsoft Office, Outlook Express has a lot of the functions you might expect from a full-featured email program.

You can start Outlook Express from an icon in the task bar or by clicking Go | Mail from the Internet Explorer window. The following figure shows an example of the Outlook Express window.

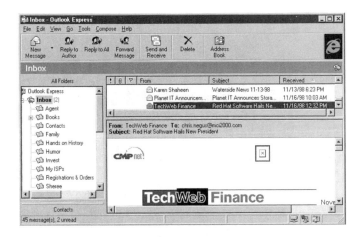

Outlook express adds mail services to the Internet Explorer suite.

The layout and buttons on the Outlook Express window are similar to the Netscape Messenger Mailbox window. Mail messages are listed in the upper pane and the current message contents appear in the lower pane. Mail folders are shown along the left column.

If you are accustomed to managing folders in the Windows Explorer window, you might notice that the layout of mail folders in Outlook Express is the same. You can create folders and subfolders that can be used to sort your mail messages.

One of the best features of Outlook Express is the Mail Rules window. With mail rules, you can set what happens to different email messages when they are downloaded. Instead of having all incoming messages sent to your Inbox, messages can be moved, copied, or forwarded to different locations based on what is in the address or subject lines.

To add rules to the mail messages as they come into Outlook Express, select Tools | Message Rules | New. The Rule Editor appears, as shown in the following figure.

You can have each email that comes in checked for a particular message size, specific words in the subject line, people in any of the address lines, or a specific mail account name. If an incoming message matches your conditions, you can take the following actions:

➤ Move or copy the message to a specific folder.

➤ Delete the message.

➤ Forward the message to specific people.

➤ Reply with a specific email message, such as "I'm on vacation so don't bother me."

➤ Flag the message or highlight it with a color.

➤ Don't download the message from the server.

➤ Delete the message from the server.

Create rules to deal with incoming mail.

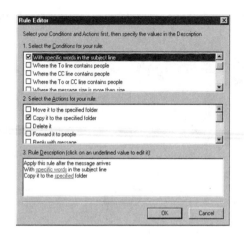

If you receive a lot of mail, you can save yourself hours of sorting and reading time using the mail rules feature. For example, if you get messages from a mailing list you can sort them to a folder that you can check later. If you have different mail accounts for work and home, those messages can go into different folders. If you have something to say to all or a few people who send you mail, you can respond to them automatically with a preset mail message.

The address book is another nice feature of Outlook Express. You can store names, email addresses, phone numbers, and other information for users with whom you want to communicate. You can also create user groups, so that by sending a message to that group you can automatically have it go to dozens or hundreds of users.

If you have multiple email accounts, you can have your messages from each account downloaded in turn when you download your mail. These accounts can exist on several different servers, as long as they are accessible from your network.

For creating new mail messages, Outlook has a stationery option that enables you to add a background to your messages. There are different motifs for birthdays, formal invitations, and holidays, to name a few. As with Netscape Messenger, you can also use HTML markup to add color, images and font changes to your messages.

Check This Out

Do you ever get a really long message in which you are looking for a specific piece of information? If so, do the following: Click in the message text, click on Edit | Find Text, type the word (or words) you are looking for in the Find box, then click Find Next. You then go right to the word you are looking for in the text.

Eudora Light

Eudora Light is the freeware email program from Qualcomm. Because Eudora has been around for a while, both Eudora Light and its commercial cousin Eudora Pro offer many features that make it compatible with older mail features. Eudora Light doesn't look as fancy as Outlook Express and Netscape Messenger, but it is extremely powerful and flexible.

The following figure shows an example of the Eudora Light window.

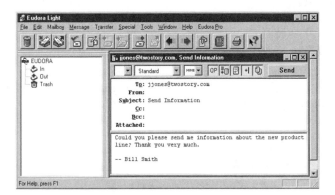

Eudora Light maintains support for legacy mail features.

The left side of the Eudora Light window shows the mail folders (In and Out, in this case). In the right frame, any features that are opened from buttons and toolbars appear. The right pane operates like a little desktop, allowing smaller windows within that area to be moved and resized.

Because of its support for legacy mail features, Eudora is a good mail program to use in a diverse corporate environment. For example, besides creating attachments in MIME (the common Internet mail attachment format), you can also use BinHex (used with Macintosh) and Uuencode (used with older UNIX systems) for attaching mail.

If you want to make changes throughout the mail message you just typed, there is a feature called Message Plug-in that enables you to do some interesting things. After you have typed a mail message, click Edit | Message Plug-ins, then select one of the following:

➤ *Sort*   Alphabetically sorts the lines in the message

➤ *Unwrap Text*   Joins the lines of text together into paragraphs

➤ *Upper Case*   Changes all text to uppercase

➤ *Lower Case*   Changes all text to lowercase

➤ *Toggle Case*   Changes upper- to lower- and lower- to uppercase

➤ *The Word Case*   Changes the case for the selected word

➤ *Sentence Case*   Begins sentences with uppercase

You can also add other plug-ins to Eudora Light that enable you to manipulate the content of the messages in different ways. If you have trouble with any of the features, Eudora Light comes with context-sensitive help. Just click on the question mark, then click on the button or window with which you need help. A pop-up box shows you a description of the item.

Understanding Email Addressing

Different kinds of networks use different forms of email addressing. Before the Internet became so pervasive, it was more of an issue than it is today. Now, most mail servers use domain-style addressing. There are, however, still some networks that use UUCP-style addressing. Both styles are described in the following section.

Domain-Style Email Addresses

By far, most email addresses today use domain-style addressing. This method assumes an address structure based on TCP/IP domains (which are used with the Internet). The form is a user name, followed by an at sign (@), followed by the domain name. For example:

```
jjones@twostory.com
```

This address directs mail to the user named `jjones` at the domain `twostory.com`. Mail can also be directed to a particular subdomain or host within the domain. For example, to send mail to the same user on a computer named `jumbo` in the same domain, you can use the following address:

    jjones@jumbo.twostory.com

If you are sending email to someone within your own domain (or subdomain), you can sometimes get away with only using the user name. So, in this case you can just type the name:

    jjones

This results in the mail being sent to `jjones` in the local domain.

UUCP-Style Email Addresses

Some of the earliest computer networking applications relied on UUCP-based networks to carry their messages. UUCP stands for UNIX-to-UNIX Copy, named after the uucp command that was used to copy files between UNIX systems.

Note

To learn more about the domain name system (DNS) and addressing, please see Chapter 17, "The Internet, Intranets, and Extranets."

Because most of the first UUCP networks relied on telephone lines to transmit messages rather than wide area networks that were always active, a store-and-forward type of addressing was used. In the email address, include the path needed to forward the email through each computer along the way.

In UUCP-style addressing, the user name is on the right and the hosts through which the message is routed appear to the left. Host and user names are separated by exclamation points. For example:

    comp1!comp2!comp3!jjones

This address tells your computer to forward the message to `comp1`, which in turn forwards it to `comp2`, then from `comp2` to `comp3`. On `comp3`, the message is placed in the mailbox of `jjones`.

The disadvantage of UUCP-style is that there is no automatic routing as there is with domain-style addressing. Computers had no sense of a structure of computers on the network; each computer sent the message to the next one over, and then lost track of whether or not the message actually made it to the final destination. Also, if one host was down along the way, an email message had to wait in a queue until the host came up again.

UUCP-style addressing was useful at the time because most messages were sent in batch mode. This means that a computer stored up a whole bunch of outgoing messages before it made the telephone call to the next computer. Sending messages in bunches made each call more cost effective.

Adding Mail Attachments

Using attachments, you can send many different kinds of information along with a mail message. For example, if you have a WordPerfect word processing file, a sound file, a video, or a graphics file, you can attach it to your mail message without it actually appearing in the text of the message.

While you are composing a mail message, look for a button marked Attach, or one that is represented by a paper clip. Click on that button, and then browse for or type the location of the file you want to include with your message.

When you receive a mail message with an attachment, a paper clip usually appears alongside the message title and within the message frame. Click on the paper clip, then select the attachment (there might be more than one). You are usually then asked either to save the message to a file or open it with a program.

Check This Out

Some mail programs, such as Netscape Messenger, enable you to attach the contents of a Web page to your email. You do this by entering the URL of the Web page.

Windows systems keeps a list of data types and applications that can run those data types. For example, it knows that a Web browser can open an HTML file and that a WAVE file plays in an audio player. The system can know the type of file it is by its file extension (such as .htm or .wav) or by its MIME type.

MIME stands for *Multipart Internet Mail Extensions*. It is a protocol designed specifically to handle file attachments used on the Internet. A MIME type consists of a category (such as audio, video, image, and so on) and a specific type within that category (such as bmp for bitmap or mov for a Quicktime movie.) Here are some examples:

Bitmap Graphics File	image/bmp
Adobe Acrobat Document	application/pdf
Intel Iphone Compatible	application/x-iphone

Most attachments are sent using MIME protocol. However, some mailers still support other encoding methods—such as BinHex and Uuencode—for managing attachments. See the following sidebar for information on BinHex and Uuencode.

Attachments with BinHex or Uuencode

Email programs that have been around for a while probably enable you to create attachments using either the BinHex or Uuencode protocols. BinHex was the first attachment style supported by Eudora. Some Macintosh mail programs still use BinHex for attachments.

Uuencode was originally used with UNIX systems to include attachments in mail messages. In UNIX, you can run an actual uuencode command on the file you want to send as an attachment. The output is an encrypted text file that can simply be pasted into a mail message. A user receiving the message can simply run the uudecode command on the attachment and the output is the attached file in its original form.

Email Protocols

Protocols are sets of rules that are used for exchanging information between two entities. There are protocols defined for transmitting email across networks that make the practice of sending and receiving mail almost invisible to end users.

The protocols used to transmit email messages across the Internet (or other networks) are referred to as *message transfer agents* (MTAs). An MTA makes sure that an email message gets from one mail server (the sender's) to another (the receiver's). *Simple Mail Transfer Protocol* (SMTP) is the protocol most often used to transfer mail across the Internet.

Not every computer is set up as a mail server. Because millions of users need to read and send mail from personal computers that are not always connected to the Internet, there are protocols that allow those PCs to download and upload mail messages from a mail server. Popular protocols for doing that are POP3 and IMAP4.

The following figure illustrates how email is transferred between mail servers and users. Here are the basic steps that go into sending and receiving email:

1. A person creates an email message (using Netscape Messenger or Eudora), and then sends the message.
2. A connection is established to the sender's mail server, possibly by dialing up an Internet service provider.
3. Using a mail drop protocol (such as POP3 or IMAP4), the email is sent to the sender's mail server.

4. The sender's mail server packages the mail message and sends it across the net-work (such as the Internet) to the recipient's mail server. This is done using a mail transfer protocol such as SMTP.

5. The mail stays in the recipient's mailbox on the server until the mail recipient calls into the mail server and requests that any messages for that recipient be downloaded.

6. Using a mail drop protocol (such as POP3 or IMAP4) the email is downloaded to the recipient, where that person can read it using a mail reader (such as Netscape Messenger or Eudora).

Mail is transferred between mail servers, and then downloaded to users.

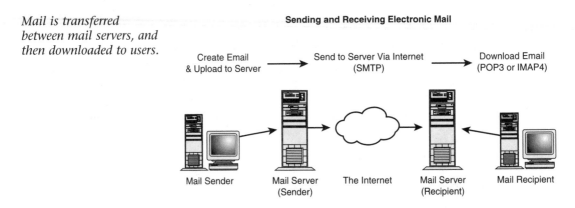

Sending and Receiving Electronic Mail

Create Email & Upload to Server → Send to Server Via Internet (SMTP) → Download Email (POP3 or IMAP4)

Mail Sender   Mail Server (Sender)   The Internet   Mail Server (Recipient)   Mail Recipient

Protocols for Downloading Email

If your computer is not a mail server—and most PCs are not—rules are needed to define how you can get the email that is being held for you on a mail server. Two protocols that are used to download messages are POP3 and IMAP4.

POP3 and IMAP4 do essentially the same thing: Authenticate the identity of a user and enable the user to pick up mail messages. Of the two protocols, POP3 is perhaps used more often whereas IMAP4 contains more features.

When you add an Internet account to your computer you might have already set up the information needed to connect to a POP3 or IMAP4 server. For example, if you are using Netscape Messenger you can check information about your mail server by doing the following:

1. From the Netscape Messenger window, click on Edit | Preferences. The Mail and Groups Preferences window appears.

2. Click on Mail Server. Information about your mail server appears, including the following:

   ➤ *Mail server user name*   The user name associated with the mailbox.

   ➤ *Outgoing mail (SMTP) server*   The name of the mail server that transfers outgoing mail to the intended recipients. This server must use an SMTP protocol.

➤ *Incoming mail server*   The name of the mail server that stores your incoming mail. This server must use POP3 or IMAP4 protocols.

➤ *Mail server type*   Choose either POP3 or IMAP4 as the incoming mail server type.

The options available for POP3 and IMAP4 servers illustrate some of the differences between the two types of servers. POP3 doesn't allow much management of the email on the server; basically, all you can do is indicate that you do not want messages to be deleted from the server after they are retrieved.

Check This Out

The option of disabling the capability to delete messages from a server after you download them is a valuable feature for people who read email from different locations. For example, you can use this option from home when you check your work email. That way, the next time you download your mail from work the messages can be permanently stored on your work PC.

The IMAP4 options in Netscape Messenger show how you can manage email messages on the server. You can set new folders for offline download, move deleted messages into a Trash folder, and use an encrypted SSL connection to communicate with the server. You can also set the locations of your local mail directory and your IMAP server directory.

When it comes to which protocol to use, as a mail recipient you probably have to use the type of protocol that is supported by your mail server. You can contact the mail server's system administrator to find out that information.

Techno Talk

If you are interested in more technical details about how POP3 and IMAP4 work, you can check out the Request for Comments (RFCs) associated with each. For POP3, see STD 53 (RFC 1725); for IMAP4, see RFC 1730.

Simple Mail Transfer Protocol

Originally, Simple Mail Transfer Protocol was designed to send simple text messages from one mail server to another over a network. Despite the fact that both the volume of mail and complexity of the Internet have increased dramatically since SMTP was created, it is still the predominant protocol for sending email messages over the Internet.

The first definition of SMTP is detailed in RFC 821: Simple Mail Transfer Protocol. Details and suggestions for implementing SMTP are contained in RFC 1123: Requirements for Internet Hosts—Application and Support. Because SMTP as it was first defined was too simple to handle the demands of today's more complex email, several extensions have been added:

➤ *RFC 1651 and 1652: Multipurpose Internet Mail Extensions (MIME)*   These RFCs describe how different types of data can be included in email messages.

➤ *RFC 1651: SMTP Service Extensions*   This RFC describes how special services can be requested between SMTP senders and receivers.

The steps that an SMTP server goes through to send a message to another SMTP server on the network are basically as follows:

1. A local user forwards a message to the SMTP server to be delivered.
2. The SMTP server checks the recipient's address and contacts the recipient's mail server.
3. The SMTP server requests a certain level of service from the recipient's server.
4. If the level of service is acceptable, the SMTP server tells the recipient's server the recipients for which it has mail.
5. For each user that is acceptable, the SMTP server sends the mail messages it has.
6. When the transmission is complete, the SMTP server can ask to send more messages, ask if the remote server has any messages for the SMTP server, or quit.

It's interesting how the SMTP server requests the level of service it needs. Remember that the first SMTP servers only supported plain text messages. Now if a server has a message that requires extensions (such as a message that includes a MIME-encrypted audio file or image), it needs a way to make a request for those extensions.

Originally, when the SMTP sender connected to the remote server, it sent a HELO message. Now, a HELO message implies that the sender has a plain text message to send (with no extensions). If it has a message with extensions, it sends an EHLO message. If the remote side can support the extensions, it responds with a 250 OK message and sends a list of supported extensions. If the remote either rejects or fails to recognize the EHLO request, the sending SMTP server can either quit or send messages without extensions.

One of the most popular implementations of SMTP is the UNIX system `sendmail` command. Although `sendmail` can require setting up some fairly difficult configuration files, it can support a wide variety of mail interfaces (such as DEC-Mail and X.400 gateway features).

Where To From Here?

After reading this chapter, you have completed the main sections of this book. Congratulations! You now have a good enough foundation of networking knowledge to enable you to delve more deeply into those aspects of computer networking that interest you.

At this point, you can check out the glossary of terms that is included at the end of this book. Or, for technical information about networking interfaces and protocols, check out some of the Request for Comments (RFCs) that interest you. You can find RFCs on the Internet at the RFC Editor site (http://www.rfc-editor.org) or a variety of other Web sites.

The Least You Need to Know

Right now, the least you need to know about what you can do with email is this:

➤ Understand some of the features that are included with popular email programs, such as adding attachments, using an address book, creating HTML messages, and managing mail messages.

➤ Know several popular email programs and some of their most important features. These programs include Netscape Messenger, Microsoft Outlook Express, and Eudora Light.

➤ Use different types of email addresses. These include domain-style addressing (most often used with the Internet) and UUCP-style addressing (used with older UNIX systems).

➤ Understand how MIME types are used to add attachments to email messages that can be stored or played (or displayed) by the email recipient. You also know about other methods of encrypting attachments, such as BinHex (used by Macintosh systems) and Uuencode (used by older UNIX systems).

➤ Understand protocols that are used to download email messages from mail servers to dial-up users. The most popular of these mail drop types of protocols are Post Office Protocol and Internet Message Access Protocol.

➤ Understand how SMTP is used to transfer email messages across the Internet to other mail servers so that remote recipients can access their messages.

Part 6
Appendix

In case you haven't had enough networking words yet, we stuck this appendix at the back of the book. It's a glossary of networking terms. Following each networking word are a few more words describing what the word means. After all, that's what a glossary is.

Speak Like a Geek: The Networking Bible

1000Base-CX   Extremely fast (1000Mbps) Ethernet, typically strung via copper wire and capable of transmitting a distance of some 75 feet.

1000Base-LX   Extremely fast (1000Mbps) Ethernet, typically strung via fiber optic cable, and capable of transmitting a distance of some 9000 feet.

1000Base-SX   Extremely fast (1000Mbps) Ethernet, typically strung via fiber cable and capable of transmitting a distance of some 1500 feet.

1000Base-TX   Extremely fast (1000Mbps) Ethernet, typically strung via copper wire and capable of transmitting a distance of some 330 feet.

100Base-FX   Fast (100Mbps) Ethernet, typically strung via fiber-optic cable and capable of transmitting a distance of some 412 meters.

100BaseT   Fast (100Mbps) Ethernet, supporting various cabling schemes and capable of transmitting a distance of some 205 meters.

10BaseT   Twisted Pair Ethernet capable of transmitting to distances of 328 feet.

10Base2   Coaxial (thinwire) Ethernet capable of transmitting to distances of 600 feet.

10Base5   Coaxial (thickwire) Ethernet that by default transports data to distances of 1500 feet.

802.2   An Ethernet frame format (probably the most common) typically used in local area networks.

AARP   *See* AppleTalk Address Resolution Protocol

AAUI   Apple AUI. Apple Computer's version of the Attachment Unit Interface. *See also* AUI.

acceptable use policy (AUP)   Originally established by the National Science Foundation, AUP once forbade use of the Internet for commercial purposes. Today, AUP refers to rules a user must adhere to when using an ISP's services.

access control   Any tool or technique that allows you to selectively grant or deny users access to system resources.

access control list (ACL)   A list that stores information on users and what system resources they're allowed to access.

ACL   *See* access control list.

active hub   The main hub in a network. A hardware device that repeats and re-propagates signals.

adapter   A hardware device used to connect devices. In networking context, an Ethernet adapter/card.

adaptive routing   Routing designed to adapt to the current network load. Adaptive routing routes data around bottlenecks and congested network areas.

AIS   *See* automated information system.

analog system   This term is generally used to describe the telephone system, which uses analog technology to convert voice to electronic signals.

adaptive pulse code modulation   A method of encoding voice into digital format over communication lines.

Address Resolution Protocol (ARP)   Maps IP addresses to physical addresses.

administrator   Either a human being charged with controlling a network or the supervisory account in Windows NT. Whoever has administrator privileges in NT can—but need not necessarily—hold complete control over their network, workgroup, or domain.

ADSL   *See* Asymmetric Digital Subscriber Line.

ADSP   *See* AppleTalk Data Stream Protocol.

Advanced Server for Workgroups   An IBM GroupWare product featuring OS/2 and Lotus Notes.

AEP   *See* AppleTalk Echo Protocol.

AIM   *See* Ascend Inverse Multiplexing.

AIX   A flavor of Unix from International Business Machines (IBM). AIX runs on RISC workstations and the PowerPC.

American National Standards Institute   *See* ANSI.

Anonymous FTP   FTP service available to the public that allows anonymous logins. Anyone can access anonymous FTP with the user name anonymous and their email address as a password.

ANSI   The American National Standards Institute. Check them out at http://www.ansi/org.

answer-only modem   A modem that answers but cannot dial out. These are useful for preventing users from initiating calls from your system via out-dials.

applet   A small Java program that runs in a Web browser environment. Applets add graphics, animation, and dynamic text to otherwise lifeless Web pages.

AppleShare   Specialized Apple Computer software used to establish and maintain Macintosh file servers.

AppleTalk   Apple Computer's networking suite that supports Ethernet and Token Ring.

AppleTalk Address Resolution Protocol (AARP)   Apple's version of ARP, this protocol maps IP addresses to physical addresses.

AppleTalk Data Stream Protocol (ADSP)   Apple's peer-to-peer streamed communication protocol for transporting large amounts of data over a network.

AppleTalk Echo Protocol (AEP)   Apple's version of the Echo protocol, used to test the network by having a remote server echo back packets you send.

AppleTalk Remote Access Protocol (ARAP)   Enabling this protocol turns your Mac server into a remote access server, allowing others to access your network from remote locations.

application gateways   Firewall devices that disallow direct communication between the Internet and an internal, private network. Data flow is controlled by proxies that screen out undesirable information or hosts.

application layer   Layer 7 of the OSI reference model, the highest layer of the model. The application layer defines how applications interact over the network. This is the layer of communications that occurs (and is conspicuous) at the user level. (For example: File Transfer Protocol interfaces with the user at the application layer.)

ARAP   *See* AppleTalk Remote Access Protocol.

ARCnet   The Attached Resource Computer Network, a LAN system by Datapoint Corporation. It supports 255 workstations in a star topology at speeds of 2.5Mbps.

ARP   *See* Address Resolution Protocol.

ARPAnet   Advanced Research Projects Agency Network. This was the original Internet, which, for many years, was controlled by the Department of Defense.

Ascend Inverse Multiplexing (AIM)   Proprietary protocol created by Ascend Communications (router manufacturer) for managing multiplexers. To learn more, go to http://www.ascend.com.

ASCII   American Standard Code for Information Interchange, ASCII is a common standard by which all operating systems treat simple text.

Asymmetric Digital Subscriber Line (ADSL)   A high-speed, digital telephone technology with fast downloading (nearly 6MBps) but much slower uploading (about 65KBps). Unfortunately, ADSL is a new technology that is available only in major metropolitan areas.

asynchronous data transmission   The transmission of data one character at a time.

asynchronous PPP   Run-of-the-mill PPP; the kind generally used by PPP dial-up customers.

asynchronous transfer mode (ATM)   An ATM network is one type of circuit-switched packet network that can transfer information in standard blocks at high speed. These are not to be confused with automatic teller networks.

attachment unit interface (AUI)   A 15-pin twisted-pair Ethernet connection or connector.

attribute   The state of a given resource (whether file or directory), and whether that resource is readable, hidden, system, or other.

ATM   *See* Asynchronous transfer mode.

AUI   *See* attachment unit interface.

AUP   *See* acceptable use policy.

authenticate   When you authenticate a particular user or host, you are verifying their identity.

authentication   The process of authenticating either a user or host. Such authentication may be simple and applied at the application level (demanding a password), or may be complex (as in challenge-response dialogs between machines, which generally rely on algorithms or encryption at a discrete level of the system).

Authentication Server Protocol   A TCP-based authentication service that can verify the identity of a user. (Please see RFC 931.)

Automated Information System (AIS)   Any system (composed of hardware and software) that allows the maintenance, storage, and processing of information.

automounting   The practice of automatically mounting network drives at boot.

back door   A hidden program, left behind by an intruder (or perhaps a disgruntled employee), that allows them future access to a victim host. This term is synonymous with the more antiquated term *trap door*.

backbone   The fastest and most centralized feed on your network. The heart of your network to which all other systems are connected.

BackOffice   A networking suite from Microsoft that packages together database, mail, and network management.

back up   To preserve a file system or files, usually for disaster recovery. Generally, backup is done to tape, floppy disk, or other portable media that can be safely stored for later use.

bandwidth   The transmission capacity of your network medium, measured in bits per second.

baseband   Audio and video signals sent over coaxial cable, typically used in cable television transmissions.

bastion host   A server that is hardened against attack and can therefore be used outside the firewall as your "face to the world." These are often sacrificial.

biometric access controls   Systems that authenticate users by physical characteristics, such as their face, fingerprints, retinal pattern, or voice.

BNC   A coaxial cable or connection used in older Ethernet networks. (BNC connectors look exactly like cable television wire connectors.)

bottleneck   An area of your network that demonstrates sluggish transfer rates, usually due to network congestion or misconfiguration.

bootstrap protocol   A network protocol used for remote booting. (Diskless workstations often use a bootstrap protocol to contact a boot server. In response, the boot server sends boot commands.)

border gateway protocol   A protocol that facilitates communication between routers serving as gateways.

bridge   A network hardware device that connects local area networks together.

broadband   A very high-speed data transmission system, capable of supporting large transfers of media such as sound, video, and other data.

broadcast/broadcasting   Any network message sent to all network hosts, or the practice of sending such a message.

bug   A hole or weakness in a computer program. *See also* vulnerability.

cable modem A modem that negotiates Internet access over cable television networks. Cable modems provide blazing speeds.

call back Call-back systems ensure that a trusted host initiated the current connection. The host connects, a brief exchange is had, and the connection is cut. Then the server calls back the requesting host.

Carrier Sense Multiple Access with Collision Avoidance (CSMA/CA) A traffic-management technique used by Ethernet. In CSMA/CA, workstations announce to the network that they're about to transmit data.

Carrier Sense Multiple Access with Collision Detection (CSMA/CD) A traffic-management technique used by Ethernet. In CSMA/CD, workstations check the wire for traffic before transmitting data.

Cast-128 An encryption algorithm that uses large keys and can be incorporated into cryptographic applications. (You can learn more by obtaining RFC 2144.)

CA-Unicenter Powerful database and network-management software from Computer Associates. Typically used in very large, enterprise-based database serving, especially over wide area networks.

CERT *See* Computer Emergency Response Team.

certificate authority Trusted third-party clearing house that issues security certificates and ensures their authenticity. Probably the most renowned commercial certificate authority is VeriSign, which issues (among other things) certificates for Microsoft-compatible ActiveX components.

certification Either the end-result of a successful security evaluation of a product or system or an academic honor bestowed on those who successfully complete courses in network engineering (such as certification as a Novell Network Engineer).

CGI *See* common gateway interface.

Challenge Handshake Authentication Protocol (CHAP) Protocol (often used with PPP) that challenges users to verify their identity. If the challenge is properly met, the user is authenticated. If not, the user is denied access. See RFC 1344 for further information.

channel In networking, a communications path.

CHAP *See* Challenge Handshake Authentication Protocol.

circuit A connection that conducts electrical currents and, by doing so, transmits data.

client Software designed to interact with a specific server application. For example, WWW browsers like Netscape Communicator and Internet Explorer are WWW clients. They are specifically designed to interact with Web or HTTP servers.

client/server model   A programming model where a single server can distribute data to many clients (the relationship between a Web server and Web clients or browsers is a good example). Most network applications and protocols are based on the client/server model.

CNE   Certified NetWare Engineer.

common carrier   Any government-regulated utility that provides the public with communications (for example, a telephone company).

common gateway interface (CGI)   A standard that specifies programming techniques through which you pass data from Web servers to Web clients. CGI is language neutral. You can write CGI programs in PERL, C, C++, Python, Visual Basic, BASIC, and shell languages.

compression   The technique of reducing file size for the purposes of maximizing bandwidth. The smaller the file, the less bandwidth you need to send it.

COM Port   A serial communications port, sometimes used to connect modems (and even mice.)

Computer Emergency Response Team (CERT)   A security organization that assists victims of cracker attacks. Find them at `http://www.cert.org`.

copy access   When a user has copy access, it means that he or she has privileges to copy a particular file.

cracker   Someone who, with malicious intent, unlawfully breaches security of computer systems or software.

CSMA/CA   *See* Carrier Sense Multiple Access with Collision Avoidance.

CSMA/CD   *See* Carrier Sense Multiple Access with Collision Detection.

DAC   *See* discretionary access control.

Data Encryption Standard (DES)   Encryption standard from IBM, developed in 1974 and published in 1977. DES is the US government standard for encrypting non-classified data.

data link layer   Layer 2 of the OSI reference model. This layer defines the rules for sending and receiving information between systems.

datagram   A packet or "...a self-contained, independent entity of data carrying sufficient information to be routed from the source to the destination computer without reliance on earlier exchanges between this source and destination computer and the transporting network..." (RFC 1594).

DECnet   An antiquated, proprietary protocol from Digital Equipment Corporation that runs chiefly over proprietary, Ethernet, and X.25 networks.

309

DES   *See* Data Encryption Standard.

digest access authentication   A security extension for HTTP that provides only basic (and not encrypted) user authentication. To learn more, see RFC 2069.

digital certificate   Any digital value used in authentication. Digital certificates are typically numeric values, derived from cryptographic processes. (There are many values that can used as the basis of a digital certificate, including but not limited to biometric values, such as retinal scans.)

discretionary access control (DAC)   Provides means for a central authority on a computer system or network to either permit or deny access to all users, and do so incisively, based on time, date, file, directory, or host.

DNS   *See* domain name service.

DoD   Department of Defense.

domain name   A host name or machine name, such as gnss.com. This is the non-numeric expression of a host's address. Numeric expressions are always in "dot" format, like this: 207.171.0.111.

domain name service (DNS)   A networked system that translates numeric IP addresses (207.171.0.111) into Internet host names (traderights.pacificnet.net).

DoS   This refers to denial-of-service, a condition that results when a user maliciously renders an Internet information server inoperable, thereby denying computer service to legitimate users.

dual-homed gateway   Configuration or machine that supports two or more disparate protocols or means of network transport, and provides packet screening between them.

EFT   Electronic funds transfer.

encryption   The process of scrambling data so it is unreadable by unauthorized parties. In most encryption schemes, you must have a password to reassemble the data into readable form. Encryption is primarily used to enhance privacy or to protect classified, secret, or top-secret information. (For example, many military and satellite transmissions are encrypted to prevent spies or hostile nations from analyzing them.)

Ethernet   A local area network networking technology (originally developed by Xerox) that connects computers and transmits data between them. Data is packaged into frames and sent via wires.

Ethernet spoofing   Any procedure that involves assuming another host's Ethernet address to gain unauthorized access to the target.

exabyte   Approximately 1,000,000,000,000,000,000 bytes.

FDDI   *See* fiber optic data distribution interface.

Fiber-optic cable   An extremely fast network cable that transmits data using light rather than electricity. Most commonly used for backbones.

fiber optic data distribution interface (FDDI)   Fiber-optic cable that transfers data at 100mbps.

file server   A computer that serves as a centralized source for files.

File Transfer Protocol (FTP)   A protocol used to transfer files from one TCP/IP host to another.

filtering   The process of examining network packets for integrity and security. Filtering is typically an automated process, performed by either routers or software.

firewall   Loosely, any device that refuses unauthorized users access to a particular host. Less loosely, a device that examines each packet's source address. If that address is on an approved list, the packets gain entry. If not, they're rejected.

frame   *See* packet.

frame relay   Frame relay technology allows networks to transfer information in bursts. This is a cost-effective way of transferring data over networks because you pay for only the resources you use. (Unfortunately, you may also be sharing your frame relay connection with someone else. Standard frame relay connections run at 56Kbps.)

FTP   *See* File Transfer Protocol.

full duplex transmission   Any transmission in which data is transmitted in both directions simultaneously.

gateway   A point on a network where two (or more) network protocols are translated into other protocols. Typical examples of such translation include TCP/IP to basic Ethernet or even proprietary protocols.

General Switch Management Protocol (GSMP)   A protocol by Ipsilon that controls ATM switches and their ports.

gigabit   Approximately 1,000,000,000 bits.

GOPHER   The Internet Gopher Protocol, a protocol for distributing documents over the Net. GOPHER preceded the World Wide Web as an information retrieval tool. (See RFC 1436 for more information.)

granularity   The degree to which you can incisively apply access controls. The more incisively a system allows controls to be set, the more granularity that system has.

group   A value denoting a collection of users. This value is used in network file permissions. All users belonging to this or that group share similar access privileges.

GroupWare   Application programs that are designed to make full use of a network, and often promote collaborative work.

GSMP   *See* General Switch Management Protocol.

hacker   Someone interested in operating systems, software, security, and the Internet, generally. Also called a *programmer*.

hardware address   The fixed physical address of a network adapter and, hence, the machine on which it was installed. Hardware addresses are sometimes hard-coded into the network adapter.

hole   *See* vulnerability.

host   A computer with a permanent hardware address, especially on a TCP/IP network.

host table   Any record of matching hostnames and network addresses. These tables are used to identify the name and location of each host on your network. Such tables are consulted before data is transmitted. (Think of a host table as a personal address book of machine addresses.)

HP-UX   A flavor of UNIX from Hewlett Packard.

HTTP   *See* hypertext transfer protocol.

hypertext   A text display format commonly used on Web pages. Hypertext is distinct from regular text because it's interactive. In a hypertext document, when you click or choose any highlighted word, other associated text appears. This allows powerful cross-referencing, and permits users to navigate a document.

hypertext transfer protocol (HTTP)   The protocol used to traffic hypertext across the Internet, and the underlying protocol of the WWW.

IDEA   *See* International Data Encryption Algorithm.

International Data Encryption Algorithm (IDEA)   IDEA is a powerful block-cipher encryption algorithm that operates with a 128-bit key. IDEA encrypts data faster than DES and is far more secure.

IDENT   *See* Identification Protocol.

Identification Protocol (IDENT)   A TCP-based protocol for identifying users. IDENT is a more modern, advanced version of the Authentication Protocol. You can find out more by obtaining RFC 1413.

IGMP   *See* Internet Group Management Protocol.

IMAP3   *See* Interactive Mail Access Protocol.

InPerson   A GroupWare product from Silicon Graphics.

Integrated Services Digital Network (ISDN)   Digital telephone service that offers data transfer rates upward of 128Kbps.

Interactive Mail Access Protocol (IMAP3)   A protocol that allows workstations to access Internet electronic mail from centralized servers. (See RFC 1176 for further information.)

Internet   In general, the conglomeration of computer networks now connected to the international switched packet telephone system that support TCP/IP. Less generally, any computer network that supports TCP/IP and is interconnected.

Internet Group Management Protocol (IGMP)   A protocol that controls broadcasts to multiple users.

Internet Protocol (IP)   The chief method of transporting data across the Internet.

Internet Protocol security option   IP security option, used to protect IP datagrams, according to U.S. classifications, whether unclassified, classified secret, or top secret. (See RFC 1038 and RFC 1108.)

Internet Worm   Also called the Morris Worm, a program that attacked the Internet in November 1988. To get a Worm overview, check out RFC 1135.

Internetworking   The practice of using networks that run standard Internet protocols.

InterNIC   The Network Information Center located at www.internic.net.

intrusion detection   The practice of using automated systems to detect intrusion attempts. Intrusion detection typically involves intelligent systems or agents.

IP   *See* Internet Protocol.

IP Address   Numeric Internet address, such as 207.171.0.111.

IP spoofing   Any procedure where an attacker assumes another host's IP address to gain unauthorized access to the target.

IPX   Internetwork Packet eXchange. A proprietary data transport protocol from Novell, Inc. that loosely resembles Internet Protocol.

IRIX   A flavor of UNIX from Silicon Graphics.

ISDN   *See* Integrated Services Digital Network.

ISO   International Standards Organization.

ISP   Internet service provider.

Java   A network programming language created by Sun Microsystems that marginally resembles C++. Java is object oriented, and is often used to generate graphics and multimedia applications, though it's most well known for its networking power.

JavaScript   A programming language developed by Netscape Communications Corporation. JavaScript runs in and manipulates Web browser environments, particularly Netscape Navigator and Communicator (but also Internet Explorer).

Kerberos   An encryption and authentication system developed at the Massachusetts Institute of Technology. Kerberos is used in network applications, and relies on trusted third-party servers for authentication.

Kerberos Network Authentication Service   Third-party, ticket-based authentication scheme that can be easily integrated into network applications. See RFC 1510 for details.

LAN   *See* local area network.

Line Printer Daemon Protocol (LPDP)   A protocol used to facilitate remote printing. (See RFC 1179 for more information.)

Linux   A free UNIX clone that runs on widely disparate architecture, including X86 (Intel), Alpha, Sparc, and PowerPC processors. Linux is becoming increasingly popular as a Web server platform.

LISTSERV   Listserv Distribute Protocol, a protocol used to deliver mass email. (See RFC 1429 for further information.)

local area network (LAN)   LANs are small, Ethernet-base networks.

Lotus Notes   A GroupWare product from Lotus.

LPDP   *See* Line Printer Daemon Protocol.

maximum transmission unit (MTU)   A value that denotes the largest packet that can be transmitted. (Many people adjust this value and often get better performance by either increasing or decreasing it.)

megabyte   Approximately 1,000,000 bytes. Abbreviated as MB.

Microsoft Exchange   A GroupWare product from Microsoft Corporation.

modem   A device that converts signals that the computer understands into signals that can be accurately transmitted over phone lines or other media, and that can convert the signals back into their original form.

Morris Worm   *See* Internet Worm.

MTU *See* maximum transmission unit.

NE2000 A standard by which network interface cards are judged. Most cards use this standard.

NetBIOS Protocol A high-speed, lightweight transport protocol commonly used in local area networks, particularly those running LAN Manager.

netstat UNIX command (also available in Windows) that shows the current TCP/IP connections and the their source addresses.

NetWare A popular network operating system from Novell, Inc.

network file system (NFS) A system that allows you to transparently import files from remote hosts. These files appear and act as though they were installed on your local machine.

Network Information System (NIS) A system developed by Sun Microsystems that allows Internet hosts to transfer information after authenticating themselves with a single password. NIS was once called the Yellow Pages system.

network interface card (NIC) An adapter card that lets the computer attach to a network cable. Also known as a NIC.

network layer Layer 3 of the OSI reference model. This layer provides the routing information for data, opening and closing paths for the data to travel, and ensuring it reaches its destination.

Network News Transfer Protocol (NNTP) The protocol that controls the transmission of Usenet news messages.

network operating system (NOS) An operating system for networks, such as NetWare or Windows NT.

NFS *See* network file system.

NIC *See* network interface card.

NIS *See* Network Information System.

NNTP *See* Network News Transfer Protocol.

NOS *See* network operating system.

offline Not available on the network.

online Available on the network.

one-time password A password generated on-the-fly during a challenge-response exchange. Such passwords are generated using a pre-defined algorithm, but are extremely secure because they are good for the current session only.

OSI reference model   Open Systems Interconnection Reference Model. A seven-layer model of data communications protocols that make up the architecture of a network.

owner   The person (or process) with privileges to read, write, or otherwise access a given file, directory, or process. The system administrator assigns ownership. However, ownership may also be assigned automatically by the operating system in certain instances.

packet   Data that is sent over a network is broken into manageable chunks called *packets* or *frames*. The size is determined by the protocol used.

Password Authentication Protocol   A protocol used to authenticate PPP users.

PCI   *See* peripheral component interface.

PCM   *See* pulse code modulation.

penetration testing   The process of attacking a host from without to ascertain remote security vulnerabilities. This process is sometimes called *ice-pick testing*.

peripheral component interface (PCI)   An interface used for expansion slots in PCs and Macintosh computers. PCI slots are where you plug in new adapter cards, including Ethernet adapters, disk controller cards, and video cards to name a few.

PERL   Practical Extraction and Report Language. A programming language commonly used in network programming, text processing, and CGI programming.

petabyte   Approximately 1,000,000,000,000,000 bytes (abbreviated as PB).

phreaking   The process of (usually unlawfully) manipulating the telephone system.

physical layer   Layer 1 of the OSI reference model. This layer deals with hardware connections and transmissions and is the only layer that involves the physical transfer of data from system to system.

Point-to-Point Protocol (PPP)   A communication protocol used between machines that support serial interfaces, such as modems. PPP is commonly use to provide and access dial-up services to Internet service providers.

Point-to-Point Tunneling Protocol (PPTP)   A specialized form of PPP. Its unique design makes it possible to "encapsulate" or wrap non-TCP/IP protocols within PPP. Through this method, PPTP allows two or more LANs to connect using the Internet as a conduit. (PPTP is a great stride ahead because previously, expensive leased lines were used to perform this task which was cost-prohibitive in many instances.)

POP2   *See* Post Office Protocol.

Post Office Protocol (POP2)   A protocol that allows workstations to access Internet electronic mail from centralized servers. (See RFC 937 for further information.)

PPP   *See* Point-to-Point Protocol.

PPP Authentication Protocols   Set of protocols that can be used to enhance security of Point-to-Point Protocol. (See RFC 1334.)

PPP DES   The PPP DES Encryption Protocol, which applies the data encryption standard protection to point-to-point links. (This is one method to harden PPP traffic against sniffing.) To learn more, see RFC 1969.

PPTP   *See* Point-to-Point Tunneling Protocol.

presentation layer   Layer 6 of the OSI reference model. This layer manages the protocols of the operating system, formatting of data for display, encryption, and translation of characters.

ProShare   A GroupWare product from Intel.

protocol   A standardized set of rules that govern communication or the way that data is transmitted.

protocol analyzer   Hardware, software, or both that monitors network traffic and reduces that traffic to either datagrams or packets that can be humanly read.

protocol stack   A hierarchy of protocols used in data transport, usually arranged in a collection called a *suite* (such as the TCP/IP suite).

pulse code modulation (PCM)   A system of transforming signals from analog to digital. (Many high-speed Internet connections from the telephone company use PCM.)

RAID   *See* redundant array of inexpensive disks.

RARP   *See* Reverse Address Resolution Protocol.

read access   When a user has read access, it means that he or she has privileges to read a particular file.

redundant array of inexpensive disks (RAID)   A large number of hard drives connected together that act as one drive. The data is spread out across several disks, and one drive keeps checking information so that if one drive fails, the data can be rebuilt.

Referral WHOIS Protocol (RWHOIS)   A protocol that provides access to the WHOIS registration database, which stores Internet domain name registration information.

repeater   A device that strengthens a signal so it can travel further distances.

request for comments (RFC)   RFC documents are working notes of the Internet development community. These are often used to propose new standards. A huge depository of RFC documents can be found at `http://www.internic.net`.

Reverse Address Resolution Protocol (RARP)   A protocol that maps Ethernet addresses to IP addresses.

RFC   *See* request for comment.

RIP   *See* Routing Information Protocol.

rlogin   A UNIX program that allows you to connect your terminal to remote hosts. rlogin is much like Telnet except that rlogin allows you to dispense with entering your password each time you log in.

router   A device that routes packets in and out of a network. Many routers are sophisticated and can serve as firewalls.

Routing Information Protocol (RIP)   A protocol that allows Internet hosts to exchange routing information. (See RFC 1058 for more information.)

RSA   RSA (which was named after its creators, Rivest, Shamir, Adleman) is a public-key encryption algorithm. RSA is probably the most popular of such algorithms and has been incorporated into many commercial applications, including but not limited to Netscape Navigator, Communicator, and even Lotus Notes. Find out more about RSA at `http://www.rsa.com`.

RWHOIS   *See* Referral WHOIS Protocol.

Secure Socket Layer (SSL)   A security protocol (created by Netscape Communications Corporation) that allows client/server applications to communicate free of eavesdropping, tampering, or message forgery. SSL is now used for secure electronic commerce. To find out more, see `http://home.netscape.com/eng/ssl3/draft302.txt`.

secured electronic transaction (SET)   A standard of secure protocols associated with online commerce and credit-card transactions. (Visa and MasterCard are the chief players in development of the SET protocol.) Its purpose is ostensibly to make electronic commerce more secure.

security audit   An examination (often by third parties) of a server's security controls and disaster-recovery mechanisms.

Serial Line Internet Protocol (SLIP)   An Internet protocol designed for connections based on serial communications (for example, telephone connections or COM port/RS232 connections).

session layer   Layer 5 of the OSI reference model. This layer handles the coordination of communication between systems, maintains sessions for as long as needed, and handles security, logging, and administrative functions.

SET   *See* secured electronic transaction.

sharing   The process of allowing users on other machines to access files and directories on your own. File sharing is a fairly typical activity within local area networks, and can sometimes be a security risk.

shielded twisted pair   A network cabling frequently used in IBM Token Ring networks. (STP now supports 100Mbps.)

Simple Mail Transfer Protocol (SMTP)   The Internet's most commonly used electronic mail protocol (see RFC 821).

Simple Network Management Protocol (SNMP)   A protocol that offers centralized management of TCP/IP-based networks (particularly those connected to the Internet).

Simple Network Paging Protocol (SNPP)   A protocol used to transmit wireless messages from the Internet to pagers. (See RFC 1861 for more information.)

Simple Network Time Protocol (SNTP)   A protocol used to negotiate synchronization of your system's clock with clocks on other hosts.

S/Key   One-time password system to secure connections. In S/Key, passwords are never sent over the network and therefore cannot be sniffed. See RFC 1760 for more information.

SLIP   *See* Serial Line Internet Protocol.

SMTP   *See* Simple Mail Transfer Protocol.

sniffer   Hardware or software that captures datagrams across a network. It can be used legitimately (by an engineer trying to diagnose network problems) or illegitimately (by a cracker).

SNMP   *See* Simple Network Management Protocol.

SNMP Security Protocols   Within the SNMP suite, there are a series of security-related protocols. You can find out about them by obtaining RFC 1352.

SNPP   *See* Simple Network Paging Protocol.

SNTP   *See* Simple Network Time Protocol.

SOCKS Protocol   Protocol that provides unsecured firewall traversal for TCP-based services. (See RFC 1928.)

SONET   Synchronous Optical Network. An extremely high-speed network standard. Compliant networks can transmit data at 2Gbps (gigabits per second) or even faster. (Yeah, you read that right! 2 gigs or better!)

SP3   Network Layer Security Protocol.

SP4   Transport Layer Security Protocol.

spoofing   Any procedure that involves impersonating another user or host to gain unauthorized access to the target.

SSL   *See* secure socket layer.

stack   *See* protocol stack.

STP   *See* shielded twisted pair.

suite   A term used to describe a collection of similar protocols. This term is used primarily when describing TCP- and IP-based protocols (when talking about the TCP/IP suite).

TCP/IP   Transmission Control Protocol/Internet Protocol. The protocols used by the Internet.

Telnet   A protocol and an application that allows you to control your system from remote locations. During a Telnet session, your machine responds precisely as it would if you were actually working on its console.

Telnet authentication option   Protocol options for Telnet that add basic security to Telnet-based connections based on rules at the source routing level. See RFC 1409 for details.

TEMPEST   Transient Electromagnetic Pulse Surveillance Technology. TEMPEST is the practice and study of capturing or eavesdropping on electromagnetic signals that emanate from any device, in this case a computer. TEMPEST shielding is any computer security system designed to defeat such eavesdropping.

terabyte   Approximately 1,000,000,000,000 bytes (abbreviated as TB).

terminator   A small plug that attaches to the end of a segment of coax Ethernet cable. This plug terminates the signal from the wire.

TFTP   *See* Trivial File Transfer Protocol.

Token Ring   A network that's connected in a ring topology, in which a special "token" is passed from computer to computer. A computer must wait until it receives this token before sending data over the network.

topology   The method or system by which your network is physically laid out.

Traceroute   A TCP/IP program common to UNIX that traces the route between your machine and a remote host.

traffic analysis   The study of patterns in communication rather than the content of the communication. For example, studying when, where, and to whom particular messages are being sent, without actually studying the content of those messages.

transceiver   An essential part of a network interface card (NIC) that connects the network cable to the card. Most 10BaseT cards have them built in, but in some cases you might have to get a transceiver for an AUI port to 10BaseT.

transport layer   Layer 4 of the OSI reference model. This layer controls the movement of data between systems, defines the protocols for messages, and does error checking.

trap door   *See* back door.

Trivial File Transfer Protocol (TFTP)   An antiquated file transfer protocol now seldom used on the Internet. (TFTP is a lot like FTP without authentication.)

Trojan Horse   An application or code that, unbeknownst to the user, performs surreptitious and unauthorized tasks that can compromise system security. Also referred to as a *Trojan*.

trusted system   An operating system or other system secure enough for use in environments where classified information is warehoused.

tunneling   The practice of employing encryption in data communication between two points, thus shielding that data from others who may be surreptitiously sniffing the wire. Tunneling procedures encrypt data within packets, making it extremely difficult for outsiders to access such data.

twisted pair   A cable that is made up of one or more pairs of wires, twisted to improve their electrical performance.

UDP   *See* User Datagram Protocol.

UID   See user ID.

UPS   *See* uninterruptible power supply.

user   Anyone who uses a computer system or system resources.

User Datagram Protocol (UDP)   A connectionless protocol from the TCP/IP family. Connectionless protocols will transmit data between two hosts even though those hosts do not currently have an active session. Such protocols are considered unreliable because there is no absolute guarantee that the data will arrive as it as intended.

321

uninterruptible power supply (UPS)   A backup power supply for when your primary power is cut. These are typically huge batteries that can only support your network for several hours.

user ID   In general, any value by which a user is identified, including his or her user name. More specifically, and in relation to UNIX and other multi-user environments, any process ID—usually a numeric value—that identifies the owner of a particular process. *See also* owner and user.

UTP   Unshielded twisted pair. *See also* 10BaseT.

Vines   A network operating system made by Banyan.

virtual private network (VPN)   VPN technology allows companies with leased lines to form a closed and secure circuit over the Internet between themselves. In this way, such companies ensure that data passed between them and their counterparts is secure (and usually encrypted).

virus   A self-replicating or propagating program (sometimes malicious) that attaches itself to other executables, drivers, or document templates, thus "infecting" the target host or file.

vulnerability   This term refers to any weakness in any system (either hardware or software) that allows intruders to gain unauthorized access or deny service.

WAN   A wide area network.

Windows NT   Microsoft's premier network operating system.

write access   When a user has write access, it means that he or she has privileges to write to a particular file.

yottabyte   Approximately 1,000,000,000,000,000,000,000,000 bytes.

zettabyte   Approximately 1,000,000,000,000,000,000,000 bytes.

Index

Symbols

3Com Corporation, 138
400 Bad Request error, 228

A

Abstract Syntax Notation, 72
account lockout, 167
account create, 160
Address Resolution Protocol, 75
administration, 29
  back up files, 182
  configuration, 29
  security, 30
  software distribution, 30
  UNIX, 103
  Windows 95/98, 99
  Z.E.N.works, 102

administration. *See* system administration
administrator, 159
Apple Computer, 81
application
  gateway, 203
  licensing, 117
  layer, 72-74
  Linux, 119
  office suite, 116
  security risks, 197
  server, 25, 80
  set, 117
  sharing, 24-26
  speed of running, 25
  Windows, 24
Archie, 276
architecture, 63
  OSI, 64-68
  SNA, 76
  TCP/IP, 73
ARCnet topology, 56
ARP (Address Resolution Protocol), 75
ARPAnet, 14, 274

attachment. *See* email, attachment
attack signatures, 202
auctions, online, 138

B

back up, 124, 177-188
  8mm tape, 185
  administration, 182
  CD-R, 185
  CD-RW, 185
  DAT tape, 185
  devices, 22
  differential, 183
  DLT, 184
  DOS, 181
  floppy disk for, 179
  full, 183
  hard drive, 184, 240
  high-density floppy, 185
  incremental, 183
  Jaz Drive, 181, 186
  library, 188

Digital Subscriber Lines, 262
directory, unable to create error, 227
Directory Services, 73
disaster plan, 122-123
diskless clients, 41
DLT (Digital Linear Tape), 184
DNS (Domain Name System), 107, 270-271
domain name, 271
Domain Name System. *See* DNS
DOS, 120
    security checklist, 204
DR-DOS, 120
DSL (Digital Subscriber Lines), 262

E

eBay, 138
Egghead.com, 137
electronic mail. *See* email
email, 26, 264, 275
    address, 292-293
    address book, 286, 290
    attachment, 27, 286, 294
        BinHex, 292, 295
        MIME, 294
        uuencode, 295
    domain-style addressing, 292
    Eudora Light, 291
    Find Text, 291
    getting, 288
    HTML, 286-288
    IMAP4, 295-297
    leave on server, 297
    links within, 27

Mail Rules option, 289
    MIME, 294
    Netscape Messenger, 287-288
    newsgroup, 286
    Outlook 98, 288
    Outlook Express, 288
    POP3, 295-297
    preferences, 296
    RFC, 299
    sending, 288
    sendmail command, 299
    SMTP, 298
    UUCP-style address, 293
equipment sources. *See* vendor
Esniff, 223
Ethernet, 9, 87
    cabling, 90
    Fast, 93
    SOHO, 142
EtherPeek, 222
ETHLOAD, 224
Eudora Light, 291
European Community Telework/Telematics Forum, 254
excessive packet collisions, 225
Excite Computer Hardware Shopping, 132
extranet, 269-270,
    certificate authority, 282
    security, 282

F

Failed DNS Lookup, 228
fat client, 41
FDISK, 238

file
    creation error, 226
    server, 26, 46, 80
    sharing, 26, 155
    UNIX, 168
File Contains No Data, 228
File Transfer Protocol. *See* FTP
File Transfer, Access, and Management, 73
firewall, 20, 272
    application-proxy, 203
    attack signatures, 202
    determining need for, 203
    intranet, 279
    mailing list, 205
    network level, 202
    router based, 203
    rules, 201
    virtual private network, 204
firmware, 39
floppy drive
    high-density, 185
    back up on, 179
Forbidden error, 228
frame, 9
frame relay, 262
Free Software Foundation, 119
freeware, 133
Frontpage Express, 100
FTAM (File Transfer, Access, and Management), 73
FTP (File Transfer Protocol), 105, 226, 264, 274

325